KABBALAH AND THE ART OF BEING

Professor Shimon Shokek, through his new approach to Kabbalah, suggests that the central ingredient in the spiritual teachings of Jewish mysticism is to be found in the Kabbalistic theme of Creation. Professor Shokek argues that Kabbalah is not just a religious phenomenon or an esoteric theology but a practical wisdom for living, creativity and well-being. Thus, he introduces Kabbalah as a spiritual Jewish way of living, an *Art of Being*.

The book skilfully reveals the core questions that emerge from the wisdom of the Jewish sages. It considers in depth the Kabbalistic meaning of Creation, mysticism, communion with God, language and speech, the human soul, messianism and repentance. Professor Shokek asks:

- What is the Kabbalistic perception of existence and being?
- How and why have Kabbalistic ideas been integrated into the lives of the Jewish people, shaping their fate and identity?
- What is the nature of Kabbalah and the truth behind it?
- Can we understand Kabbalah and Jewish mysticism in the light of world philosophy and contemporary psychological theories?

At a time when the study of Kabbalah and Jewish mysticism is attracting a growing number of students, *Kabbalah and the Art of Being* opens an accessible and lively avenue of debate, for both the academic student and the interested general reader.

Shimon Shokek received his PhD from the Department of Jewish Philosophy and Kabbalah at the Hebrew University of Jerusalem, where he taught for several years. He is currently Professor of Jewish Philosophy and Mysticism at Baltimore Hebrew University, and has lectured at the Smithsonian Institution, Washington, DC. He is the author of *Jewish Ethics and Jewish Mysticism in Sefer Ha-Yashar*, 1991 (English), and *Repentance in Jewish Ethics, Philosophy, and Mysticism*, 1995 (Hebrew).

KABBALAH AND THE ART OF BEING

The Smithsonian Lectures

Shimon Shokek

הקבלה ואמנות ההויה
שמעון שוקק

Edited by Michael Leavitt

London and New York

First published 2001
by Routledge
11 New Fetter Lane, London EC4P 4EE

Simultaneously published in the USA and Canada
by Routledge
29 West 35th Street, New York, NY 10001

Routledge is an imprint of the Taylor & Francis Group

© 2001 Shimon Shokek

Typeset in Garamond by
Prepress Projects Ltd, Perth, Scotland
Printed and bound in Great Britain by
St Edmundsbury Press, Bury St Edmunds, Suffolk

All rights reserved. No part of this book may be reprinted or reproduced or
utilised in any form or by any electronic, mechanical, or other means, now
known or hereafter invented, including photocopying and recording, or in
any information storage or retrieval system, without permission in writing
from the publishers.

British Library Cataloguing in Publication Data
A catalogue record for this book is available
from the British Library

Library of Congress Cataloging in Publication Data
Shokek, Shimon.
Kabbalah and the art of being : the Smithsonian lectures / Shimon Shokek ;
editor, Michael Leavitt.
p. cm.
Lectures originally presented at the Smithsonian Institution.
Includes bibliographical references and index.
1. Cabala – History. 2. Creation. 3. Spiritual life – Judaism.
I. Leavitt, Michael. II. Title.
BM526.S55 2001
296. 1'6–dc21   01-034484
ISBN 0-415-24044-1 (hbk) 0-415-24045-X (pbk)

This book is dedicated with love to my family,
Dalia, Ori, and Tali, and to my friends
Leo Lubow and Mark Komrad

CONTENTS

List of illustrations viii
Preface ix
Acknowledgments xii
Epigraph xiv

1 The mystery of creation 1

2 A note on creation in philosophy, mythology and Gnosis 15

3 Kabbalah on God's intent and language in creation 24

4 Creation and *imitatio dei*: Lurianic Kabbalah and Hasidism 38

5 Kabbalah and God's individuation 62

6 Kabbalah and the art of being 78

7 Waiting for Godot and the Jewish art of waiting 103

8 *Teshuvah*: the conclusive return to God 127

Notes 149
Glossary 163
Bibliography 168
Index 173

LIST OF ILLUSTRATIONS

1	Devekut, the Communion of Heaven with Earth	14
2	Toho Va-VoHu, Creation out of Chaos	23
3	The Ten Sefirot in Kabbalah	37
4	Tzimtzoom, God's Contraction in the Creation according to Lurianic Kabbalah	61
5	From Ayin to Yesh, God's Individuation	77
6	SHEKHINAH, the Kabbalistic Divine Presence	102
7	Waiting for the Messiah	126
8	TESHUVAH, Repentance	148

All the illustrations are prints of original artworks by Smadar Livne.

PREFACE

This book is based on a series of lectures and seminars that I delivered at the Smithsonian Institute in Washington, DC, during 1994–8. Thus, the text retains the style of an oral discourse to make it easy to read and understand. The eight chapters in this volume can be read either as independent essays or as interrelated lectures. These lectures reflect different aspects of the central theme of this book: creation and being in Jewish spirituality. On the one hand, the reader who is interested in learning mainly about the Jewish concept of waiting for the Messiah, for example, is invited to study the seventh chapter, whereas one who is interested in learning about repentance is welcome to explore the eighth chapter. On the other hand, substantial literary and theological ingredients bind together the entire book: first, all eight chapters focus on the affinity between the Creator and His Creation, and, second, they all introduce integrated building blocks in Jewish spirituality that when studied concurrently will reveal the inner structure of the Jewish mystical mind.

The literary point of departure of this book and its philosophical model was not intended to satisfy a rigid academic taste. This is not because the book lacks an academic framework. In fact, its scholarly framework reflects the best current academic research, and its attention to cultural and historical context is sound. At the same time, the book proposes to open a new window for those interested in Jewish spirituality. It uses a new lens that renders its subject more comprehensible and less complicated.

Here readers will find an invitation to inquire "why things are the way they are," but at the same time they will be required to take long leaps between themes and across historical periods. This ride into the mystical texts of Kabbalah, on the Jewish road of hyper-reality, uses as its vehicle the inspiring myth that the Jewish mystics have created regarding the Creation of the world. I call it in the book the Kabbalistic creation myth. I explore it in diverse classic texts of Kabbalah, and I define it as the existential and psychological foundation of Jewish spirituality. Whereas the existential dimension of this myth is shown by the Kabbalists to be divine oneness, an extension of the One into the many, its psychological dimension is revealed as the human soul's desire to be reunited with this unity. The abundant implications of this formula bind the book's chapters together from the first to the last.

PREFACE

Ironically, despite the fact that many researchers in Jewish studies are immersed in scholasticism and the debates in current literary theories – phenomenology, ontology, terminology, and methodology – they are often chained by the ordinary methods and procedures of the academic world. They are haunted by the rigid historical context, by heritage, ancestry, and culture, to the extent that they may even confuse significance with insignificance. The academic framework thus becomes the core, while the core becomes bland. In this book, although the philosophical method preserves the boundaries of scholarship, the core is not hidden under piles of footnotes or lexical points. For this book is aimed at those who are willing to learn with an open mind and an unchained intellect. My intent is to present as its core the wisdom of Kabbalah as a map illustrating the intersections of human thoughts, feelings, and actions; that is, as an esoteric doctrine and an intellectual philosophy that is an art of being. This, I believe, has always been the purpose of the Jewish sages who composed the treasury of masterpieces of Jewish mysticism and Kabbalah.

The process of thinking – what we call "intellectualizing" – can become a flight into abstractions that have no meaningful, experienced relevance. This book looks at the central themes of Kabbalah as accessible components for practical living. It proposes that the spiritual, psychological, and existential modules of Kabbalah have not only shaped the essence of Jewish identity, but also sustained the Jewish people through centuries of exile. The book does not suggest that the reader become a Kabbalist, but it definitely emphasizes that Kabbalah, as the major spiritual force of Judaism, has played a central role in the collective experience of the Jewish people. Hence, the book examines some of the focal themes of Kabbalah not merely as themes of a mysterious tradition, but rather as efficient, pragmatic, and even sacred themes of life, i.e. as an inseparable part of the Jewish ritual, ceremony, and liturgy.

When Aristotle asked what kind of problems his predecessors, the early Greek thinkers, contemplated, he concluded in the opening pages of his *Metaphysics* that they were always motivated by the sense of wonder: "For it is owing to their wonder that men both now and at first began to philosophize; they wondered originally at the obvious difficulties, then advanced little by little and stated difficulties about greater matters, e.g. about the phenomena of the moon and those of the sun and the stars, and [finally] about the genesis of the universe." The Jewish mystics and philosophers also first investigated obvious difficulties and only then ascended to wonder at the genesis of the universe. In the classic texts of the early Kabbalah that were composed in the Middle Ages in Provence and Gerona, in the magnum opus of the Kabbalah of thirteenth-century Spain known as the *Zohar*, in the influential Kabbalah of sixteenth-century Spain from the schools of Cordovero and Luria, and in the compelling teachings of Hasidism in the eighteenth and nineteenth centuries, the theme of the genesis of the universe emerges as the primary Kabbalistic mystery: as *Sod Be'riat ha-Olam* (the mystery of the creation of the world). The thoughts, the debates, the dialectics, and the sublime implications of this mystery are the focal point of this book.

PREFACE

There are many threads that run through the tapestry of Kaballah. However, the Jewish mystical sense of wonder about the genesis of the universe has occupied the heart and the core of the most penetrating and influential texts of Kabbalah and Jewish spirituality. Thus, in this book, *Sod Be'riat ha-Olam* is presented as the eternal ingredient of Jewish spirituality that eternally sustains the spiritual way of living.

Shimon Shokek
November 2000

ACKNOWLEDGMENTS

I should like to express my deep gratitude to the Smithsonian Institution for encouraging my writing of this book. Their enthusiastic permission to include their name in the subtitle of this book is greatly appreciated. I am grateful to the hundreds of students who participated with devotion in my classes at the Smithsonian Institution and contributed a great deal to the enhancement and crystallization of my thoughts and presentations.

I am thankful to Mark Komrad, MD, a senior psychiatrist at Sheppard Pratt in Baltimore, an instructor of psychiatry at the Johns Hopkins University and at the University of Maryland, and an expert in Jungian thought, who has studied Jewish mysticism and Kabbalah with me for many years. During the last twelve years, Dr Komrad has become my friend and colleague. Together, we co-taught a few stimulating courses at Baltimore Hebrew University on Kabbalah and Jungian analytical psychology. These courses remarkably enhanced my scholarly interest in the psychology of religion and led to my research on Kabbalah and existential psychology. Dr Komrad also read earlier versions of the manuscript for this book, particularly the sections on Jungian psychology, and contributed most insightfully.

This book could not have been written had it not been for the support and dedication of my editor, Dr Michael Leavitt. Dr Leavitt has participated in every step of the preparation of this book and has contributed to it significantly, both linguistically and conceptually. It is with pleasure that I express my thanks to him. Most of the classic Hebrew sources quoted in this book are Dr Leavitt's and my own English translations, unless mentioned otherwise in the book. The quotations from the Bible are based on the Bible's Soncino edition and on *The Holy Bible: The Old and New Testament* (Collins Clear Type Press).

I am grateful to the publishers who most generously granted permission for me to quote from the following books: Thomas Aquinas, *Summa Contra Gentiles, Book I: God*, translated by Anton C. Pegis, and *Summa Contra Gentiles, Book II: Creation*, translated by James F. Anderson, both published by The University of Notre Dame Press, London, 1955–6; permission was granted by Doubleday, a division of Random House Inc. Aniella Jaffe', *Was Jung a Mystic*, Daimon Verlag, 1989; permission was granted from Dr Robert Hinshaw, Publisher.

ACKNOWLEDGMENTS

Anselm of Canterbury: The Major Works, edited by B. Davies and G. R. Evans, Oxford University Press, 1998. Kurt Rudolph, *Gnosis: The Nature and History of Gnosticism*, translated by R. McLachlan Wilson, Harper & Row, Publisher 1984; permission was granted from T&T Clark Ltd., Publishers, Edinburgh, Scotland. G. W. F. Hegel, *Phenomenology of Spirit*, translated by A. V. Miller, Oxford University Press, 1977.

Many gifted individuals have done much to make this book a success. I wish to thank the editor at Routledge, Dr Richard Stoneman, the book's project manager, Mr David MacDonald, the copy-editor, Ms Ann Grant, and the entire dedicated editorial staff for making the process of the publication of this volume a pleasurable experience.

Finally, I thank my student and friend, the Israeli artist, Smadar Livne, for her kind permission to use her Kabbalistic illustrations on the cover of this book and among its chapters.

This book received the Baltimore Hebrew University Fellowship Award.

[God] wished that there be creatures who could recognize His attributes and deeds, and that He be called "Compassionate," "Gracious," and "Long-suffering." All this could only have been realized in a world in which there are creatures. Thus, it was His will to create such a world so that creatures could recognize His greatness.

Menakhem Nakhum of Chernobyl, *Me'or E'nayim*

1
THE MYSTERY OF CREATION

The "stem cell" called creation

This book looks at the treasures of the doctrine of Jewish mysticism of the last millennium, known as Kabbalah, from *existential* and *psychological* points of view. It examines some of the major and profound components of Kabbalah as they emerge from the complex descriptions of the classic texts of the Jewish mystics, the Kabbalists, who created and crafted a new religious and spiritual force in the Jewish faith. This study does not reject the accepted scholarly assumption that divides the major trends in Kabbalah into the *theosophical–theurgical* and the *ecstatic*, but it is not based on this scholarly assumption. For the goal of this book is not to present a Kabbalistic historical or conceptual survey of the major schools of Jewish mysticism. Nor is it to divide Kabbalah into *theoretical mysticism* as opposed to *experiential mysticism*, and thus separate the unifying elements that tie together the various ingredients of Jewish mysticism and Kabbalah. Instead, this book aims at looking into the teachings of Kabbalah as a religious phenomenon and a way of life; it aims to explore Kabbalah as the exemplary teaching of the mystical Jewish wisdom that has shaped the spirit of the Jewish people for centuries; that taught the Jew how to survive in strenuous times, how to become an actualized and fulfilled human being, and how to flourish and live a complete and healthy life. Thus, this work asks the following questions: What is that "thing" which is depicted in the spirit of the Jewish mystics and Kabbalists that enraptures the hearts and the minds of the Jewish people? How and why have the ideas of Jewish mysticism and Kabbalah been integrated into the lives of the Jewish people and shaped their identity and spirituality? What is the secret behind the fascination of Kabbalah that has caused it to become the major force of Jewish spirituality, and, what is the nature of the truth behind its reality? Can we understand Jewish mysticism and Kabbalah, which is after all the creation of the human spirit, in light of contemporary psychological theories? And finally, can Jewish mysticism and Kabbalah be considered as an *art of being*, a practical wisdom of the sages that has opened a new path of spiritual and psychological life for the Jewish people?

These questions lead eventually to an individual search, for, when a student of Kabbalah enters into the mystery of the *pardes*, the domain of the spirit, there necessarily emerges a personal relationship between the subject and the object; between the person and God, who are separate in the beginning of their relationship but can be inseparable as one reveals himself to another.

The reader who studies this book will discover that the end of this book is already in its beginning, since according to Kabbalah every reality is composed of a dialectical ontology comprising an entity and its opposite simultaneously. I will return to this point in its own chapter below. Here and now I am determined to present a primary Kabbalistic point of departure that, I believe, can serve as the existential and psychological foundation for the core teachings of Jewish mysticism and Kabbalah; I call it the Kabbalistic *creation myth*.

If all the mystical, scholarly, and scientific knowledge were to be shattered and destroyed and only one sentence passed on to the succeeding generations of humanity, what statement would contain the most significant information from the world of Jewish mysticism and Kabbalah? I believe it is the Jewish creation myth, that *all things come from the One, depend on the One, wish to imitate the One, and yearn to return to the One*. The Neoplatonic quality of this statement embraces the "stem cell" of the major teachings of Kabbalah; for in Kabbalah everything stems from this belief, whether physical or metaphysical, concrete or abstract. Most importantly, the Kabbalistic creation myth determines in Jewish spirituality the character of the two major "partners" in the "partnership" of existence: God and Man. And thus, every aspect of the creation myth should be studied, for it is the key to the understanding of the true essence of Kabbalah.

Since "all comes from the One and all returns to the One," all Jewish mystics and Kabbalists agree that the center point of Kabbalah, which is cleaving to God, knowing Him, and uniting with Him, must be contemplated through the study of the relationship between God and the creation.[1] I therefore wish to begin with a few remarks that may shed some light on the relationship between God and creation in Jewish mysticism and other religions. This will illuminate the crucial assumption that the *pneuma* of the Kabbalistic teachings is rooted in the distinctive meeting point of the Divine and the universe.

However, I invite the reader to look not only at the creation itself, but also at the Godly *intent* that led to the creation. The classic descriptions that reveal the notion of creation in Kabbalah do not concentrate on the cosmology only but rather on the *cosmogony* and *theogony*. Cosmology, cosmogony, and theogony ought to have an in-depth discussion, but I will limit my explanation of these terms and say here only the following: cosmology describes the acts that occur at the time of the creation, cosmogony describes the processes that led to the creation, and theogony describes the rise of awareness in God's mind even before the rise of the processes that led to the creation. Thus, theogony is the birth of God's consciousness: it is the genesis of genesis and the initiation of His intent in creation that pre-existed the genesis of the creation of the world.

Indeed, exploring the processes that led to the creation and the intent of

THE MYSTERY OF CREATION

God before the creation of the world is a task involving risk. Our Rabbis warned us in the Mishnah not to speculate about anything regarding what preceded the creation of the world: "Whoever speculates upon four things, a pity for him! He is as though he had not come into the world: What is above? What is beneath? What is before? What is after?"[2] The Jewish mystics and Kabbalists did enter, however, into a long path of investigation in this obscure area: what is *before* the creation has become one of the most sensitive issues among the esoteric teachings of Kabbalah. Thus, the mystery of creation has become the central theme in the texts of the medieval classic Kabbalists of Provence, Gerona, Safed, and even among the masters of Hasidism of the last three centuries. These Kabbalists and Hasidic masters arrived at some fascinating and startling conclusions: a small part of their heritage is what I wish to share with the reader of this book.

The existential element in the Kabbalistic creation myth

I opened with the emphasis that the treasures of Jewish mysticism and Kabbalah, some of whose premises I intend to examine in this book, should be looked upon from *existential* and *psychological* points of view. But why is this point of departure so central in the teachings of the Jewish mystics and Kabbalists? And what is the denotation of the terms existential and psychological in the context of the Kabbalistic creation myth? These are essential questions for this book.

I shall answer them as follows: first, the creation myth of Jewish mysticism and Kabbalah is by my definition existential, for the Godly act of the creation is defined by the Jewish mystics as the performance of God in the world – *existentiating* it! according to the Kabbalah, within the Godly act of the creation, four worlds are created simultaneously; they are known in Hebrew as the worlds of *Atzilut*, *Be'riah*, *Ye'tzirah*, and *Assiyah* ("Emanation," "Creation," "Formation," and "Making"). God emanates from His own *existence* to these four worlds, and thus they are considered as the four Godly hierarchies that establish the chain of being between Heaven and Earth. But the act that sparks the relationship between God and the four worlds does not existentiate the four worlds alone, it also existentiates God Himself; that is, *through the creation of the worlds God reveals both His own Persona and the persona of the worlds, existentiating both Himself and the worlds*. Hence, within the process of the creation all aspects of existence are disclosed, above and below: the Creator is created, and the worlds are created with Him.

The Godly act of creation is understood in Jewish mysticism and Kabbalah as the one and only "thing" that the Creator could not *not* do, since the name "Creator" cannot be applied to Him unless there is something that He has created, and since creativity is inherent in His Divine "Nature." Therefore the Kabbalistic creation myth involves both the manifestation of the creation of God as the Creator of the worlds and the King of the universe, and the manifestation of the composition of the worlds below. Hence, the Kabbalistic Godly act of creation is twofold; it is the *esoteric creation* of God Himself, who desires to create the world but is first faced with the manifestation of Himself; and it is the *exoteric creation* of the worlds which are created by God while He manifests Himself.

Furthermore, according to the teachings of the Jewish mystics and Kabbalists, the cosmogonial tools that are used by God in order to create the worlds – language and speech – and even more so the theogonial tools that serve Him in the process that lead to the creation – Divine Thought and Will – determine the *Personae* of both the Creator and the created worlds. Although God Himself is a singular Oneness, while the created worlds are composed of many parts, both the Creator and the creation share the *birth of existence* within the framework of their linguistic act of creation, for everything is created by thought, language, and speech. This is a central component in the Jewish Kabbalistic creation myth that I will discuss at length below.[3]

Here I would like to sharpen and deepen what I mean by the existential element in the Kabbalistic creation myth: *It is the element that reflects both the Godly nature and the human need for partnership and for an existence-related search*; *It is both the Godly and the human yearning for the self-transcendent self as the basic element of life*. And, therefore, the existential element in the Kabbalistic creation myth deals with both God's and man's inner search for authenticity and self-actualization.

In the religious–existential nucleus of Jewish mysticism and Kabbalah there is a mutual yearning between God and man for partnership and relationship. Man explores his existential solitude in this earthly world of corporeality, and gradually reveals the endless symbolic dimensions of spirituality that lie beyond the surface of the world. He recognizes the one basic alternative to the temporal frustrations of his life; during his growth and development he discovers that as a finite entity he can cleave to the Infinite and become one with Him. And God who appears in the Bible as the ultimate Being, who introduces Himself with the Name "I Am that I Am," reveals the Infinite-Being of Himself by His yearning to unite and become the Creator of man. Thus, in the history of the Jewish people a shared relationship is established between God and His people. This relationship is a mirror-image of the intimacy between the Creator and His creation. It is a *shared principle* that constitutes that man is in search of God since by his nature he looks above to unite with the *concealed* God who grants him life, while God is in search of man since by His "Nature" He looks below to unite with the *revealed* man who had received life from Him.

The existence of God as the Creator of man begins, therefore, with the existence of man who is created by God. This is the most fundamental principle that determines the Kabbalistic *co-existence* of God and man who *share* the same destiny. They are "united together" in the peak events of their mutual history: in the covenant between God and Abraham; when Moses hands down the Torah to the people of Israel in Sinai; when the Kingdom of the people of Israel is established by David; and when the Temple is built by Solomon. However, they are also "separated together." Thus, when the people of Israel are rooted out of their homeland and go to exile, God exiles with them. The ancient Midrash teaches us that "to every place where the Jewish people were exiled, the *Shekhinah* [the Divine presence], exiled [herself] with them."[4] From here we learn that the covenant of God and His people dictates a *co-existential* and *co-independent* form of life; it is their *symbiotic* union, for their existence lives "together," in *symbiosis*, as in the existential relationship between a mother and the fetus; who are two and yet they are one. Within this symbiosis, as much as the mother feeds and protects the fetus, her own life is enhanced by the fetus. She becomes a "mother" only because of her fetus; and her fetus will become a "human being" only because of its mother. These are core beliefs in Jewish mysticism and Kabbalah regarding the existential relationship between God and His people.

But the nature of existence itself is complex and dialectical. It may be compared to the state of atoms. An eminent contemporary physicist describes atoms as small particles that move around in an endless motion; on one hand they attract each other when they are a little distance apart, but on the other hand they reject each other when they are squeezed into one another.[5] The relationship between God and man as reflected in Kabbalah functions in a fashion similar to the motion of the atoms – similar but not identical. For it permits God and man to move around each other in perpetual motion, to attract each other and to cleave to one another. But the question is, once God and man seek one another, do they necessarily repel and reject and renounce each other to the extent that there is always some distance between them? Is there a complete unity or an incomplete unity between God and man according to Kabbalah? Is it existentially necessary that God and man keep "a little distance apart" as in the case of atoms, or is it built into the nature of both that they unite without boundaries? I suggest an answer to this primary, existential question below when discussing the concept of communion with God, known in Hebrew as *Devekut*. But first I would like to present in this brief introduction a few remarks on the psychological element in Kabbalah.

The psychological element in the Kabbalistic creation myth

Complementing the existential element in the Kabbalistic creation myth is its psychological element. It is the stratum that presumes that God and man share the *passion* for their relationship as their mutual desire, which is the most powerful striving force that bonds them together. What is the meaning of this passion and what sort of desire does it treasure? There is a natural passion that keeps the human race "together." This natural passion is reflected in the idea of the "couple," in the form of the "family," the "tribe," the "society," and in the entire notion of human "togetherness." Men and women in every society look for an interpersonal fusion. But the subject of their search is usually "someone unknown": thus, their search begins at a point of confusion and their confusion continues to grow as they enter into an unknown relationship, sometimes with fear and trembling and with the hope that they walk on the right path and eventually make the right choice. But in the relationship between God and man the movement for "togetherness" is significantly different; it is not a walk "forward" toward something unknown, but rather a walk "backward" to something known. The person who is in search of God already knows God, for according to Kabbalah his spirit was hewn from the spirit of God. God is the only partner who has always been taking part in the life of every man and every woman. Therefore, the movement toward God is "backward"; it is a movement of return; it is not bound to the future discovery of the "unknown" but rather to the rediscovery of that which is already "Known and All Knowing"; for God has always been in the spirit of the seeker.

Furthermore, according to the classic teachings of Kabbalah, God and man have a shared identity, i.e. God is an entity existing at the realm of Himself and at the realm of man, since man is created in His image. Hence, God and man are *Isomorphic*, i.e. they share the same structure and are logically equivalent. This shared identity creates a powerful *intrinsic* quality between them: It means that God and man are identical not because they are dependent on the existence of some further, *extrinsic* thing, but rather because they are mutually dependent on one another. Thus, the psychological element in the Kabbalistic creation myth promises the human being that in the relationship with God a great covenant *ad infinitum* is signed. It is a bond that provides the human being with immense reassurance and comfort. It is a bond that establishes a heavenly marriage between the human being and the Divine, a marriage of unification (*Yikhud*), which reassures commitment for eternity, joy and delight forever in both this world, *Olam ha-Zeh*, and in the world to come, *Olam ha-Ba*. In Kabbalah the *Mitzvah* of marriage, *Nissui'n*, incorporates the obligation of procreation. However, its ultimate basis is not found in the earthly "coupling" but rather in the heavenly counterpart. The earthly marriage of "togetherness" serves as temporal compensation and merely as a *symbol* of a greater, ontological marriage of "togetherness," which is the heavenly, everlasting unification of man and God.

One very important aspect of the psychological element in the Kabbalistic creation myth is bound up in the person's fundamental sensation of being fractured and his equally fundamental yearning to achieve completion and become whole. The Kabbalists describe the human being as a "half" entity in search of his other missing "half." Whereas the first "half" represents the psychological condition of the human being, the second completing "half" is always found in the bosom of God Himself. This Kabbalistic psychological sensation of incompleteness and the yearning to become whole, appear in central texts of Kabbalah, such as in the Kabbalah of Provence and Gerona, in the *Zohar*, in the ecstatic mysticism of Abraham Abulafia, and in the Safedian Kabbalah.[6] The sensation of "half" searching for the other "half" is a Kabbalistic psychological marvel that describes the recognition of man's incompleteness, and the aspiration of man's need for culmination and self-realization. But the unique point of this mystical search for completion is that it ends with man's comprehension that a similar eagerness for completion and partnership lives in the hidden life of God Himself, his ultimate partner.

This psycho-mystical sensation of God's and man's *co-existence* and *co-dependency* is not limited to the teachings of Kabbalah. It is also a central perception emphasized by the great philosophers of western civilization. For example, in his *Phenomenology of Spirit*, Hegel strongly emphasizes that any entity that thinks and sustains consciousness can exist only in being acknowledged by another entity that also thinks and sustains consciousness. Since God is in Himself consciousness, He seeks another consciousness to be united with.[7] This "other" consciousness is the consciousness of man. Similarly, the psychological element of the Kabbalistic creation myth demands that the bond between God and man unites their conscious minds as one. I call this synergy of the two conscious minds *consciousunity*. In Kabbalah one of the forms of communion with God is called *Hishtavut*, equanimity, which means that since God's consciousness is in search for man's consciousness who seeks freedom, and since man's consciousness longs to unite with God's consciousness who seeks recognition, the unification of the conscious minds of God and man is the fulfillment of both man's freedom and God's recognition. *Hishtavut* is thus reached through the meeting of the minds of the Divine and the human being; it is a process that correlates equanimity between the Creator and His creature.

Devekut and the breaking of the One into the two

Thus we understand that the Kabbalistic creation myth includes two major elements: the existential element, which claims that the very existence of both the Creator and man is based on their co-existence and co-dependency. And the psychological element, which claims that there exists a passion and a desire in both God and man to unite, a yearning for consciousunity.

Here I return to the question of the nature of the unification of man and God that was left unanswered above. Whereas the creation is the departure of man from God, the act of cleaving to Him is the return of man to his Divine source. Thus, Kabbalah teaches that God and man are partners in the same venture, for they both seek to unite and become One. Is that unity complete or limited? Does Kabbalah require that God and man keep "a little distance apart," as in the case of atoms, or is it built into the "nature" of both God and man that they unite totally and without boundaries? This issue has been one of the central disputes among scholars of Kabbalah. In his *Kabbalah – New Perspectives*,[8] Moshe Idel eruditely describes varieties of *Devekut*, proposing a typology of concepts and images that the Kabbalists developed and incorporated in their mystical experiences in reference to man's communion with God. His typology includes three main types of *Devekut*: Aristotelian, Neoplatonic, and Hermetic.

The Aristotelian type of *Devekut* is the intellectual type that was adopted by many Jewish Kabbalists and even by some Hasidic masters. Its main character is based on union with the *Active Intellect* or with God Himself. The Neoplatonic type of *Devekut*, which was also popular among many Kabbalists and Hasidic masters, is mainly interested in the union of the human soul with her root. It is the union of the spirit, unlike the Aristotelian type, which emphasizes the union of the intellect. And in the Hermetic type of *Devekut*, which is the main domain of the ecstatic Kabbalah of Abraham Abulafia, we learn about a special kind of unification of the human being with God, mainly by means of mystical combinations of the Hebrew letters and their recitation.

Professor Moshe Idel sharply disagrees with the late professor Gershom Scholem, who claimed that only in extreme and rare cases in Kabbalah does the Kabbalist unite with God without boundaries, in a mystical union known as *unio mystica*.[9] The Kabbalist, Scholem claimed, rarely experiences *unio mystica*, for he almost always intends to keep a certain distance between God and himself. Idel brings vivid examples from the vast teachings of Kabbalah that prove that Scholem's assertion about *unio mystica* in Kabbalah was wrong.[10]

There is no doubt in my mind that the concept of *unio mystica* is a critical theme in Kabbalah. Indeed, there are Kabbalistic texts of different Jewish mystical traditions that clearly demonstrate that the Divine nature of man allows him to commune with God, completely and without boundaries. But the question before us is what is the driving force that makes the concept of *unio mystica* necessary in the Jewish mystical texts? What is the essential factor behind the existential need for unification without boundaries? And, what is the ontological nature of the Jewish psychological theology of *unio mystica* as described in the teachings of the Kabbalah? I believe that the answer to these questions can be found at the center of the Jewish creation myth.

According to the Hebrew Bible beginning with the first chapter in Genesis, the creation of the world signifies a unique process; it is the "breaking" of the One into the two:

> In the beginning God created the <u>Heaven</u> and the <u>Earth</u> .... and God divided the <u>Light</u> from <u>Darkness</u>. And God called the light <u>Day</u>, and the darkness He called <u>Night</u>.[11]

This formula of the creation, i.e. the "breaking" of the One into the two, establishes from the dawn of history the "opposite couples" of every existent thing: the Heaven versus the Earth, the Light versus the Darkness, and the Day versus the Night. It is the most fundamental characteristic of the created world, and it bears profound significance in the theology of Jewish mysticism and Kabbalah. This formula is not limited to the creation of the world; it also establishes the duality of the human being, who is created in the image of God, as male and female. Thus, the first chapter of the book of Genesis states that:

THE MYSTERY OF CREATION

> God created man in His own image, in the image of God created He him; *Male* and *Female* created He them.[12]

This primary biblical statement has shaped the original formula inherent in the biblical creation myth; accordingly, the human being is an entity of duality. It establishes the mystery of the creation as the developmental process from singularity into plurality and from timelessness into time. Furthermore, it represents the "breaking" of the One into the two; it is the beginning of the cosmogonic cycle, the dawn of consciousness in the mind of God, and the beginning of wisdom in the mind of man. Most importantly, it is a formula that implies that since man was created in the image of God and man is "bisexual" from the first moment of his creation, God also is "bisexual" in nature.[13]

In the history of Jewish thought, the motive of the "breaking" of the One into the two is almost 2,000 years old. We find this fundamental principle already in the philosophy of the first century Philo of Alexandria, emphasizing how the Creator God divides primordial matter by means of His *Logos*. The Creator God is described by Philo as the Artisan who fashions the world first into two sections that are called "Heavy and Light," which are divided into "Air and Fire," and then into "Water and Earth" until the world is established on the basis of opposites.[14] But without any doubt, the interesting point in Philo's theory is that he identifies the Creator's unique ability to break the One into the two, not just as a geometrical quality but as a moral quality. Because God is the only entity who is unequivocally just and moral, He has the ability to divide the One into *two exact halves*, says Philo: "divide [exactly] in the Middle." Through this exclusive act, God's goodness is revealed and recognized in the creation.[15]

In the Jewish Scripture the formula of the breaking of the One into the two determines not only the androgynous embodiment of man, who is subsequently separated by God into a man and a woman, as described in the book of Genesis,[16] it also establishes an anthropological principal of duality and opposites, a principal that occupies the throne of honor in the consciousness of both the Divine and humanity. This principal is the fundamental concept of separation that necessitates unification; it is a Jewish belief that establishes the most basic *psycho-anthropological* truth: that man who is created in the image of God should not be limited to Aristotle's definition as being *animal rationale*,[17] nor should he be limited to Cassirer's definition as being *animal symbolicum*;[18] for the definition of man must be first and foremost *animal dualismus*.

The dualistic character embodied in man who was created in the image of God is equal to the dualistic character embodied in the world that was created in the same creation by the same God. This is the precise meaning of the Jewish theory that while it behooves us to relate to the world as the *macro cosmos*, it behooves us to relate to man as its *micro cosmos*. Human beings are "small worlds" because they carry within their ontological definition the nature of the duality of the created world. One should not relate this conception to Neoplatonic influence on Judaism, for it is a Jewish biblical concept *par excellence*.

But here we are faced with an even more far-reaching Jewish idea. The dualistic character that defines both man and the world also equates to the primordial *dualistic persona* of God Himself, for God is the One who created all. He created the world by the formula of the breaking of the One into the two. He created the human being as the Male versus the Female, and He himself is characterized as a dualistic persona. Thus, the classic texts of the Kabbalah teach that God, known in Hebrew as *Ein-Sof*, the Infinite, acts in the creation of the world through a process of emanation, which causes the revelation and the manifestation of both Divine aspects, the Male and the Female. This duality is the core characteristic of the Divine world of emanation, called by the Kabbalists the world of *Atzilut*, or the world of the *Sefirot*. This important point will also be discussed at length.[19]

The formula of the breaking of the One into the two, which is the foundation of God, man, and the universe according to the Jewish creation myth, is the essential factor behind the concept of *Devekut* and *unio mystica* in Kabbalah. *Devekut* (from the etymological Hebrew root DaBaK) means in Hebrew literally, "gluing," that is consciousness yearning for reunification of the two parts that broke from the One. It is a concept asserting that the two parts of the whole, the "halves" that broke during the creation, the Heaven and the Earth, the Man and the Woman, and even the Masculine and the Feminine aspects of the Divine, desire to return to their pristine position and become whole again. But what is the "thing" that generates this desire? Kabbalah claims that all created things are "halves" and all created things *realize by their nature* that they came from the One who broke to the two and the many. Since the consciousness of all "halves" urges them to recognize that they are incomplete, and since completeness is the end that all things yearn for, all things depend on the One, wish to imitate the One, and yearn to return to the One. In other words, all things seek *Devekut* by their nature.

The Hebrew term DaBaK appears for the first time in Judaism in the story of the creation of man in the Torah:

> And the Lord God caused a deep sleep to fall upon the man, and he slept; and He took one of his ribs, and closed up the places with flesh instead thereof. And the rib, which the Lord God had taken from the man made He a woman, and brought her unto the man. And the man said: "This is now bone of my bones and flesh of my flesh; she shall be called woman [*Isha'*] because she was taken out of man [*Ish*]." Therefore shall a man leave his father and his mother, and shall *glue* {DaBaK} unto his wife, and they shall be one flesh.[20]

These biblical verses are of a primary significance to the understanding of the concept of *Devekut* and *unio mystica* in Kabbalah and Jewish spirituality. It is true, though, that the verb DaBaK is not used here in the context of man's cleaving (or "gluing") himself to God but rather in the human context, i.e. man's cleaving to a woman. But this does not change the basic etymological denotation of the verb DaBaK and its religious definition, since it always denotes *a desire of a part – which once was One, and then broke into the two and the many – to return into becoming One again.*

It is of great interest that the Bible puts a strong emphasis on the natural philosophy of *Devekut*; i.e. every man and every woman yearn to cleave to one another not because they are ordered to do so, nor because it is an accepted custom of society, not even because of procreation, but rather because *Devekut* is inherent in their own nature. The "two parts" known as a Man and a Woman seek their authenticity that can be found only in their return to wholeness. The conception of the two separated "parts" evolves from a consciousness that recognizes its inner voice out crying: "I am 'half'; I will have neither peace nor tranquility until I find my second 'half'; and then I will cleave to it and commune with it and we shall be one flesh again."

If this formula applies to the relationship of a man and a woman, all the more does it apply to the relationship of man and God: for the Bible explicitly commands:

> After your Lord your God shall ye walk, and Him shall ye fear, and His commandments shall ye keep, and unto His voice shall ye hearken, and Him shall ye serve, and unto Him shall ye *cleave* [tiDaBaKun].[21]

This biblical verse sets the tone and the successive conditions for *unio mystica* in Kabbalah, and places it in its precise framework. It unambiguously teaches that *Devekut* is inseparable from the commandment of the imitation of God, "after your Lord your God ye shall walk"; that *Devekut* is interconnected with the "fear of God," "and Him shall ye fear"; that it is conditioned on the fulfillment of all of the laws of the Torah, "and His commandments shall ye keep"; that it requires obedience, "and unto His voice shall ye hearken"; that it obligates worship, "and Him shall ye serve"; and, above all, it commands *Devekut*, "unto Him shall ye cleave." Cleaving to God stands, without a doubt, at the height of the Jewish religious requirements. Thus, *Devekut* is the most pertinent and intrinsic psycho-mystical element that emanates from the creation myth. For it is during the creation that man "broke" from oneness to two while losing his authenticity; and in a new process of creation man will regain his oneness, when he will walk toward wholeness and authenticity. Since man cannot create his original state, he creates a point of return that facilitates his renewal and celebrates his wholeness by cleaving to God. Through *Devekut* he recovers his freedom; he overcomes his sensation of being a "half," and he moves from the ailment of incompleteness into the wellness of wholeness. Hence, *Devekut* with God is the bliss that God has bestowed upon man as described in many Kabbalistic texts.

In the classic medieval Kabbalah of Rabbi Isaac of Ako, for example, we learn about different modes of *Devekut* that enlighten the human being and bring him an abundant, good life in this world and in the world to come:

> It is possible [for a man] to connect his thought to God, and when [he] would do so constantly, there is no doubt that he would be worthy of the world to come, and the Name of God will be with him all the time, in this world and in the world to come ... When a man is worthy of the secret of *Devekut* ("cleaving"), he will also be worthy of the secret of *Hishtavut* ("equanimity") ... he will also be worthy of *Hitbodedut* ("aloneness") ... he will also be worthy of *Rua'ch Ha-Kodesh* (Holy Spirit) ...
>
> [A man] who is worthy to arrive at the domain of *Hitbodedut* has peace in his life. To arrive at this domain [he] must attach himself to three traits: ... Rejoice in his portion ... love contemplation ... [and] distance himself from position and honor.[22]

The importance of this Kabbalistic teaching is that it emphasizes that one mode of communion with God has the power to lead the mystic to a higher one. Thus, *Devekut* leads to *Hishtavut*, and *Hishtavut* leads to *Hitbodedut*. *Devekut* is the general mode of communion with God; it is the mystical method of concentration with a deep sense of intention to achieve unity and wholeness. *Hishtavut* is a unique method of communion, where the seeker of God yearns to have his will ascend to the high level of the exalted Will of God and thus achieve equanimity of the two wills. *Hitbodedut* is a mode of communion through solitude, which allows the mystic to desire and experience unity with God while isolating himself from the company of other human beings. One can find additional modes of communion with God in Kabbalah. These include communion through the mystical act of the permutation of the Hebrew letters and the Names of God, known as *Tzeruf*, which was the well-known mode of communion in the ecstatic Kabbalah of Rabbi Abraham Abulafia and his school. Another important mode is communion through the visualization of the Names of God, known as *Hitbonenut*, which was popular in medieval Kabbalah and among Hasidism, as in the Hasidic teachings of Rabbi Nachman of Bratslav. But perhaps it is even more important to emphasize that the Kabbalist quoted above, Rabbi Isaac of Ako, like many other Kabbalists and Hasidic masters, stresses strongly the ethical deeds which must accompany the mystical act of communion with God. Hence, true communion with the Divine is inseparable from good ethical behavior; for the Deity responds to the human being in communion only when the seeker of God is ethical and righteous; when he worships God and loves his fellow man; when he enhances the lives of the people around him with his humility, charity, responsibility, and good deeds.

To conclude this chapter I would like to return to the concept of the creation myth in Kabbalah and emphasize four particular points, *and the enlightened will shine like the Zohar of the sky.*[23]

1. The creation myth in Kabbalah is the "stem cell" of Jewish spirituality since it uncovers the intent of God before the creation, His active performance during the creation, and the relationship between God and His creation after the world came into being. Indeed, all aspects of life stem from the theogonial, cosmogonial and cosmological phases of the creation myth; it shapes the nature of God, the character of the world, and the destiny of humanity.

2. The Kabbalistic process of the creation myth involves forceful existential and psychological elements. In Kabbalah, these elements play a central role not only in the hidden life of God but also in the purposeful nature of the world, and in the *telos* of man who is created in the image of God. Man becomes a partner with His Creator, and thus bears an enormous cosmic responsibility that expands far beyond the scope of his limited obligation for himself only.

3. The Kabbalistic process of the creation of the world is based on dialectical motion and maneuver: all things come from the One, instantaneously "break" into the two, and yearn to return to the One. The quality of this dialectical maneuver decrees a duality of being and meaning in every aspect of existence: from the metaphysical life of the Divine to the physical reality of humanity. Thus, God of the Kabbalah appears in His revealed manifestation as the duality of the Supernal Father and the Supernal Mother. The world emerges as the duality of the Light and the Darkness, and humanity arises as the duality of the Masculine and the Feminine.

4. The Kabbalistic act of creation is twofold: it is the *esoteric* creation of God Himself through the manifestation of His emanation, and it is the *exoteric* creation of the world after God had manifested His emanation. Therefore, the creation of the world is absolutely dependent on the Creator God. For God sustains the world, upholds it, and sanctifies it by means of His Divine creativity and providence. The world, on the other hand, reflects these relationships with its Creator. Hence, God and the creation are inseparable; they maintain mutual conscious relationships with each other. Similarly, God and man are intimately linked, for God desires to create, and man to imitate his Creator.

These major points create the Kabbalistic dialogue between God, man and the world, and they all emerge from the creation myth. In later chapters I will examine different aspects of this dialogue in various Kabbalistic and Hasidic texts. As an introduction to that examination, I will first consider in the next chapter some remarks on the theological problems of creation according to Jewish philosophy and other religions and cultures.

Devekut, the Communion of Heaven with Earth

2

A NOTE ON CREATION IN PHILOSOPHY, MYTHOLOGY AND GNOSIS

Creation in the philosophy of Judaism, Islam, and Christianity

The classic rationalistic theology of the three monotheistic religions that were influenced by Aristotelian philosophy tended to avoid the problem of theogony and cosmogony. Questions such as: where was God *before* the creation, what was His original intent that motivated His will to create, and what were the causes and processes that led to the creation, remain sealed and concealed in the rationalistic classic sources of the philosophy of Judaism, Christianity, and Islam. The Torah that claims to begin "In the Beginning" also does not reflect the beginning of the theogony and cosmogony but only the beginning of the cosmology. One could almost say that there is a "missing chapter" in the book of Genesis, which is the one chapter that could have revealed how God rose to the dawn of creation.

Maimonides, the prominent Jewish rationalist philosopher of twelfth-century Spain, teaches in his *Guide for the Perplexed* that any kind of attribute should be denied to God, "For He, may He be exalted, has no causes preceding to Him that are the cause of His being and by which, in consequence, He is defined."[1] Even the greatest master of knowledge, Moses, who asked God "to let him know His essence and true reality," received the answer that human intellectual capacity is unable to comprehend the Divine; at best, the human mind may learn about "His ways and actions" in *this* world, whereas "His true essence" and, even more, His intent in the creation of the world are beyond the comprehension of the human mind.[2]

The problem of Maimonides' position on the relation of God to the world has been one of the most controversial enigmas among scholars of Jewish thought. Some scholars have held the opinion that Maimonides maintained the classic doctrine of creation from "nothing," *ex nihilo*,[3] a doctrine that was claimed by the leading Jewish philosophers of the Middle Ages, such as Saadia Gaon of tenth-century Egypt, and Bachya Ibn Paquda of eleventh-century Spain. Other scholars believe that Maimonides accepted the doctrine of the eternity of the world.[4] Professor Sara Klein-Braslavy suggests a new and an original perspective to this problem: instead of looking in Maimonides' *Guide for the Perplexed*, as other scholars did, she looked at his biblical exegesis, particularly his interpretation of the Hebrew verb *bara* ("created") in Genesis 1:1. She concluded that Maimonides' point of departure in reference to the concept of creation was to abstain from judging this matter, which he was, apparently, unable to decide logically or philosophically.[5] According to Braslavy, Maimonides interpreted the "six days of creation" as the order of priority referring to the *cause* and the *nature* existing simultaneously, and not as a sequence of six different units of time. Therefore, his biblical account on the story of creation, she claims, "is not a *cosmogony* ... but rather the *cosmology*," i.e. it does not tell us about the way in which the world came into being in time, but rather about the structure of the created world. Furthermore, she states, Maimonides explains that the Hebrew verb *bara* means "bringing into existence out of nonexistence." However, it is an *equivocal term* (in Hebrew, *shem meshutaf*), and therefore it requires an equivocal explanation: it can either mean "bringing into existence out of nothing," *ex nihilo*, or "bringing into existence out of matter." The latter interpretation is of great significance, for it could mean that Heaven and Earth were created *all at once* from an antemundane matter, a position which is tantamount to the Platonic position of the creation of the world, or that Heaven and Earth were not created *all at once*, and thus the creation is rather a *process of the action of eternal matter*, a position which is tantamount with the Aristotelian concept of the creation of the world.

It is beyond doubt that the Jewish philosophers perceived the notion of creation as a significant theological problem. Indeed, they have considered *Ma'asse' Be'Re'shit* (the "account of creation") to be a very challenging and even dangerous issue in the Jewish religious philosophical world. Even Maimonides had to use ambiguous language in dealing with this concept in his philosophy. And who is greater than Maimonides among the Jewish philosophers? It is not my intention to examine the complex treatment of Maimonides' concept of creation within the context of this discussion, but rather only to reflect upon its difficulty in Jewish rationalistic thought as well as in Islamic rationalistic philosophy and Christian scholasticism.

Indeed, the theme of creation was a challenging subject not only for the Jewish thinkers. It was also a major problem in classic medieval Islamic theology. In the philosophy of one of the prominent Muslim thinkers of the tenth century, Alfarabi (who greatly influenced important Jewish philosophers and had a strong impact on the way that Maimonides thought[6]), God is perceived as the Creator of the world, despite the fact that the world is seen as equal to God in time and eternity. Following Aristotle's teachings, Alfarabi claims that from the *First Being* comes forth the first intellect called the *First Cause*. From the *First Being*'s act of thinking flows forth a second intellect which gives life to the third intellect, and the process goes on in necessary succession to the lowest pure intellect, the tenth, called the Active Intellect. Here the chain of the "separate intellects" ends, and the lower level of the supersensible world is reached. The Active Intellect constitutes a bridge between Heaven and Earth; above it are the high intellects, and on top of them is God. Alfarabi, unlike another great medieval Islamic thinker, Averroes (Arabic, Ibn Rushd), thus believed that God must have had materials to work upon in order to create the world. God, says Alfarabi, produced the world out of matter, but the world was not created *ex nihilo*. Instead, God fashioned the universe from an eternal, uncreated matter. This matter contained many forms *in potentia*. If there had been no such matter in existence, then God's creation of the world would have represented a fundamental change in His nature because of the novelty of that matter. His intention to make this kind of basic change could suggest that God was initially imperfect. But since God is flawless, it would be inconceivable to imply that He has any such intention. For God, says Alfarabi, is perfect; in fact, He is so perfect that paradoxically He could not have created the world *ex nihilo*, for, had He done so, that would have marked a change in Him, which would imply an imperfection on His part. The conclusion of Alfarabi's position is that God and the world exist alongside each other and that the creation of the world can relate only to God fashioning it but not creating it out of nothingness.[7]

We find another approach in the Islamic philosophy of a contemporary of Alfarabi, the eminent Muslim philosopher Avicenna (died 1037). In Avicenna's theology there is a striking similarity to Maimonides' interpretation of the verb "created." He claims that the word "created" in the Arabic language has two distinct meanings that should not be confounded. I shall not discuss this similarity to Maimonides' treatment of the verb *bara* in this context, but only state briefly a few remarks about Avicenna's main point with reference to God and creation. Avicenna held the belief that the world may be eternal according to *essence*, but it may also be eternal with respect to *time*. It is possible to conceive that God the Almighty is omnipotent and at the same time is not the Creator of the world *ex nihilo*. But how could this be possible? Avicenna formulates the following answer: because it is possible to assume that the world is eternal, and because God gives forms to pre-existent matter since He is the "Giver of Forms," only when a new disposition makes matter ready to receive a new form does the old one disappear and the new one appear. Thus, God the Almighty is the *Artisan* who forms matter from pre-existence but at the same time does not create it *ex nihilo*.[8]

The concept of God and creation also occupied the Christian theologians. I would like to briefly discuss two prominent examples: Anselm of Canterbury and Saint Thomas Aquinas.

Anselm is the acclaimed eleventh-century Christian theologian, the monk from Bec, who contributed some of the great theological treatises to the Christian world of spirituality. His proficiency in the vast fields of physics, metaphysics, ethics, and logic is a challenge to every student of philosophy. In his *Monologion* he begins with the assumption that the creation of everything comes out of nothing. He claims that when a "thing" is made out of A, A is the cause of that "thing." But then, if the cause is made out of nothing, nothing *is* the cause of A. How is it possible that that which has no existence at all would contribute to something coming into existence? Surely, we know that out of nothing will come only nothing. Anselm's conclusion is that that which comes to be, comes to be out of *something*. But what is the nature of that "something" that is called by Anselm "nothing" and is the God of the world? Anselm claims: "nothing" *turns out to be* "something," and because of this, the superlative "something" *turns out to be* "nothing."[9]

There are three ways of looking at Nothing according to Anselm:

1. Nothing is nothing; hence, the world was not made at all.
2. Nothing is something; as if Nothing was something that had existed before the world was made.
3. Nothing is something; in the sense that it has *been made*, but there is not something from which it *was made*.

Anselm's God is *the* Nothing, the "Supreme Essence," as he calls it, that gives life to everything. It is the Essence that makes everything out of itself, of "nothing"; neither the nothing that is nothing 1, nor the nothing that is something 2, but rather the Nothing which has the supreme nature to exist through itself while other things exist through it.

Anselm's theory on creation is interconnected with his "ontological argument," his well-known proof of the existence of God. The "ontological argument" appears in his *Proslogion*, which was the sequel to the *Monologion*, for he was looking for the *unum argumentum* to establish his teachings on the existence of God and His relation to the universe. The argument holds, as scholars formulate it, "that nothing greater than God can be conceived to be and that God cannot even be conceived *not* to be."[10] God is "something-than-which-nothing-greater-can-be-thought." If you contemplate this idea you will have to admit that for this to exist in reality would be greater than for it to exist in the mind alone. "Something-than-which-nothing-greater-can-be-thought," Anselm argues, must therefore exist in reality as well as in the mind. For Anselm, the concept of God is built into the mind of each and every human being. Even those who deny God's existence can nevertheless be thought of as having some concept of God, since they surely have some idea about that which they deny. Thus, they have some idea of what it is whose existence they deny, and therefore God cannot fail to exist not only in the minds of those who have an idea of Him, but also in the minds of those who "have no idea" of Him, namely He surely exists in reality. Anselm determines and says:

That God cannot be thought not to exist

> And certainly this Being so truly exists that it cannot be even thought not to exist. For something can be thought to exist that cannot be thought not to exist, and this is greater than that which can be thought not to exist. Hence, if that-than-which-a-greater-can-not-

be-thought can be thought not to exist, then that-than-which-a-greater-cannot-be-thought is not the same as that-than-which-a-greater-cannot-be-thought, which is absurd. Something-than-which-a-greater-cannot-be-thought exists so truly then, that it cannot be even thought not to exist.[11]

The text before us is unique among the many arguments of the classic medieval theologians who sought to create a bridge between religion and logic in reference to the problem of creation. We find similar intellectual efforts among the writings of the Jewish philosophers, such as the "four arguments" in the first chapter of *The Book of Beliefs and Opinions* by Saadia Gaon; the "arguments" in *Sha'ar Ha-Yikhud* in *Duties of the Heart* by Bachya Ibn Paquda; and the "arguments" in the second part of *The Guide for the Perplexed* by Maimonides. But instead of analyzing these arguments, I would like to turn to another example from Christianity, that of Saint Thomas Aquinas.

Aquinas, without any doubt one of the most brilliant and influential theologians in the history of Western civilization, contributed a great deal to the problem of creation. He is the father of Christian Aristotelianism who attempted to assimilate Christianity and philosophy, for he believed that the truth is one and came from God. On the theological issue of creation, he owes much to his predecessors but he differs from them all. In a sense, the Thomistic position on creation lies midway between that of the Muslim thinker Averroes and the Christian theologian Augustine. Averroes maintained the eternal existence of the world as a matter of rational demonstration, whereas Augustine held that a beginning of the world in time was not only a matter of rational demonstration but a matter of revelation as well. Aquinas, however, maintains *the possibility of a beginning of the world in time*, along with *the possibility of its eternity*, denying that either possibility can be shown by reason to be the fact. Two major philosophical assumptions constitute his position on the creation of the world: first, that the creation is not a *change*; and, second, that there is no *passive potency* in God.

In his *Summa Contra Gentiles*, Book Two: *Creation*, he says:

> It is evident that God's action, which is without pre-existing matter and is called *creation*, is neither a motion nor a change ... for all motion or change is the "act of that which exists potentially, as such." But in the action which is creation, nothing potential pre-exists to receive the action ... therefore creation is not a motion or a change ....
>
> In every change or motion there must be something existing in one way *now* and in a different way *before* ... but where the whole substance of a thing is brought into being, there can be no same thing existing in different ways, because such a thing would not itself be produced, but would be presupposed to the production. Hence, creation is not a change.[12]

In his *Summa Contra Gentiles, Book One: God*, he says the following:

> If God is eternal, of necessity there is no potency in Him. The being whose substance has an admixture of potency is liable not to be by as much as it has potency; for that which can be, can not-be. But, *God, Being everlasting in His substance cannot not be*. In God, therefore, there is no potency to being ... God is through Himself a necessary being. He is, therefore, in no way a possible being, and so no potency is found in His substance.[13]

The above illustrations demonstrate the centrality and complexity of the problem of God and creation in the monotheistic rational theology of the Middle Ages. These are central and substantial chapters by some of the most prominent philosophers and theologians of Judaism, Islam, and Christianity who tried to solve the problem of creation by using logic and philosophy alongside theology. But the problem before us has not been merely the fundamental predicament of the leading thinkers of the three religions of monotheism. The same problem appears in world mythology and in Gnosis, the religion that held a significant influence on Jewish mysticism and Kabbalah. I will briefly discuss the theme of creation in some short examples from world mythology and Gnosis; the reader, however, must recognize that this is but a drop in an enormous ocean.

Creation in mythology and Gnosis

The ancient Egyptian creation myth as recounted by Plutarch, the Greco-Roman historian, teaches that the god Ra emerged from chaos and gave birth to Shu and Tefnut. From his tears, Ra created men but instantly regretted having created that ungrateful and troubled race which plotted against him. So he called a council of the gods and designated the goddess Hathor to destroy mankind and he, Ra, was so dreadfully sick of the world that he retreated into the heavens, leaving Shu to reign in his place. The interesting element in this myth is that here the creator god, Ra, realizes that he had made a mistake by creating mankind, and thus, he regrets it and "escapes back" into the heavens.

The ancient Babylonian *Epic of Creation* justifies Marduk's rule over gods and men; it reflects the political supremacy of Babylon in Mesopotamia, since Marduk was the chief god of that city. In this myth it is Marduk who slays the monster goddess Tiamat and orders the cosmos. We learn that Marduk appears as a great warrior armed with bow, arrows, a special net, and with the lightning, the winds, and the hurricane; he traps Tiamat in his net; then, he cuts Tiamat's body, and divides it in two "halves." He makes from one half of her body the dome of the heavens, and with the other half he makes the earth; from the blood of Kingu, the general of Tiamat's army, he creates humankind.

Similar catastrophic cosmogonies appear in the Babylonian *Gilgamesh Epic* and also in the Greek mythology. In the latter, there seems to be a compelling dialectical movement; the fundamental powers generate their opposites; vacancy creates solidity, darkness creates light, the earth creates the sky, and crime creates love.

A major rule is included in the creation myth; that is, *the principle of the creation of the universe is preconditioned not only in the will of its Creator but mainly in the revolting and abhorrent character of that which is created*. I will examine this rule in the following chapters when presenting selective paragraphs on creation in Kabbalah. Before that, I would like to close this chapter with a few comments on the theme of creation in Gnosis because of the significant influence of Gnosticism on Jewish mysticism.[14]

At the foundation of Gnosis there is the dualistic view of the world, which sets its religious ideology on a cosmological and anthropological level. The dualism of Gnosis is first and foremost "anti-cosmic"; that is, its conception includes an unequivocally negative evaluation of the visible world together with its Creator, both of which represent the realm of evil and darkness. At the same time there is a positive pole in Gnostic dualism, there is an otherworldly God who dwells beyond the visible world and is the real Lord of the universe. This God is the counter-God, remote from the universe, the "alien." He is free from any kind of relation with the world. According to the Nag Hammadi Codex or Codices,[15] the origin of the world comprised an extraordinary myth, involving mythological entities such as "chaos," "shadow," "physis," "pistis," "sophia," "aeon," "dynamis," and others; whereby "shadow," also called "darkness," preceded "chaos."[16] The *pre-existence* of "darkness" in Gnosticism is of great significance, for it determines a cardinal "dark" element not only in its religion but also in its theogony. The Nag Hammadi anonymous treatise *On the Origin of the World* describes the following theogony:

> Shadow derives from a work which was there from the beginning, [and] it is therefore evident that *it was already there* when chaos had not yet come into being .... But when the Nature (*physis*) of the immortals had been completed out of the boundless one, there flowed a likeness out of Faith (*pistis*) which was called Wisdom (*sophia*). It willed and became a work which is like the light which first existed, and immediately its will became manifest: a heavenly image of inconceivable greatness, which is now between the immortals and those who came into being after them according to the fashion of the things above: it is a curtain which separates men and the heavenly things. But the region (*aeon*) of truth has no shadow in its inward part, for the immeasurable light fills it entirely. But its outward part is shadow and therefore it is called "darkness." A power (*dynamis*) appeared over the darkness. The powers which came into being thereafter however called the shadow "the boundless chaos." From it sprouted the race of the Gods ..., so that a race of dung appeared after the first work. The abyss, thus, originated from the Pistis ...."[17]

In another Gnostic text "Sophia ... wished to create her work alone ... her work became an image of heaven ... a curtain exists between the heavenly and the lower region ... and a shadow came into being ... and that shadow became matter."[18] Again we see how "shadow," the dark element in Gnosis, constitutes the bedrock of reality.

It seems, however, that an even greater interest is to be found in another Gnostic text regarding the origin of the world. This text provides a fragment describing the consciousness of "shadow," its psychological self-recognized inferiority and, even more importantly, its sexuality. In the following example "matter" originates from a very negative psychic sensation on the part of the "shadow":

> Thereupon the shadow took note that there was something stronger than itself. It became envious and immediately it gave birth to envy, after *it had become pregnant from itself* ... as with a woman who gives birth to a child all her superfluous matter falls away, so the matter (*hyle'*) which originated from the shadow was cast into a part of chaos ...."[19]

The spectrum of the traditions briefly discussed above is a compendium that suggests a unique rule: *The relationship between the Creator, any Creator, and the creation, any creation, is the central mystery in all cultures and religions.* We may say, therefore, that the stories about the creation of the world do not signify solely "the beginning," i.e. the *chronos genesis* of the universe as its ultimate starting point; rather they establish a central principle to every creation, that is *creation is a yearning to make something new; but at the same time it always involves a dramatic, even catastrophic, and unexpected element.*

In the next chapter I invite the reader into the palaces of the minds of the Kabbalists – the abodes of the Jewish mystics – who challenged with fortitude the pivotal questions of existence: the existence of the Divine as well as their own existence. As we shall see, the Kabbalistic challenge was not limited to the question of the relationship between the Creator and the creation, but penetrated into the esoteric conundrum of God's *intent* before the creation of the world.

Toho Va-VoHu, Creation out of Chaos

3

KABBALAH ON GOD'S INTENT AND LANGUAGE IN CREATION

Ein-Sof, Sefirot, and *Atzilut*

The early Kabbalists of twelfth-century Provence and thirteenth-century Gerona coined the name *Ein-Sof* ("Infinite") to the ultimate, exalted God of Kabbalah. *Ein-Sof* "extends without end," has no beginning and no end; has no gender, no attribute, no quality, no quantity. It is "that which thought cannot attain"; "a pure concealed light." It is the absolute perfection and the "indistinguishable unity," for It comprises a unity in which all opposites are equal and in which there is no differentiation. Every existing thing is in *Ein-Sof* and yet *Ein-Sof* is the source of non-existence. It is immeasurable, nameless, ineffable, and, most importantly, It is beyond all perception, for It signifies that which is beyond the limits of human intellectual capacity. Thus, we learn from the magnum opus of the Kabbalah, the *Zohar*, that:

> It [*Ein-Sof*] comprehends all, but there is no one that understands It ... "That which is exceedingly deep, who can find it?" (Eccl. 7:24). There is no light that can look at It without becoming dark ... It [*Ein-Sof*] encompasses all worlds, and no one but Itself surrounds them on every side, above and below ... and no one may go beyond Its domain.[1]

Ein-Sof of the Kabbalah portrays a new image of God in the history of Judaism. It is not only the Lawgiver and Ruler as depicted in the Torah, the Mishnah, and the Talmud; nor is it merely the awesome King and the Almighty as described in early Jewish mysticism called *Merkabah*[2]: It is also the hidden source; the singular concealed unity who emanates multiplicity; the creative force that resembles an infinite fountain that flows endlessly and provides vitality to everything that exists.

Because of the concealment of *Ein-Sof*, It does not appear outside Its own domain. Instead, It governs the world through the act of emanation (*Atzilut*), which brings forth ten emanated Divine spheres (*Sefirot*) that constantly flow from Its fountainhead. Through the act of *Atzilut* the *Sefirot* flow from *Ein-Sof*, and by the *Sefirot*, *Ein-Sof* governs and shapes the world. Thus, *Ein-Sof* is a concealed reality, the ten *Sefirot* are Its hyper-reality, and through them *Ein-Sof* dictates the world's reality. Before anything emanated, there was *Ein-Sof* alone. It was all that existed. Now, through the act of *Atzilut*, the concealed turns into the revealed and singularity becomes plurality. Indeed, one of the major problems of creation in Kabbalah is bound up with the "place" and "time," where and when, *Ein-Sof* transposes Its concealment into revelation. This is the point where and when *Ein-Sof* appears in a form of ten emanated manifestations, ten *Sefirot*, beginning with *Keter*, which is the first *Sefirah*, which the Kabbalists identify as the Will of wills (*Ra'va de-Ra'avin*). From *Keter* flow *Hokhmah, Binah, Hesed, Deen, Tife'ret, Netzakh, Hod, Yesod*, and *Malkhut*.

These ten *Sefirot* are the powers and the attributes of *Ein-Sof*, inspired by the biblical verse "Yours, O Lord, is the *greatness* and the *power*, and the *beauty*, and the *victory*, and the *majesty* ... Yours is the *kingdom*."[3] They are the display of the spiritual pattern of categories embodied in concealment in *Ein-Sof*, and they reveal the symbolic system of the spiritual forces that are the means of activity within the Godhead. The essence of the *Sefirot* is the Divine influence that sustains both the *Sefirot* and the worlds. This influence existentiates through *Atzilut*, which is the process of the *One giving from Itself to the other without the giver having lost anything Itself*; it is like light passing from one candle to another without the first candle losing anything, a metaphor used frequently by the Kabbalists.

The ten *Sefirot* constitute the revealed spiritual attributes of the Godhead but they are revealed only to *Ein-Sof*. Thus, they are the Kabbalists' pre-eminent subject of inquiry, the motivating force behind the Kabbalists' spiritual curiosity, and the source of the Kabbalists' mystical attraction. The first *Sefirah*, *Keter*, also called *Ayin*, "nothingness," is the power of the initial awakening within the Godhead; it is the source and the initiation that ignites the genesis of everything that passes from "nothing" into "something." The second *Sefirah*, *Hokhmah*, "wisdom," is the supernal masculine emanation of *Ein-Sof*. It is the fountain of the Divine thought, the root of faith (*shoresh ha-emunah*) and the beginning (*reshit*), the "Supernal Father" of the seven lower *Sefirot* and the "husband" of *Binah*. The third *Sefirah*, *Binah*, "understanding," is the "supernal mother." It is the origin of birth and separation; it is repentance (*teshuvah*), the Divine "womb" and the supreme source of all human souls, the origin of every existence, the "mother" of reality, and the "wife" of *Hokhmah*.

From the unification of the "Supernal Father," *Hokhmah*, with the "Supernal Mother," *Binah*, the world of the lower seven *Sefirot* is emanated. *Binah* "gives birth" to the seven lower *Sefirot*, beginning with *Hesed*, "loving kindness," on the right, and its opposite, *Deen*, "judgment," on the left, balanced with *Tife'ret*, "beauty," in the middle. Below them are *Netzakh*, the emanation that manifests the "endurance" of *Ein-Sof*; *Hod*, the emanation of "glory"; *Yesod*, the emanation of "foundation," and finally *Malkhut*, which stands as the great symbol of the "lower kingdom" of *Ein-Sof* and also as the symbol of the feminine Divine Presence, called in Hebrew the *Shekhinah*.

KABALLAH AND THE ART OF BEING

Since the reality of *Ein-Sof* is above and beyond any perception, Its "movement" from concealment to revelation has nothing but a symbolic meaning within the language of the Jewish mystics. The dialectical language of mysticism cannot be applied to God's true essence, and thus it merely describes a symbolic process of emanation. Therefore, it is important that we ask what the meaning of this symbolism is. Is there an ontological reality to *Ein-Sof*, who emanates Divine *Sefirot* ten in number? Is there any difference in essence of any kind between the Emanator and Its emanations? And how does the process of emanation, which according to Kabbalah determines the fundamentals of both the worlds above and below, shape the *Persona* of God Himself and the vitality of every human being on earth?

In the coming chapters I examine the focal problems regarding the "movement" of *Ein-Sof*, shifting from Infinity into Emanation and Creation. By examining central Kabbalistic texts dealing with God and the creation I ask what caused *Ein-Sof* to rise up and emanate His *Sefirot*. Did the God of the Kabbalists create just once, or is there a process of recurrence in His act of creation? What is the nature of the relationship between the Creator and His creation? Does the creation of the world reflect any need or any lack in His "lonely" godly world prior to the creation of the world? Did He shift from potentiality into actuality? Did He change, mature, or individuate? And, finally, what are the implications of the Kabbalistic creation myth for those created in His image? Exploring these questions will unfold not only the mystery of the creation in Kabbalah but also teach an important lesson about the Kabbalistic essence of human life and its destiny.

God's intent in creation

The Kabbalistic investigation into the mystery of the creation of the world emerges at the turn of the thirteenth century as one of the major problems in Kabbalah. The problem arises in the mystical teachings of the chief Kabbalist of Provence, Rabbi Isaac the Blind, in the Kabbalah of the leading Kabbalists of Gerona, Rabbi Moshe Ben Nachman (Nachmanides), Rabbi Azriel and Rabbi Ezra of Gerona, and especially in the *Zohar*, which was composed during the last two decades of the thirteenth century in Spain. I would like to begin our journey into the Kabbalistic world of the creation myth through a perusal of a thirteenth-century book that attempted to create a merger of Jewish ethics and mysticism: I refer to *Sefer Ha-Yashar* (*The Book of the Righteous*) attributed to Rabbenu Tam.

Sefer Ha-Yashar enjoyed outstanding popularity, wide influence, and continuing dissemination. It was published in more than eighty editions, and occupied the interest of many scholars who wished to reveal its true authorship. The major literary problem of this book is that, although it has a mystical grounding, it has no explicit mention of the symbolism of the Kabbalah. It does not refer to God as *Ein-Sof*, nor does it make any use of the Kabbalistic *Sefirot*. Instead, there are other Kabbalistic ingredients in its concept of God and of evil, in its understanding of anthropology and cosmology, in its conception of ethics, and particularly in its dealing with the cosmogony, i.e. the mystery of the processes that led to the creation of the world. In my book on *Sefer Ha-Yashar*[4] I examined at length the many Kabbalistic ingredients that make *Sefer Ha-Yashar* qualify as a book of Kabbalah, and I concluded that we are confronted with an ethical work that contains Kabbalistic material, yet its decisive tendency is to conceal Kabbalistic sources.

The work before us is uniquely important. It is one of a handful of classic Hebrew ethical texts and also one of the best examples of a book of Kabbalah where an anonymous author wishes to reveal neither his identity nor his tendency to Kabbalah. This was because at the time and place of its composition, mid-thirteenth-century Gerona, the writing and teaching of Kabbalah was still considered among some Jewish mystics an esoteric doctrine that should not be revealed to the public. In the first chapter, entitled *Sod Be'riat ha-Olam*, the anonymous author analyzes the "Secret of the Creation of the World" and emphasizes the following ideas that will become the cornerstones of the Kabbalistic creation myth:

> We know and acknowledge that our Creator did not create the world for the sake of evil men, (*resha'im*), or those who anger Him … but He created it for the sake of the pious, (*hasidim*), who acknowledge His divinity and serve Him correctly. *And His sole intent was to create the hasidim, but the resha'im were created by the power of the nature of Creation.* … Just as we see that the intention of the sower of the seed is to cause wheat alone to grow, but that the power of the sprout will bring forth noxious weeds with the wheat, and with the rose, thorns. *Thus it is the intention of the Creator to create the hasidim, but by power of the nature of creation, the resha'im are brought forth with the hasidim* …..

And the author continues:

> His power forced the creatures to come forth *ex nihilo*. And if you say, why did He force them [to come forth *ex nihilo*]? [the answer is] *In order to make His divinity acknowledged, and to show the honor of His greatness, and that {He} be happy in His acts.* Since when the Creator creates a pious man, [a *hasid*], He is happy in him, as a father is happy when he begets an intelligent and wise son, who acknowledges and respects his father properly … and because of this it is said (Psalms 104:31) "Let the Lord rejoice in His works".

Here the author determines his deepest Kabbalistic ideology:

> We can say that the world was created for a great reason and this reason is the worship of the Creator, Blessed be He, *for just as a King is not called King until he has a people*, as it is said (Proverbs 14:28), "In the

> multitude of people is the glory of a King," likewise the name Creator cannot be attached to one unless there is something He has created. *He is not called God until He has people*, as it is said (Leviticus 26:12) "And I will be your God and ye shall be My people."

Now the author further deepens his Kabbalistic ideology by emphasizing the following:

> Even if the Divine Name is not missing anything because of the lack of men, nor does It gain by them, nevertheless, in the creation of the world, it was appropriate that the Name of the Creator should be God [Elohim] .... Thus with the Creator, nothing was lacking in His power before the world was created, BUT *in the creation of the world, His perfection was augmented*. And this is the reason why the world was created, so we know and acknowledge that *the creation of the world is the perfection of God's name* ....

Finally the author concludes:

> And as we know that every artisan who does some work, his intention is to do the best work of his ability ... and all of his intention is to make very pretty vessels [*kelim nai'm me'od*], and if one of them comes out ugly or crooked or imperfect [the artisan] will despise it and will not put it altogether with the pretty vessels, but will throw it away or break it; similarly the Creator, Blessed be He, intended to create in His world only the good and the pious. And if there exists *resha'im*, God despises them for they do not represent the best of his skillful work of creation. Just as the wise artisan, when he produces a pretty piece of work, he proudly shows it to all who see him, so does the Creator, Blessed be He, glories in His pious ones, as it is said (Isaiah 44:23) "And He doth glory Himself in Israel" and it says further, (Isaiah 49:3) "Israel in whom I will be glorified."[5]

The text before us presents a complex set of ideas; it suggests four cardinal components in God's intention in the creation of the world. On the one hand we are taught that God's intent was:

1 to create only the pious men, i.e. the *hasidim*;
2 to rejoice in His pious men and to be glorified by them;
3 to make His divinity acknowledged; and,
4 to augment His name, i.e. to earn the titles "Creator" and "King."

On the other hand we are taught that God could *not* fulfill all four of His components of intent, which He planned in the creation of the world. First, He intended to create the pious men, but the wicked were created as a byproduct of the "power of the nature of creation." Second, He intended to rejoice in His pious men, but the wicked surely "disturb" His initial intent to create the pious men only and rejoice in them alone. Third, He did, indeed, fulfill His intent to be acknowledged; for even if the wicked were created altogether with the pious men, He still can relate to the people who confirm His divinity, who worship Him and accept the terms of the covenant that state "I will be your God – and ye shall be My people." However, even though the pious men acknowledge Him, the wicked *do not*! Lastly, He did augment His name in the act of creation; for now He is finally called "Creator" and "King" by His people. The conclusion is, therefore, that through the act of the creation of the world God's perfection was augmented.

This discussion raises critical questions with regard to God's omnipotence. Is it possible for the creation to oppose God's original intent to create only the pious men? Why were the wicked created with the righteous? Does the nature of the creation stand contrary to the will of the omnipotent God? What is the meaning of the "power of the nature of creation," i.e. the power responsible for the creation of the wicked? Was it included *ab initio* in God's will or was it entirely antithetical to God's purpose in creation? Does the author of *Sefer Ha-Yashar* present evil and the creation of the wicked as a necessary part of the nature of existence itself? The radical consequence of this position is that the first meeting point between God and the world failed to fulfill His initial intent in creation. Thus, the creation of the world is, in effect, the result of a battle between internal cosmogonic events: a crisis occurring between opposing forces; the intent of God the Creator on one hand, and "the power of the nature of creation" on the other hand. Through this process, filled with conflicting forces, the "power of the nature of creation" constitutes a startling element.[6]

Furthermore, there are two major issues in this cosmogony that require cautious investigation; the first is the issue of the name of God, *Elohim*, a name that He receives only through the creation of the world; and the second is the emphasis that the completion and perfection of the Divine name is in actuality the *telos* of creation. The name *Elohim*, which denotes the Creator, has been a central concept in Jewish thought. According to an ancient Midrash, God said to Moses, "What would you like to know [about Me and My names]? According to my deeds I am called *El-Shaddai*, *Tze'va'ot*, *Elohim*, or *HaShem*. When I judge my creatures I am called *Elohim*."[7] This Midrash teaches that God appears in different name manifestations at different times and purposes. It also teaches that the ultimate name of God is not yet complete, as we also learn from another ancient Midrash: "As long as the descendants of Amaleq are in the world, neither the name nor the throne is complete. When the descendants of Amaleq are gone from the world, the throne is complete and the name is complete."[8] We find a similar notion in the teachings of classic medieval Jewish mystics. Rabbi Yehudah ha-Barceloni writes: "After His glory created beings and produced them by *Elohim*, He was called *'Elo'ha'* over all, through His having actually acted."[9] Further, ha-Barceloni states: "Of all His names He was called in the creation *Elohim* and not *HaShem*, until He completed the production of Heaven and Earth and all they contained."[10] The Kabbalist Rabbi Isaac the Blind of Provence writes: "'These are the generations of the Heaven and the Earth' [Genesis 2:4], the Divine name was not complete when the generations of the above and the below were created ... 'In the day that the Lord God created Earth and Heaven' [Ibid., 2:4] ... indeed the Divine name was not complete until man was created in God's image, only then was the seal complete."[11]

In the Kabbalah of the *Zohar* we read how the letters that create the name of the Creator (*Eloh.* and *mi.*) are joined together and become the name *Elohim* within the process of the creation:

> At the moment that the most hidden of all hidden things sought to be revealed in one point [*nequdah*] ... it portrayed in it all the pictures ... and engraved into the holy concealed light the engraving of the concealed picture ... that departed from thought and was called *mi* [i.e. the third *Sefirah*, *Binah*, was not called by the name unique to it, *Elohim*, but rather by the appellation *mi.*, which means "who" in Hebrew and signifies its hiddenness] ....
>
> It sought to be revealed and to be called a name ... and It created *elh*. And *elh*. arose as a name [i.e. the appellation *elh*. became *elohim* through being joined to the name *mi*]; the letters became attached to each other and reached completion in the name *Elohim*.[12]

The above examples are compatible with the conception held by the author of *Sefer Ha-Yashar* that the creation of the world is synchronic with the creation of the names of God; that is, the creation is a process which brings God toward *His Own* completion, a concept already found in ancient Midrashim. But an even more important emphasis is embodied in the Kabbalistic idea that God is inseparable from His names; namely, His names are not merely His attributes, but rather His essence, for God is equal in essence to the Hebrew letters and words. Thus, the revelation of the world is concurrent with the revelation of all His names, as suggested by Gershom Scholem when he writes about one of God's names, *HaShem*:

> The name, *HaShem*, is the reality of the supreme power that embraces all traces of existence and of creation in an ideal inclusion of all there is. For what does "all that exists" reveal in the long run? It reveals the supreme power expressed in it; the power expressed in it is nothing but the name of God. The name that we use in human speech is only a distant echo of the real name which is beyond human ability to express.[13]

Thus, God's names are identical with His essence, for both God and His names reflect the same Divine ontology; and since it is the augmentation of His names that God seeks in the creation, the creation of the world is synonymous with the creation of Himself. The creation of the world was not intended only to create the pious men and to benefit them, but also to have God acknowledged and recognized by His pious people. The God of *Sefer Ha-Yashar* is, as its author claims, like a father who is eager to be recognized and to become happy; He is the God who comes to be the Creator only through the creation of the world, since it is the creation that enables Him to be in partnership with His creatures, who recognize Him as *Elohim* and make him happy as their father. But *Ein-Sof*, the Creator God of Kabbalah, does not seek recognition only from His creatures on earth; He also seeks recognition from Himself; i.e. from His own *Sefirot*, who were emanated from His Divine substance. And therefore, the recognition for which God yearns is twofold: it is (a) an external recognition from His creatures and (b) an internal, self-recognition from His *Sefirot*, who manifest the substance of His divinity.

On this idea the *Zohar* teaches:

> [*Ein-Sof*] manifests everything from potentiality to actuality ... It is He that arranges the *Sefirot* in their pattern ... each one in its proper place in the sequence, but in Him there is no order. He created everything with *Binah*, and nothing created Him. He is an architect [and He] designed everything with *Tife'ret,* but He has no design nor an architect. He fashioned everything with *Malkhut,* but nothing fashioned Him. Since He is within these ten *Sefirot*, He created, designed, and fashioned everything through them. [In the ten *Sefirot*] He established His unity so that they [the *Sefirot*] would recognize Him.[14]

Kabbalah and language: thirty-two paths of wisdom

"The process of creation takes place on two levels," says the *Zohar*, "one above and one below, and thus the Torah begins with the letter *Bet*, with a numerical value of two."[15] The lower creation corresponds to the higher: one produced the world of the *Sefirot*, and the other produced the material world. But all creations, teaches the *Zohar*, occur simultaneously. To the Kabbalists, then, creation has a twofold character: it presents the cosmogony which is the internal creation that takes place *in* God, i.e. inside the realm of the *Sefirot*, and the cosmology, which is the external creation that takes place in the material world, i.e. outside the realm of the *Sefirot*. But it also signifies a crisis in the hidden life of *Ein-Sof*, since the introspective God, who until now was hidden in the world of "nothingness," begins to externalize and "dress up" into the world of "everythingness." This is the most crucial shift in the hidden life of *Ein-Sof*: it involves the gradual unfolding of the hidden *Ein-Sof* into the world of the *Sefirot* through the act of emanation. At this point *Ein-Sof* shifts from being undifferentiated into being differentiated. Here He breaks from the One to the two and the many, and thus plurality emerges from singularity.

The transformation of God in the creation is an illustration of a chain whose links are revealed as unfolding levels of many different worlds.[16] It is an illustration where "everything is linked with everything else down to the lowest ring on the chain, and the true essence of God is above as well as below ... and nothing exists outside Him," as formulated in *Sefer Ha-Rimmon* by the great Kabbalist Moses de-Leon.[17] This transformation is a godly act of expansion; it is God's exit from His own infinity and His entrance into space and time. And at the same time it is a theory that establishes the Kabbalistic foundation of pantheism, for the expansion of God causes Him to be everywhere, *pan-theos*, i.e. to reside in all spiritual *and* material things, above and below.

The transformation of God in the creation, however, is first and foremost a godly mental conversion. It is the transposition of God's *Self* from unconsciousness to consciousness, since during the process of the creation He undergoes a change of mind. The Kabbalists teach that the Hebrew word for "nothingness," *Ayin* (written in Hebrew *aleph yud nun*, AIN), has the same consonants as I (written in Hebrew *aleph nun yud*, ANI). God departs from His hidden "nothingness," AIN, and acquires His revealed I, ANI; although this is revealed only to Himself. It is this I that subsequently is transformed into ANOKHI when God reveals Himself to the people of Israel in the first commandment: "I Am (ANOKHI) the Lord thy God."[18] Thus, in His very first commandment He introduces Himself as a fully conscious God who requires recognition and demands acknowledgement of His unity. In the classic teachings of the Kabbalists of Spain, in the Kabbalah of the *Zohar* and in the Hebrew works of the master Kabbalist, Moses de-Leon, the transformation of God from the *Ayin* to the I is described by means of the symbol of the primordial point, *nequdah*. *Nequdah* is the pristine seed of emanation; it expands and grows by its motion, and it eventually creates the line and the surface until it is manifested into the ten *Sefirot*. Thus, the expansion of the *Sefirot* manifests the expansion of God's mind; that is, through the godly act of expansion He becomes aware and conscious.[19]

The expansion of God's mind is described in Kabbalah as a mystical Divine pregnancy. According to the *Zohar*, the *nequdah* that emanates from the *Ayin* enters into the *Yesh*; that is, it flows from the first *Sefirah*, *Keter*, and enters into the second *Sefirah*, *Hokhmah*. *Hokhmah* emanates the third *Sefirah*, *Binah*, and together, *Hokhmah* and *Binah* represent the male and the female aspects of God in the upper world. *Hokhmah*, being the supernal Father, uses the *nequda* to impregnate *Binah*, the supernal Mother. *Binah*, on her part, accepts the *nequdah* and transfuses it into Her "womb," from which the seven lower *Sefirot* are born and all differentiations begin. Thus, *Binah* is the core of everything that exists: It represents division (in Hebrew, *Bin*), the differentiation of things, since from her Divine "womb" singularity gives birth to plurality.[20] Now, each *Sefirah* of the lower seven *Sefirot* signifies a different aspect of *Ein-Sof*; finally,

GOD'S INTENT AND LANGUAGE IN CREATION

God's mind is expanded and "nothingness" is transformed into "being"; the concealed *Ayin* is at last revealed as *Yesh*.

But what is the meaning of the symbolic transformation of *Ein-Sof* into the ten *Sefirot*? The answer to this question is complex, since there are many Kabbalistic meanings embodied in this process. The primary symbolism, however, is that of language. Since the dawn of history the Creator God appears first and foremost as a Speaker. He is the Divine Creator who creates through speech, explicitly emphasized ten times in the first chapter of Genesis, as, for example, in the biblical verse that reads: "And God said, 'Let there be light', And there was Light."[21] These biblical verses inspired the Kabbalists to ontologize speech as the central mechanism of God's transformation from the *Ayin* to the *Yesh*. Speech has become God's ultimate tool in the creation myth of Jewish mysticism and Kabbalah, particularly since it was emphasized in the influential *Sefer Ye'tzirah* (*The Book of Formation*), which was composed in the sixth century. *Sefer Ye'tzirah* based the entire process of creation on letters and numerals.

Its first chapter reads as follows:

> In 32 wondrous paths of Wisdom (*32 netibot peli'ot Hokhmah*)
> engraved Yah, the Lord of Hosts, the God of Israel, the living God,
> King of the universe, *El Shaddai*, Merciful and Gracious,
> High and Exalted, Dwelling in Eternity,
> Whose name is Holy, Lofty and Holy,
> He created His universe
> with three "books" (*Sepharim*)
> with text (*Sepher*)
> with number (*Sephar* or *Mispar*)
> and with verbalized speech (*Sipur*).

The thirty-two paths of wisdom, explains *Sefer Ye'tzirah*, are manifest as the twenty-two *otiyot*, letters of the Hebrew alphabet, and the ten *misparim*, digits. The letters and the digits are the basis of creation, for the letters are the *quality* and the digits are the *quantity* of everything that was created by the speech of God. The Midrash tells us that the name *Elohim*, the name through which God is revealed as the Creator, appears exactly thirty-two times in the first chapter of Genesis, which describes the account of creation. The expression "God said" appears ten times in this chapter, exemplifying the *Assara Ma'amarot*, the ten sayings of God in the creation as alluded to in the Mishnah: "In *Assara Ma'amarot* was the world created,"[22] and these ten sayings, according to the Kabbalists, parallel the ten *Sefirot*.[23] The original linguistic way in which *Sefer Ye'tzirah* treats the "three books" that served God as His tool in creation has a special significance. The root-word S-Ph-R serves in Hebrew as the etymological root for a text (*sepher*), a digit (*mispar*), and a verbalized speech (*sipur*). The mystical author of *Sefer Ye'tzirah* grasps all three meanings in this one etymological root, claiming that by the act of speaking God brought all "three books" from potentiality to actuality; that is, God spoke – *a text*, *a digit*, and *a speech*, all at once – and the world came into being; or, as described in Hebrew in *Sefer Ye'tzirah*, through speech God *assa et aino yeshno*, meaning through speech God "made nonbeing, being."[24] The world, according to *Sefer Ye'tzirah*, is founded, then, on intangible beings. It is a world created and sustained by thought transforming to letters and digits. It is a world of *Logos*. One may borrow the accurate words of the Gospel of Saint John declaring: *"In the beginning was the word, and the word was with God, and the word was God."* This teaches that the word pre-existed the world, that the word is identical to God, and that the world is nothing but a "material dress" to the spiritual word, which *is* God. Similarly, we find in ancient Jewish Midrash that "God looked at the Torah and created the world,"[25] meaning that the Torah not only pre-existed the world but is also the blueprint that serves the Creator in the making of the world. This Midrash taught the Kabbalists that the Hebrew language of the Torah is not the same as any other language. For the Hebrew language it not merely a general structural language (synchronic), nor is it a general historical language (diachronic); it is rather a *meta-language*, a language rich enough from which all languages emerge. If we may apply Kant's terminology (in his *Critique of Pure Reason*) to the Hebrew language we can say that the Hebrew language is not a *phenomenon* created by humanity, but rather the *noumenon*; it is "the thing in itself." This linguistic concept is the focal point of God's transformation from the *Ayin* to the *Yesh*. The *Ayin* is the prehistoric Thought of God, signifying the *theogonial* period in the Godhead when the creation is in potentiality in the mind of God. It is the *non-verbalized* era in the hidden life of *Ein-Sof*. The *Yesh*, on the other hand, is the original Speech of God, signifying the *cosmogonial* period in *Ein-Sof* when the Thought of *Ein-Sof* passes from potentiality to actuality. Thus, the *Yesh* is the *verbalized* era in the life of *Ein-Sof*; it is the genesis of God's consciousness, and the entire process of the creation is an internal transformation, occurring inside the mind of God Himself, shifting His unconsciousness into consciousness. And, therefore, the creation of the material world, our *cosmological* world, is but a marginal byproduct, a tenuous result and a shallow reflection of the ontological transformation that occurs in the mind of God as He moves from the *Ayin* to the *Yesh*. Here God is conceived as a spiritual being who is a Thought that thinks Himself; He is a *Word* who manifests Itself from undifferentiated infinity, i.e. from *nequdah* to a differentiated finitude of letters, words, sentences, language, and speech. He uses the *Word* that pre-exists the creation as a means of expression and as an instrument of self-creation, until finally by means of His speaking He, the *Word*, and the World emerge from the darkness of *Ayin* and see the light of the *Yesh*. Hence, the transformation of God from the *Ayin* to the *Yesh* is purely mental and linguistic. When God begins to speak, language is created, worlds are created, plurality is created, and the Creator is created. Thus, the essence of God and the essence of everything that exists is a *Word*, and life in its deepest Kabbalistic meaning is a godly state of mind. This doctrine is portrayed in the life of the Kabbalist as a spiritual reality, for the entire vitality of the universe symbolizes for him the dynamic activity of God's mind.

This Kabbalistic perception was embraced by the leading Kabbalists of the last millennium. In his Kabbalistic treatise, *The Process of Emanation*, Rabbi Isaac the Blind interprets the first biblical word in the Torah, which describes the account of creation, as the emanation of the Hebrew letters that correlate the *Sefirot*. The first Hebrew word in Genesis (which is translated into English in three words: "In-the-Beginning") is *Be'Reshit*. Rabbi Isaac teaches that in this one word two *Sefirot* are hidden: *Keter* and *Hokhmah*. *Be'* ("In-the") stands for "the most elevated Crown," i.e. it is the first *Sefirah*, called *Keter*, whereas *Reshit* ("Beginning") is the second *Sefirah*, called *Hokhmah*. "In truth" says Rabbi Isaac, "two *Sefirot* [*Keter* and *Hokhmah*] are included in [the first] one word [*Be'Reshit*]."[26] This means that the first theogonial thought that occurred in the mind of God crystallized into the first animated word, *Be'Reshit*. This word caused the emanation of the first two *Sefirot*, *Keter* and *Hokhmah*. When *Keter* and *Hokhmah* appeared, everything else began to emerge. But it also means that the first word in the Torah, *Be'Reshit*, is not a word denoting only time: it is a Divine emanation, even two Divine emanations. Thus, everything emanates from *Ein-Sof* into *Keter* and from *Keter* into *Hokhmah* and from *Hokhmah* into the rest of the ten *Sefirot*. In other words, the creation is the expansion of God's consciousness, but at the same time it is tantamount to the expansion of the Hebrew letters; it is identical to the origin of the world, but at the same time it is matching the birth of language.

In the *Zohar* the shift from the *Ayin* to the *Yesh*, or from "nothingness" into "being" is also equivalent to the shift from silence to voice.[27] The following passage describes the chain of the *Sefirot* and the means by which they are born as a result of God's speech in the creation:

> "And God said 'Let there be light' and there was light" (Genesis 1:3) ... When the emanation moved through the heavenly palace, the mystery of *Elohim*, it is described as speech ... *Va-yomer* ["And He said"] was a force that ascended, and the ascent was in *silence*, from the mystery of *Ein-Sof* through the mystery of *thought*. "And God said," now it brought forth that palace that was conceived from the holy seed, and it was brought forth in *silence*, and [the *voice*] of the newborn [the *Sefirah*] was heard outside. That which brought it did so in *silence*, so that it could not be heard at all. When that which emerged emerged from it, a *voice* ascended through this mystery.[28]

This example illustrates the Kabbalistic deep belief in the spoken word as the primary force in which all beings and doings originate, including God Himself. Thought and speech are usually regarded as one, for the mind that thinks and the tongue that speaks belong essentially together; but in Kabbalah, thought

(*Makhashava*) precedes the spoken word (*Dibbur*), as the silence precedes the voice. Hence, in the theogony of Kabbalah, the movement of the godly transformation from thought to speech parallels God's shift from silence to voice. But creation in terms of speech does not merely crystallize the thought into newborn words, it also constitutes a unity between the created thing and its name, to the extent that the thing and its name become one and the same. This is the reason for the significance of the naming of a newborn in Judaism; before the name is given to a newborn, he or she lacks an identity, but when the name is given, the person becomes an individual, conferred with creativity, vitality, content, and with the ability to modify his or her personality and destiny. Thus we learn that the very first creative act of Adam after his creation is naming the newly born creatures of the world: "And Adam gave names to all cattle, and to the fowl of the air, and to every beast of the field."[29] This means that the godly transition from thought to speech was already being imitated by Adam, signifying his uniqueness as the one and only creature on earth who was created in the image of God. Adam, like God, celebrated the birth of language from thought and the emergence of voice from silence. Adam himself was named Adam because his body was created from the *Adamah*, the "dust of the earth," to which his body eventually returns. In the Jewish faith each person is named in accordance with his or her origin and destiny. When a change in the destiny of the human being occurs, the name is changed accordingly. Hence, we learn from the Torah that the name of the father of Judaism was augmented from Avram to Avraham, the name of the mother of Judaism was changed from Sarai to Sarah, and the name of Jacob was changed from Jacob to Israel. We read in the book of Genesis that God says to Jacob: "Thy name shall be called no more Jacob but Israel, for thou has striven with *Elohim* and with men and hast prevailed."[30]

The Kabbalistic belief that portrays God's intent in the creation as His yearning to become the Creator and to be recognized by His creatures, together with the belief that the creation of language is identical with God's shift from the *Ayin* to the *Yesh*, are essential innovations of Kabbalah, despite the fact that their roots can be found in ancient Midrashim. These conceptions set the crucial grounds for the anthropomorphic psychology in Kabbalistic literature. These are the core esoteric concepts that establish the mystical belief in Kabbalah that *Ein-Sof* is a mind and a consciousness, yearning to grow and be actualized.

In the next chapter I present central texts on the creation of the world from Lurianic Kabbalah and Hasidism that deepen our understanding of this mystical anthropomorphic psychology as it was taught by the famed masters of Jewish spirituality. The ideological implications of those texts and their audacity, as exemplified in the next chapter, are indeed remarkable.

The Ten Sefirot in Kabbalah

4

CREATION AND *IMITATIO DEI*

Lurianic Kabbalah and Hasidism

The creation myth in the Kabbalah of Cordovero and the Ari

In the entire history of Kabbalah and Jewish spirituality there has not been a more significant and influential school of Jewish mysticism then the sixteenth-century Kabbalah of Safed. Here, Kabbalah merged decidedly with Jewish ethics by emphasizing the Kabbalistic creation myth as the focus of Jewish religious life. In truth, sixteenth-century Safed Kabbalah concentrated so much on the creation myth that it would not be improper to ascribe to it the signature "the Kabbalah of Creation." But since this book does not focus on the history of Kabbalah, I do not attempt to describe the development of this magnificent center of Jewish mysticism, nor do I aspire to describe its charismatic Kabbalists and their powerful works: Instead, I present selective Safedian texts dealing specifically with creation.

Many great Kabbalists from Safed left their legacy on the Jewish people and their spiritual life. But none became as famous and influential as Rabbi Moses Cordovero, known as RaMaC, and as Rabbi Isaac Luria Ashkenazi, known as the Ari. I begin our journey into the Safedian Kabbalistic concept of creation by entering into the *Pardes* of Moses Cordovero.

Rabbi Moses Cordovero's most famous work is *Sefer Pardes Rimmonim* (*The Book of the Orchard of Pomegranates*), one of the few truly classic books in Kabbalah, which he wrote when he was only twenty-seven years old. It includes a systematic commentary on the Kabbalah of the *Zohar*, illuminating with great brilliance the *Zoharic* conceptions of *Ein-Sof* and the *Sefirot*, and in particular the relationship between the substance (*atzmut*) of *Ein-Sof* and Its vessels (*kellim*). Cordovero analyzes in depth the problem of emanation and produces a comprehensive thesis on the subject of creation. He teaches that the transcendental God who is sublime and hidden in the depth of His exalted self, *seeks to reveal Himself to the creatures of the world so that they worship Him.* Therefore He emanates a world of graduated levels of *Sefirot* that bridge the chasm between Himself and His creatures. He shifts from being a transcendental and "lonely" God into a personal God who develops active and actual relationships with His people.

CREATION AND *IMITATIO DEI*

Cordovero writes:

> Before the emanation [occurred], the greatness of the Necessary-Being [God] was not known to anybody else, for there was nobody else except Him. *The emanation occurred so that the creatures recognize His power and exaltedness* ... and [His] reality comes down and emerges from His face and descends by way of a graduated ladder in which its head touches the Infinite God and its lower part reaches the earth ... *The intent of the emanation was that through Him, His greatness will be revealed and the world will be ruled by Him* ... and thus the conclusion is that the main reason for the rise of the Will [of God to emanate the world] was for [His] Kingdom to rule the world ... [God's Will rises] to bring forth His emanation so that He reveals to the eyes of the creatures His greatness *in order that He be recognized by His creatures and comprehended by His Sefirot*.[1]

In another famous Kabbalistic composition, *Elimah Rabbati*, Cordovero develops a novel approach to the mechanism of creation. The reason for creation, he claims, is not the result of any change occurring in God, but rather the result of an "active potentiality" that resides in God and has always been hidden in His Will. This "active potentiality," says Cordovero, has always been an essential and inseparable part of God's nature. Indeed, God is the Creator of the world and from His active potentiality the world is nurtured. But how can this be possible? Is not potentiality a "thing" that signifies a desire for a future change? Does not His passage from potentiality to actuality inscribe changes in His form and shape and perhaps even in His substance? Cordovero's answer is that although in every created thing potentiality signifies necessarily a future change, in God it is not so. For God's potentiality *and* actuality are one and the same. God constantly passes from potentiality to actuality and thus creates His world unceasingly. Therefore no change occurs in Him: *He is in potential actuality and in actual potentiality*; *He is potentially actual and actually potential*; He emanates His Divine emanations *all the time*; He brings forth his potentiality *all the time*, and, therefore, there is no difference or change of any kind in Him or in His actions in the present, the past, or the future. Only if God ceases to emanate and create would a change be found in Him. But then again this is impossible; for God is unchanging; for God never ceases to emanate and create. He *is* the Creator; He has always created in the past, always creates in the present, and will always create in the future. In Cordovero's Kabbalistic opus we hear the echo of the voice of the Jewish rationalist philosopher, Maimonides, who rejected any kind of anthropomorphism and change in reference to God. This doctrine held that whereas change is the epitome of the human quality, it is contrary to God's essence. Whereas the human being constantly changes in substance, form, and shape, God is immutable.

Here we face another problem: if God creates *all the time*, does this mean that there was no beginning? What then would be the difference between Cordovero and Aristotle? Aristotle spoke of the "First Cause" that causes everything to be, but *never began* to cause the world to be, for the world is eternal and "was always there." Cordovero's concept of creation, however, is as distant from Aristotle's as is the distance of east from west. Cordovero's God is the *conscious* Creator of the world, who creates for the specific purpose "that the creatures recognize His power and exaltedness ... so that His greatness will be revealed and the world will be ruled by Him." Whereas human beings have a narrow epistemological view of God and His creation, God's own perspective, claims Cordovero, is decidedly different. God has an "active principle" that causes the creatures to come into being. From His perspective, His grace emanates even if there is no one to accept those emanations, "even if there are no creatures at all." The fact that the creatures are created at a certain specific time is not a proof that God shifts from potentiality to actuality, because God's "active principle" is active at all times. Thus, God's "active principle" means that "God's [actuality] and His potentiality are one" and, therefore, God is unchanging.[2]

Cordovero's concept of creation teaches us that God's will to create the world is inherent in Him and is identical with His essence. Hence, God is not a Creator by attribute, but rather a Creator *by definition*, i.e. the word "Creator" does not only describe what God *does* but what God *is*, for "Creator" is His *ontological definition*. Furthermore, because He and His will are one and the same, because the potential to create is inherent in His will – as His "active principle," because there is no change in Him, and because the "active principle" of His potentiality operates all the time, this ontological definition of God includes His being the *All-Time Creator*, since creating is not only what He *is*, it is also what He does *all the time*, and that is why God is unchanging.

Cordovero's original ideas in his *Pardes Rimmonim*, *Elimah Rabbati*, and his other Kabbalistic works led to his primacy among the Kabbalists of Safed. But the Jewish spiritual world in Safed sharply changed when Rabbi Isaac Luria, the Ari, came to Safed in 1570. The Ari is without a doubt the most stimulating, influential, and revered Kabbalist of all time. Unlike Cordovero, the Ari regarded his Kabbalistic teachings as esoteric and did not intend them to be published and become the beliefs for the Jewish masses. His disciple, Rabbi Hayyim Vital, dedicated all his intellectual and spiritual efforts to writing down the Kabbalistic teachings of his admired teacher, which he, Vital, kept in secret. Legend has it that the books that Vital wrote "from the mouth" of the Ari were stolen from Vital's house while he was sick and then disseminated and copied.

The central work of the Ari's (or Lurianic) Kabbalah is *Sefer Etz Hayyim* (*The Book of the Tree of Life*). In the heart of this book stands the problem of creation. According to the Ari and his school, the nature of the Creator is manifest through His twofold character: expansion and contraction (*Hitpashtut* and *Tzimtzoom*). The meaning of this conception is that the Divine realm is alive with dynamics of vitality and perpetual movements. It is a Divine entity composed of spiritual motions of ascents and descents that determine two "mental" states: an expanded state and a contracted state. This dialectical movement is described by the Ari as a Godly "passion" to be revealed and concealed, a passion inherent in the nature of God who alternates between the *Ayin* and the *Yesh*. This concept is similar to the findings of physics which claim that light (energy) can be shown to be simultaneously in two contradictory states: a particle and or a wave. Energy alternates between these states depending on the perspective of the viewer. God's alternation between the *Ayin* and the *Yesh* has much the same character, for God is simultaneously in both states. The question is, what is the source of this idea in Judaism?

The idea of God's duality of movements originates in the prophet Ezekiel's vision of the "Chariots of God." Ezekiel declares that he saw the following vision of the *Pleroma*:

> And I looked and behold, a stormy wind came out of the north, a great cloud with the fire flashing up, so that a brightness was round about it; and out of the midst thereof as the color of electrum (*Hashmal*), out of the midst of the fire. And out of the midst thereof came the likeness of four living creatures. And this was their appearance; they had the likeness of a man. And every one had four faces, and every one of them had four wings ... they had the face of a man; and they four had the face of a lion on the right side; and they four had the face of an ox on the left side; they four had also the face of an eagle ... And they went every one straight forward whither the spirit was to go, they went; they turned not when they went. As for the likeness of the living creatures, their appearance was like coals of fire, burning like the appearance of torches; it flashed up and down among the living creatures; and there was brightness to the fire, and out of the fire went forth lightning. And the living creatures ran and returned (*ratzo va-shov*) as the appearance of a flash lightning.[3]

These "four living creatures" described by Ezekiel illustrate the dynamics of vitality in the Godhead. They signify the *Pleroma*, the angelic world of fullness in the abode of God. God Himself is described as a Divine entity with the "appearance of a man" sitting on a throne "above the firmament." But the important element in this mystical description is the movement inherent in the nature of the Divine creatures, a movement that enraptured the imagination of the Jewish mystics for generations. This movement is called *Ratzo va-Shov*, "run and return"; it teaches that there is an inherent dynamism within the world of God. Indeed, *Ratzo va-Shov* has become a symbol in Jewish mysticism and Kabbalah that not only denotes the understanding of "run and return" but also of ascent and descent, expansion and contraction, revelation and concealment, realization and annihilation, being and non-being. This dialectical movement of the "living creatures" is interpreted by the Jewish mystics as being the core motion in the Godhead and the primary characteristic of God Himself. God embodies in His Divine nature a duality of perpetual movement, i.e. in God's consciousness "to be or not to be" is not the question, it is rather the *answer*, for since He is everything that there is, He is the ultimate being *and* non-being. This mystical principle is essential to our understanding of the process of creation according to the Ari and his Kabbalistic school.

Contemporary scholars of Jewish mysticism have emphasized three major phases in the Lurianic process of creation: Contraction (*Tzimtzoom*), Breaking (*Shevirah*), and Mending (*Tikkun*). I would like to introduce the meaning of each phase and also to challenge this accepted scholarly formula. As discussed in the previous chapters, the question of how the world came into being became a central problem in the Kabbalah of Provence and Gerona. But the Provencal and Geronese Kabbalists concentrated on the theme of creation principally through the mystical interpretation of *Ein-Sof* emanating the *Sefirot*. This process of creation can be defined as the progressive revelation of *Ein-Sof*, emanating Its lights from the highest stage to the lowest stage until the lights "thicken" and reach our earthly world. In Lurianic Kabbalah, however, the notion of creation is much more complex. Before the beginning of creation, *Ein-Sof* was everything that was and everything that "was not." In order for something other than *Ein-Sof* to come into being, *Ein-Sof* had to withdraw into Itself, i.e. to retreat within the depth of Its hidden divinity, in order to create an empty space into which creation could be brought forth. This shift of *Ein-Sof* from Infinity into withdrawal describes the first cosmogonial act of *Ein-Sof*, an act known in Lurianic Kabbalah as *Tzimtzoom*.

The following is the classic passage on *Tzimtzoom* from Hayyim Vital's Lurianic Kabbalah, *Etz Hayyim*:

> Know, that before the emanations were emanated there was a simple higher light [*Or Elyon Pashut*] that filled all of existence, and there was no empty space whatsoever ... but all was filled with the simple light of *Ein-Sof*. *Ein-Sof* did not include any form of finitude but everything in It was one simple light ... And when [an awakening] in Its simple will arose to create worlds and emanate emanations in order to realize Its perfect actions, Its names and Its attributes, for this was the reason for the creation of the worlds, [*Ein-Sof*] contracted [*tzimtzem*] Itself in the middle point of Itself, and withdrew [*tzimtzem*] that light, removing it from every direction toward the center point.
>
> And then remained an empty space ... The Tzimtzoom was concentrated around that central point so that the space left empty was completely circular .... Ein-Sof withdrew Itself [*tzimtzem atzmo*] in a completely circular shape ...
>
> Thereafter the *Tzimtzoom* emerged a single light ... that came down into the empty space ... there remained a place in which there could emerge what would subsequently be emanated, and into that space

[*Ein-Sof*] emanated, formed, created and made all the worlds. Before the emergence of these four worlds [Emanation, Formation, Creation, and Making] *Ein-Sof* was One and His name was One [*Ehad u-Shemo Ehad*] in a marvelous, hidden unity of a kind beyond the comprehension even of those angels nearest to It. For there is no created mind which can comprehend It, since It has neither place nor limit nor name.[4]

Among the many significant implications of the act of *Tzimtzoom*, I would like to emphasize the following three points. First, *Tzimtzoom* in Lurianic Kabbalah means that *Ein-Sof* moves from one position to another. According to Mach's Principle,[5] "every body's inertial mass depends on the mass of every other body in the universe." When the inertia of one body is changed, all other bodies change along with it. And thus, metaphorically speaking, as in Mach's Principle, when God's "inertial mass" changes in the act of *Tzimtzoom*, space is created for other bodies and the world comes to be. However, the created world in *actuality* is what was the created world in *potentiality* since the newly created world is merely a new Divine form; it is not God's change of essence but rather His *metamorphosis*. Second, *Tzimtzoom* means that *Ein-Sof* "exiles" Itself into Its contracted "limited" Self, leaving behind It Its authentic "unlimited" Self, for the sake of creation. In other words, *Ein-Sof* gives up a part of Its wholeness in order to enable the creation. The act of *Tzimtzoom* epitomizes, therefore, God's morality; for God "sacrifices" His primordial wholeness for the sake of the creation of the world and its creatures. This is unquestionably an ethical Godly act that attests to His Divine benevolence. And finally, since *Tzimtzoom* is a creative act of *Ein-Sof*, it should be emphasized that this act is a "negative" act rather than a "positive" one, for *Ein-Sof* does not begin Its process of creation by "giving" something, but rather by taking something away. Its withdrawal surely signifies some sort of internal separation or even some sort of self-diminishment. Furthermore, the process of *Tzimtzoom* in Lurianic Kabbalah is not a linear one. It is a process that demonstrates at each stage the need for both contraction and expansion, a force of limitation and a force of emanation, since without limitation everything would immediately revert to *Ein-Sof*, and without emanation nothing would come into being. Thus, retreat and propagation are the dialectical basis of the first phase called *Tzimtzoom*.

The act of *Tzimtzoom* enables a space for the worlds to come into being, and after the *Tzimtzoom Ein-Sof* can send Its lights and begin to shape the creation. *Ein-Sof* emanates the *Sefirot*, pouring and sculpting them into limited shapes or "vessels," ten in number, from *Keter* to *Malkhut*, and they yearn to absorb the Divine light into themselves. Now *Ein-Sof* does not remain in Its contracted state but performs Its expansion. But here Lurianic Kabbalah takes a very different course from the early Kabbalah: here, when the Divine light of *Ein-Sof* enter the "vessels" in order to take a form appropriate to their function in creation, an unexpected event occurs. The vessels cannot contain the powerful energy of the Godly light, and they break. This is the second phase in Lurianic Kabbalah, which the Ari calls *Shevirah* or *Shevirat ha-Kellim* ("breaking of the vessels"). What is the consequence of these shattered vessels? The Divine light is dispersed. Some of it returns to Its source in *Ein-Sof*, and the rest of the light – called *Nitzotzot* ("sparks") – falls downward and becomes imprisoned in the material world. There is no doubt that the myth of the "breaking of the vessels" introduces a catastrophic aspect into the process of creation. If God's *Tzimtzoom* could be explained as God's "exile" into Himself, all the more does the myth of *Shevirat ha-Kellim* explain the placement of the entire reality in exile, imprisoned by the forces of evil. After the "breaking of the vessels," everything is damaged and ruined, nothing is in its proper place, neither in the world above nor in the world below. The picture of the broken world is a morbid symbol for the total ruin of all; it is a somber myth about the descent and the downfall of a spiritual world that falls into the material abyss. It is the myth of annihilation and pain; the myth of cosmogonial crisis and of cosmological failure; it symbolizes the exile of the Jewish people, the exile of the physical cosmos, and the exile of the Divine Presence, known in Hebrew as *Galut ha-Shekhinah*.

Now that the broken "sparks" fell into the abyss of the forces of evil and impurity and are imprisoned in the realm of darkness, which the Lurianic Kabbalists call *Qelipah* ("shell"), they yearn to be redeemed and they cry to be mended. Here the destiny of the people of Israel enters into the cosmological events of history. For the people of Israel are called to fulfill the cosmological task of repairing the broken worlds. The predicament of the people of Israel is thus inherent in the process of the world's creation, and it is in Israel's power to repair the cosmological flaw. Their destiny, says the Ari, is to liberate the imprisoned "sparks" and uplift them back into the Divine realm, to redeem the *Shekhinah* from exile, and restore the damage caused in the creation. But how would the people of Israel restore the broken world? At this precise point the Ari's answer merges Kabbalah with ethics. For his answer is *the people of Israel restore the broken worlds through Torah and Mitzvot*. Every commandment in the Torah includes *ab initio* the secret remedy for the broken worlds. Each and every Jew is obligated to adhere to the word of God in the Torah, not just for self-recovery but mainly for the total redemption of the worlds above and below. For it is in the hands of the people of Israel to bring about the end of suffering; and it may be that the time for the very last deed required for this redemption is right now. Therefore, every deed counts, until the moment arrives and the Messiah stands at the gates of Jerusalem. This is indeed, a powerful eschatological message that puts a tremendous responsibility in the hands of every individual of the people of Israel. It is the third phase in Lurianic Kabbalah that the Kabbalists call *Tikkun* ("mending").

This discussion raises serious questions with regard to God's omnipotence and intent, even more profound ones than the questions that we asked above when we discussed *Sefer Ha-Yashar*. What is God's initial intent in creation, according to the Ari and his Kabbalistic school? Is the process of the breaking of the vessels, i.e. the process responsible for the catastrophe in creation, included *ab initio* in God's Will, or is it entirely antithetical to God's intent in creation? Is it possible for the character of the creation to be contrary to the original intent of the omnipotent God? Does God intend the world to break so that His people would enter into partnership with Him by restoring it? Is this the destiny and *telos* of the Chosen People? These questions have occupied the minds of the most prominent Kabbalists and Hasidic masters over the last four centuries. These are the focal theological problems of religious Jewish life both in post-Lurianic Kabbalah and in the mystical literature of Hasidism. In fact, these religious problems are very much alive among the hundreds of thousands of Hasidic and Orthodox Jews living today.

One of the superb scholarly works ever written on Lurianic Kabbalah is Professor Isaiah Tishby's, *The Concept of Evil and Qelipah in the Kabbalah of the Ari*.[6] Tishby's scholarly work not only deals with the concept of creation in Lurianic Kabbalah, but it also reveals the crucial Lurianic solutions to the problem of the existence of evil. Tishby concludes that there is more than one way in which the myth of the breaking of the vessels was interpreted by post-Lurianic Kabbalists. Of special interest is the interpretation of the Catharsis myth. According to this explanation, the intent in the creation was to purify God from the impurity of evil, i.e. to root evil out of *Ein-Sof*, and then to cast evil away from the essence of divinity and expel it down into the darkened dungeon where it belongs. Ramchal, the important eighteenth-century post-Lurianic Kabbalist, teaches in his Kabbalah that the act of *Tzimtzoom* in God was not a one-time event, since there were many *Tzimtzoomim*; each one uncovering more of the *Qelipah* than the previous one in order to purify God's divinity and separating It from the powers of evil. Thus, the creation was aimed at sanctifying and cleansing *Ein-Sof*, and the process of the breaking of the vessels had existed *ab initio* in God's intent. Why, then, would evil be uncovered in the process of *Tzimtzoom?* According to another post-Lurianic Kabbalist, Emanuel Chai-Riqqi, the root of evil exists as the putrid element in reality and is a necessary byproduct of every existence that is outside the realm of the Divine life of *Ein-Sof*. Every *Tzimtzoom*, therefore, in itself is evil, because *Ein-Sof* contracts Itself into an "exiled" world, and thus enables evil to rise up. But without *Tzimtzoom* there would be no existence at all except for the existence of God, and, therefore, there could be no existence outside the realm of God without evil.

On one hand, there are two possible ways to look at the initial existence of evil in Lurianic Kabbalah: either that evil was in *Ein-Sof* before the *Tzimtzoom*, or that evil is created after the *Tzimtzoom* as its byproduct. In both cases evil could not have been prevented. On the other hand, if *Ein-Sof* had not initiated the *Tzimtzoom*, evil would not have been uncovered and the world would not have come into being. Furthermore, had *Ein-Sof* not initiated the *Tzimtzoom*, *Ein-Sof* would not have cleansed Itself and could not be separated from evil. Thus, God initiates the *Tzimtzoom*, uncovers evil, emanates His lights, permits the vessels to break, drives evil down, creates the people of Israel, gives them the Torah, guides them to *Tikkun*, and then, when the people of Israel adhere to the word of the Torah, He brings the Messiah and erases evil forever. This is the eschatological agenda in the mind of God according to Lurianic Kabbalah.

When dealing with God's intent during creation in Lurianic Kabbalah, there are central passages from the teachings of the Ari that exemplify the Lurianic theory of creation. The following text is the primary passage about God's intent in creation as formulated in *Sefer Etz Hayyim*:

> In regard to the intent and the goal of the creation of the world we shall now explain ... that which the first and the last sages investigated in order to know what was the reason for the creation of the worlds. What inner cause was intended? And they determined, confirmed, and decided [*nimmnu, ve-gammru, ve-gazzru*] that the reason was because He, Blessed Be He, *must be complete in all His actions and powers and names of greatness and exaltedness and honor: And had He not made and actualized His actions and powers, it would be as if* [*ke-vayachol*] *He could not be called complete, not in His action nor in His names and not {in His} attributes.*
>
> For the Great Name that is of four letters YHVH [*HaVaYaH*] is called so because of His eternal existence [*HaVaYaHto*] and His everlasting life: [*HaVaYaH*] was, is, and will be, [*Haya, Hoveh*, and *Yihe'yeh*]; before the creation, and at the time of creation, and after He transposed to what He became. *And if the worlds and everything in them had not been created, His true guiding existence could not be seen,* [i.e.] the Eternal One in the past, and [the Eternal One] in the present, and [the Eternal One in the] future: and He could not be called by the name YHVH ... Hence, the attribute Mastership [*ADNut*] is called so because a Master has slaves and He is a Master [*ADoN*] of them, *and if He did not have creatures, He could not be called a Master .... Only when the worlds are created, His actions and powers, Blessed Be He, come into actuality and He is called complete* ....[7]

This conclusion in *Sefer Etz Hayyim* summarizes centuries of investigations of "the first and the last sages" of Jewish wisdom regarding the question of the intent of God in creation. The *Sefer Etz Hayyim* of sixteenth-century Safed arrives at the same conclusion that is found in the thirteenth-century *Sefer Ha-Yashar*, in the teachings of the *Zohar*, and in many other classics of Jewish spirituality, claiming that the creation of the world is intended to complete God's name, to enable Him to become *Adon,* and allow Him to bring forth His actions and powers. The intent behind the creation, according to the Ari, permits, authorizes, and validates God as He gives birth to the depth of His hidden Self, and thus becomes recognized by the world and Self-recognized by His Divine *Sefirot*.

Scholars of Jewish mysticism have emphasized that *Tzimtzoom, Shevirah,* and

CREATION AND *IMITATIO DEI*

Tikkun maintain the three major components in the Lurianic formula of creation.[8] I would like to suggest an additional component to this formula, an essential missing piece that when put together with these three components reflects a more accurate and comprehensive description of Lurianic Kabbalah. I call this missing part *Hitore'rut*, "Awakening," and I place it as the first component in Lurianic Kabbalah, even before the *Tzimtzoom*. Why *Hitore'rut* and what is it in the context of Lurianic creation? *Hitore'rut* is the first theogonial phase that causes God to "wake up" from His world of *Ayin*. It is the Genesis of every genesis; the theogonial state that none of the Kabbalists describes, not even in esoteric language. It is the state that pre-existed everything in the mind of God, even the *Tzimtzoom*, i.e. the state that causes the commencement of the Godly shift from the *Ayin* to the *Yesh*. Whereas *Hitore'rut* is the *cause* in Lurianic Kabbalah, *Tzimtzoom* is the *effect*. And thus, *Tzimtzoom* is not the first act in Lurianism but the second one. *Hitore'rut* is usually described in Lurianic Kabbalah in the simple Hebrew words *ke-she-alla bi-re'tzono*, meaning literally "when His Will emerged." The Kabbalists, however, are never explicit about the reason for that emergence which arose in God's Will. It seems that the only explanation which makes sense in this repeated formula is that *Hitore'rut* is the inception of God's yearning to become the Creator, because God *must be complete in all His actions and powers and names of greatness and exaltedness and honor*, as explicitly stated by the Ari.

Since the *Hitore'rut* arises in God, we may conclude that the entire journey of creation in Lurianic Kabbalah is a psychological one. It is the one and only kind of "Awakening" by which God "rises up" and develops an awareness, desire, and urgency to create and to be created. It is the necessity to grow and mature, to be born and to give birth, to acknowledge and to be acknowledged. This process unavoidably invites opposing forces and crisis, and at the same time it invites the need for *Tikkun*. In other words, *Hitore'rut* is the component that establishes both the "Awakening" of God and His departure from Oneness. Lurianic Kabbalah should be perceived, therefore, as the best example in the history of Jewish spirituality of illustrating a religious eschatology that emphasizes a psychological yearning to return to the Oneness that God has left when He "awakened." It should be perceived as the esoteric Jewish school of thought, which confirms that the deepest meaning of our lives is to be found in the journey whose beginning is in the end and whose end is in the beginning, for all existing things yearn for *Tikkun*; for all things walk toward the future until they arrive at their pristine point in the past.

Thus, in Lurianic Kabbalah there are *four* rather than three major phases in the creation myth:

1   *Hitore'rut*, which is the first theogonial phase, dealing with the rise of awareness in God's mind, the birth of His consciousness, and the initiation of His *intent* in creation.
2   *Tzimtzoom*, the first cosmogonial phase, which transforms God's awakening

and intention into His first Godly act of withdrawal.
3   *Shevirah*, the first cosmological phase, which illustrates the crisis of the hyper reality in God's heavenly world and the crisis of the lower reality of man's earthly world, i.e. the crisis of the "broken vessels." And,
4   *Tikkun*, the first eschatological phase, which brings back God and humanity together, striving toward mending and redemption.

However, these four phases of the Lurianic creation myth do not constitute a straight line, but rather a circular sequence of events, an eternal recurrence. For every *Hitore'rut* necessarily leads to an act of *Tzimtzoom*, which necessarily leads to *Shevirah*, which necessarily leads to *Tikkun*, which causes another *Hitore'rut*. Therefore, each of the four phases of the Lurianic creation myth necessarily creates a sequence of circular events that involves all the other three phases. This circular pattern means that the creative act and the creation itself are continual, permanent, ongoing, and eternal. For at every given moment, man, like God, creates and destroys, as implied by Rabbi Abbahu in the Midrash: "The Holy One blessed be He, creates worlds and destroys them."[9] This Midrash significantly inspired the teachings of the Kabbalists. In one of these Kabbalistic texts, *Masekhet Atzilut* (*The Tractate of Emanation*), a composition that was written long before the rise of Lurianic Kabbalah in thirteen-century Catalonia, we find the idea that "The Holy One, blessed be He, initially created worlds and destroyed them, [created] trees and uprooted them, since they were hasty and envious of one another."[10] The text goes so far as to claim that each "tree" (or world) that was created by God desired to rule over all other trees, "to draw all the moisture from the soil, so that all of them thereby become dried out." Hence, God caused all of them to dry and die: "And the Holy one blessed be He removed His light from them, and they became darkness in which the wicked would be punished."[11]

These Kabbalistic perceptions raise serious difficulties. Why does God create and destroy? How is it possible that the somber act of destruction would emerge from the same God whose definitive skill is in being the Creator? Kabbalah's answer to these questions is dialectical and mysterious. The Law of Creation, the Kabbalists claim, requires that everything hidden in the concealed life of God comes into complete fruition. God yearns to create and reveal His hidden life, since revelation and creativity are inherent in His Divine "Nature." However, in every active process dwells an internal struggle between two opposing forces: one force desires to be revealed, whereas the other strives to remain concealed. These two forces were described by the Kabbalists in different mystical and psychological patterns and terminology. In the Sabbatean Kabbalah of the seventeenth century, Nathan of Gaza calls the first force *Or she-Yesh Bo Makhashavah* ("a light that contains thought') and the second force *Or she-Ain Bo Makhashavah* ("a light that does not contain thought").[12] Both forces are concealed in the essence of *Ein-Sof* before the *Tzimtzoom*. The act of *Tzimtzoom* is aimed in advance at bringing forth all forces from God's innermost hidden

CREATION AND *IMITATIO DEI*

self. These forces are the true essence of God's infinity; however, one of them – "the light that does not contain thought" – is a rebellious and a resentful force. Whereas "the light that contains thought" desires to be revealed, "the light that does not contain thought" desires to remain concealed. As a result, the process of *Tzimtzoom* sparks a struggle between *Or she-Yesh Bo Makhashavah* and *Or she-Ain Bo Makhashavah*; a struggle that purifies God by cleansing Him from all impurities. And, therefore, Creation itself and every act of creation is a dialectical act of purification. It is the refinement of *Ein-Sof* in the world above, and the refinement of humanity in the world below. The conclusion of this internal conflict in the mind of God results with a creation that is both a struggle and an integration between two opposing forces, between consciousness and unconsciousness, between awareness and unawareness, between the part that desires to see the light and the counterpart that desires to remain in darkness. In Kabbalah, creation is always the culmination of the struggle between "the thing and its opposite," but at the same time it is the integration between "the thing and its opposite." These opposites constitute God's "unconscious-conscious" mind, which is the dialectical root and the synthesis of being and non-being, of creation and destruction, and of good and evil. Although creation is the oasis of duality, it is also striving for harmony and unity; for everything yearns to arrive at the sanctuary of integration in order to become One again.

The creation myth in Hasidism

The beginning of Hasidism as a religious movement marks a new phase in the history of Jewish spirituality, particularly because of Hasidism's new social and historical structure. But again, since this book does not focus on the history of Kabbalah or Hasidism, I shall not attempt to describe the development of Hasidism in Judaism, nor shall I attempt to describe the leading masters (*Tzaddikim*) of Hasidism and their powerful works. Instead, I shall discuss some Hasidic ideas dealing specifically with creation.

But first I would like to identify with scholars who hold the following general position on the relationship of Hasidism to Kabbalah; that is, that Hasidism *is* an essential part of Kabbalah.[13] It is the latest developed phase of Kabbalistic ideas that were crystallized and absorbed into the complex "new world" of Judaism in east Europe during the last three centuries. Ever since Hasidism was established by its father and founder, Rabbi Israel Ba'al Shem Tov, known as the Besht, during the first half of the eighteenth century, it has flourished and changed. It became controversial and even gained an opposition, known in Hebrew as *Mitnagdim*. But despite the many different interpretations that Hasidism has given to Kabbalistic ideas, it has always been faithful to the fundamentals of Kabbalah, in particular to the Kabbalah of the *Zohar* and the Kabbalah of the Ari. Therefore, as we stand at the gate of the teachings of Hasidism, we must bear in mind that most of the ideas that we have discussed earlier in the classic texts of Kabbalah on creation have been internalized into the Hasidic world and accepted with reverence.

The focal Kabbalistic perception that views God and His creation, above and below, as having two opposing aspects also stands at the heart of Hasidism. In fact, the perception of duality in regard to every being and meaning is the pulse of the Hasidic heart. It can be seen metaphorically as the zigzag line of an electrocardiogram, a line with dual directions, ascending and descending, engraving every aspect of existence with a dual reality. The dual elements in the Kabbalistic classic formulae, *Ratzo va-Shov* ("ran and return"), *Yesh* and *Ayin* ("being and nothingness"), *Hitpashtut* and *Tzimtzoom* ("expansion and contraction"), *Ribbuy* and *Akh'dut* ("plurality and singularity"), are but a few examples of this main Kabbalistic principle that was absorbed into Hasidism with great enthusiasm. This dialectic perception of life is not limited in the Hasidic world to mystical speculation. Since it has been adopted by the *Tzaddikim*, the "Hasidic Rebbes," it has become a way of life for every simple *hasid*. For the *hasid* this duality means that his life is not linear, for life is real only when a thing and its opposite exist side by side: life is built of "ups and downs," mountains and valleys, successes and failures, health and sickness, good and bad. And if, God forbid, life becomes like the straight, linear line of an electrocardiogram, it would mean death.

In the philosophy of the sixteenth-century mystic the Maharal of Prague, a prolific Jewish mystic whose ideas heavily influenced Hasidism, we find the ideology of the duality of existence in reference to the central question of the exile. The Maharal perceives the *Galut* (exile) of the people of Israel as the "best" reassurance for their *Geu'llah* (redemption), since "the good thing is known [only] from its opposite … [and since] the exile is but a temporary change from God's arrangement … there is no doubt that the exile is the clear proof for [the coming] of the redemption."[14]

In Hasidism we find again that the purpose of the creation is for the Diety to achieve His Divine intent of full actualization, similar to what was described previously (pp. 26–31) in the texts of the classic Kabbalists. Rabbi Schneur Zalman of Liadi, the founder of Habad Hasidism writes in his *Tanya*:

> It is known to all that the purpose of the creation of the world is for the sake of the revelation of His kingdom, may He be blessed, for "There is no king without a nation" …., Only "In a multitude of people is the glory of the king," [as said in Proverbs 14:28].[15]

This passage teaches that Rabbi Schneur Zalman, one of the major speakers of Hasidism, accepts the classic Kabbalistic perception of God creating the worlds in order to be revealed as the King of the Universe. The prominent Hasidic masters also accept the three phases of Lurianic Kabbalah in creation: *Tzimtzoom*, *Shevirah*, and *Tikkun*. They agree with the concept of *Hitore'rut* as mentioned above (see p. 47) despite the fact that they do not use this term. However, these Hasidic Rebbes add a significant layer of human psychology to Kabbalah: whereas the notion of *Hitore'rut* in Kabbalah emphasizes that awakening is the first theogonial phase dealing with the rise of the awareness in *God's* mind, in Hasidism the awakening emphasizes the human condition required from every *hasid* who is determined to imitate his Creator. Awakening in Hasidism signifies not just the awareness in God's mind, but the awareness in man's mind; not just the birth of God's consciousness, but in particular the birth of man's consciousness. But how is the perception of the awakening shifted from God to man? The *hasid* participates in the process of the mending of the broken worlds. He studies the Torah, fulfills its commandments, and participates in good deeds. But he is also required to walk in the ways of God and imitate His *Hitore'rut* and *Tzimtzoom*. Unlike the Lurianic Kabbalist, the *hasid* not only participates in the work of the *Tikkun*, but also identifies with the awakened mind of God, who discovers at the original point of His Awakening the dual meaning of existence. For what does Awakening mean? Awakening *generates duality*. It means that in every creation there is an immediate shift from singularity to plurality. It means that at the very moment that the desire to create arises, the breaking of the one into the two arises with it. The *hasid* identifies not only with the broken creation that he is committed to repair, but also with the Creator, who rises up from singularity to plurality, from pre-thought to thought, from pre-will to will, from pre-intent to intent, from expansion to contraction; and from *Ayin* to *Yesh*. God's shift from singularity to plurality does not mean for the *hasid* that God, the One, becomes many: it means for him that God's Oneness expands into the various aspects of the *Sefirot*. For if God would duplicate Himself from His Oneness to another identical Oneness, the world would not come to be. Thus, *Ein-Sof* emanates the *Sefirah* of *Keter*, which immediately emanates the sefirotical couples: *Hokhmah* and *Binah*, *Hesed* and *Deen*, *Netzakh* and *Hod*, *Tife'ret* and *Malkhut*.[16]

However, the path that God engraved in creation which headed *forward* is repeated by the *hasid* who paves his path *backward*; whereas God shifted from the *Ayin* to the *Yesh*, the *hasid* shifts from the *Yesh* back to the *Ayin*. In Habad Hasidism, the purpose of the descent of the Divine emanation to the world is identical to the purpose of the descent of the Divine soul into the body of the *hasid*. Both cases represent the manifestation of *Ein-Sof* in the lower realm. Both the world and the *hasid* are created to absorb this Divine manifestation. But there is a difference of essence between the world and the *hasid*: whereas the world cannot and does not recognize the Divine, the *hasid* recognizes the Divine with all his soul and might. When he comprehends the Divine nature of his soul, he begins to discover the duality and opposites in his nature. This is the *hasid*'s *Hitore'rut*. Now he arrives at the recognition of his duality of being, which guides him toward his actualization. Now he shifts from singularity to plurality and gains Wisdom, Understanding, and Discernment (*Hokhmah*, *Binah*, and *Da'at* = *HaBaD*). Now he discovers that there are two major tasks that remain incomplete after the creation. First, God did not complete the creation of the world as He intended it, for the Divine light shattered the vessels; and, second, God did not culminate His own completion since the incomplete creation did not enable Him to fulfill His own actualization. The task of the *hasid* is, therefore, twofold: to complete the unfulfilled world and to complete the "unfulfilled" God. Furthermore, the *hasid* remembers that although God in creation "walked forward," he is required to "walk backward"; a walk which Habad Hasidism defines as "reversal." The *hasid* who is in search of his discovery finds out that his spiritual entity, i.e. his soul, belongs to a higher realm, and he strives to return it to its source. His process of completion is, therefore, a "return" to his pristine core, and only by returning to his core can he redeem himself and repair the unfulfilled world above and below.

In a recent work on Habad Hasidism, one scholar properly concludes that the initial purpose of the creation of the world according to Habad is interpreted as "a stage toward achieving the Divine goal of the full actualization of all its manifestations through its reversal."[17] Here, the main belief is that God did not complete the realization of His intention in creation, but instead left the task of completing the world in man's hands. The *hasid's* participation in the *Tikkun* is based first and foremost on "awareness of the double meaning of reality." He unfolds the Divine essence in his own soul and gradually recognizes its ontological dual reality.

Hasidism accepts without any hesitation the Lurianic principles in the process of the creation. But one should not infer from this statement that the major phases of Lurianism in creation were absorbed in Hasidism without a new flavor. Hasidism has expanded, for example, the original concept of *Tzimtzoom* and suggested that there is not only one *tzimtzoom* in the creation but many *tzimtzoomim*. The Maggid Dov Baer of Mazheritch writes in his *Maggid Devarav le-Ya'akov*:

> That the brightness [of the light] of God, the world cannot endure, therefore He does a *few tzimtzoommim* so that they are able to endure Him.[18]

Even more important in this context is the question of "nominalism versus realism." Is the content of the Lurianic phases of creation, as described by the Hasidic masters, a symbolic content (nominalism) or a literal one (realism)? Has this content been perceived by the Hasidic masters as an epistemological phenomenon, i.e. a human description that does not abide God's true involvement in the process of creation, or has it been perceived as an ontological occurrence, i.e. something real that occurs in the Godhead? According to central texts in Hasidism, the Ari and his school of Kabbalah are correct in describing the process of creation as their classic phases of creation: *Tzimtzoom*, *Shevirah*, and *Tikkun*. However, it would be a severe error, claims one of the Hasidic Rebbes, to understand the Lurianic principles literally. Rabbi Schneur Zalman of Liadi writes the following on the concept of Lurianic *Tzimtzoom*:

CREATION AND *IMITATIO DEI*

> It is possible to comprehend the mistakes of some people who are scholars in their own eyes, may God forgive them, who erred and were confused in their study of the writing of the Ari, of blessed memory, and understood the concept of *Tzimtzoom* ... literally ... it is impossible to interpret the concept of *Tzimtzoom* literally, [for then it] is a phenomenon of corporeality.[19]

But if the Lurianic conception of creation is accepted by Hasidism epistemologically but not literally, then what is its value? If *Tzimtzoom* is an epistemological perception of man, and it did not occur literally during the process of creation, then how does it reflect the religious life and the beliefs of the *hasid*? Here we are confronted with one of the central problems of Hasidism, a problem not associated merely with the Hasidic perception of the relationship between God and cosmology, but also with the Hasidic perception of the *Tzaddik*, the spiritual and religious leader of the Hasidic circle. In Habad Hasidism, as in other circles of Hasidism, the perception of God is purely pantheistic. This means that the Divine essence is immanent and existent everywhere in the world. But the immanence of God "everywhere in the world" suggests an even more far-reaching conclusion: since God is "everywhere," the world itself has no reality, it is *Acosmic*. The only entity that does have a true reality is that of God Himself, whereas all other existence is an illusion devoid of substance. Thus, Rabbi Schneur Zalman of Liadi declares that "even the most sublime worlds are esteemed as truly *naught* before Him [*ke-la mamash hashive'y kame'y*]."[20] This conception establishes two important Hasidic beliefs: (a) God is the only ontological reality, and (b) the world is a veil of illusion, a "non-materialistic" entity.[21] The immediate implication stemming from these beliefs is that Hasidism sets its ideology on the platform of an illusory nature of existence that is based on man's mind and imagination. The reality of God and the reality of the cosmos does not dwell in an external, independent sphere of wisdom, but rather in the mind of the *hasid*. The process of creation in Lurianic Kabbalah is thus transposed into a psycho-mythical understanding in the spiritual life of the *hasid*. The fundamentals of Hasidism are based, therefore, on human perceptions; that is, on an epistemological and psychological foundation. It is not only God who "wakes up" and creates, the *Tzaddik* too "wakes up" and creates; it is not only God who performs *Tzimtzoom*, the *Tzaddik* too performs *Tzimtzoom*, a concept that is known in Hasidism as *Katnut* ("smallness") and *Gadlut* ("greatness"). On the *Tzimtzoom* of the *Tzaddik*, Rabbi Nachman of Bratslav writes:

> When the *Tzaddik* speaks to the wicked, he raises his mind and unites with God, and then he also raises the [wicked people's] minds, from wherever they are, and unites them with God. The True *Tzaddik* brings sinners to repentance as he "diminishes [*metzamtzem*] his mind," and by speaking to them with great wisdom.[22]

The *Tzaddik* is to the sinner, then, as *Ein-Sof* is to creation. Both participate in the act of *Tzimtzoom* and thus diminish themselves to permit others to be and become. Because the *Tzaddik* imitates His Creator and performs Godly acts, Hasidism opens itself up to the psychologization of Kabbalah. Thus, it is not surprising that we find in Hasidism a strong tendency toward magic and ecstasy, which are strictly psychological phenomena. In central texts of Hasidism we find that the *Tzaddik* is described as a "magician" who is able to cleave to God in a mystical union and afterward bring down spiritual forces. He receives an influx of Divine light from the upper worlds and then becomes "the vessel" who collects these spiritual forces. Rabbi Ya'akov Yosef of Polnoy describes the *Tzaddik* as the "vessel" of the *Shekhinah*, the Divine Presence, presenting the *Zohar* as the proof text for this theory:

> The *Tzaddik* is called a vessel of the *Shekhinah*, as it is written in the *Zohar* that "they [the people of Israel] are His [God's] broken vessels [*Ma'anin Tevirrin*]."[23]

These examples demonstrate how Hasidism reconstructed the main Kabbalistic principles. The ultimate meaning of Lurianic Kabbalah was somewhat elusive for the orthodox Hasidic Kabbalists, and thus the principles of Kabbalah and in particular of Lurianic Kabbalah were reorganized, and, even more importantly, psychologized in Hasidism.[24] But here we must return to our discussion on creation. As we have seen, the main belief that the early Kabbalists and the Lurianic Kabbalists share in reference to the purpose of the creation of the world is that the world was created first and foremost for the completion of God Himself, for His recognition by His *Sefirot*, and for the sake of the glorification that He receives from His people. The strong tendency of Hasidism to psychologize the principles of Kabbalah only strengthens this Kabbalistic belief, and it places the concept of the completion of God in creation at the core of Hasidism.[25] This belief can be found in the Hasidic teachings of the focal masters of Hasidism; such as in the teachings of Rabbi Schneur Zalman of Liadi and the Maggid, Rabbi Dov Baer of Mazheritch. In *Likutei Moharan* of Rabbi Nachman of Bratslav we find the following Hasidic saying:

> The *Tzaddik* always seeks and searches to reveal the will of God, because God's will is immanent in everything. This is true of the creation, because God wanted to create the whole world. There is an essence of God's will in every detail of the creation, since God wanted it to be exactly the way it is; in this specific depiction, power, and nature .... For the whole world is created for the people of Israel, as it is said (Genesis 1:1) "*Be'Reshit*" ["In the Beginning,"]; for Israel is called "*Reshit*" [beginning], because Israel emerged in [God's] thought first, so that God, blessed be He, envisioned the glorification He would receive from Israel, as it is said (Isaiah 49:4) "Israel of whom I will be

glorified" …. Thus for this reason He created the entire world, *only for the glorification that He will be glorified in Israel*.[26]

These words of Rabbi Nachman are among the many examples in the texts of Hasidism which sustain the Kabbalistic belief that the idea of the creation of the world is inseparable from God's intent to be actualized and recognized. However, in Hasidism, God's intent to be actualized and recognized is a continual process, since "He, in His goodness, renews *every day* the works of Creation," as is said in the morning prayer. Thus, Rabbi Levi Yitzkhak of Berdichev teaches us that the world is created anew *ad infinitum*:

> The Creator, blessed be He, created everything and He is in everything. His abundance never ceases, for every moment He sends His abundance to all His creatures and to all the worlds … This is why we say "He makes light and creates darkness" … in the present tense, *for He creates continually*, giving life to every living being, and He is the source of all.[27]

The Jewish way of imitating God

The strong Hasidic tendency to perceive Kabbalah and the religious life as the domain of man's mind, as we have seen, creates a powerful foundation for relating human psychology to Jewish spirituality. This tendency, however, has its roots in earlier Jewish spiritual teachings: in the Mishnah, the Talmud, in the ancient Midrash, in the classic books of Jewish philosophy, and even in the Torah.

The most prominent psychological pattern that we find in all of these Jewish texts is that of *Imitatio Dei*, the imitation of God. The psycho-religious notion of *Imitatio Dei* is a basic belief in Judaism since the Jewish faith is founded on the paradoxical notion that we are destined to be like God. "The fundamental reason for the creation of man," claims one of the major Hasidic books, "is that he is to make himself as much like his Creator as he can."[28] The book further cites Rabbi Hizkiah, the son of Rabbi Hiyya, who said in the Midrash: "Happy are the pious prophets who liken what is formed to He who forms, and what is planted to He who plants,"[29] and interprets it in the following way:

> They make themselves like their Creator by unifying all their limbs to resemble His unity, and driving all parts of evil out of themselves that they may be perfect with the Lord … That is why God said (Genesis 1;26) "Let us make man in our image and after our likeness" – out of His love for man He created him in His own image, so that man should be able to make himself like his Creator.[30]

When Maimonides composed his *Laws Concerning Character Traits*, he included eleven major commandments for the Jewish people, and he placed "the imitation of God" as the first and elevated commandment among them.

Maimonides writes:

> Laws concerning character traits, they include altogether eleven commandments ... *to imitate His ways*, to cleave to those who know Him, to love neighbors, to love converts, not to hate brothers, to rebuke, not to put anyone to shame, not to afflict the distressed, not to go about as a talebearer, not to take revenge, and not to bear a grudge.[31]

Further, Maimonides teaches:

> The prophets applied all these terms of God: slow to anger and abundant in loving-kindness, just and righteous, perfect, powerful, strong and the like. They did so to proclaim that these ways are good and right, and a man is obliged to train himself to follow them and to *imitate Him*, according to his strength.[32]

These words of Maimonides, placing the imitation of God on the top of the list of the Jewish commandments in the book of Jewish laws that has become "Second to the Torah" (*Mishneh Torah*) have established the religious tradition of *Imitatio Dei* as the chief *Mitzvah* in Judaism. This Jewish belief has its roots in earlier Jewish spiritual teachings. In fact, it occupied a position of great significance already in the Torah.

We read in Leviticus:

> Speak unto all the congregation of the children of Israel, and say unto them; Ye shall be holy, for I the Lord your God am holy.[33]

Later on, we learn in Deuteronomy that if the people of Israel fulfill the commandment of the imitation of God and "walk in His ways," love Him and cleave to Him, they shall inherit the Promised Land and become the greatest nation on earth:

> For if ye shall diligently keep all this commandment which I command you to do it, to love the Lord your God, *to walk in all His ways*, and to cleave unto Him, then will the Lord drive out all these nations from before you, and ye shall dispossess nations greater and mightier than yourselves: Every place whereon the sole of your foot shall tread shall be yours: from the river, the river Euphrates, even unto the hinder sea shall be your border: There shall no man be able to stand against you: the Lord your God shall lay the fear of you and the dread of you upon all the land that ye shall tread upon, as He hath spoken unto you.[34]

CREATION AND *IMITATIO DEI*

One of the ancient Rabbinic works, *Siphre*, interprets the commandment of the imitation of God ethically and literally: "Just as He is called 'Merciful' be thou merciful, just as He is called 'Compassionate' be thou compassionate."[35] Following this tradition, Rav Hama Bar Hanina presented in the Talmud the commandment of the imitation of God as a central paradox in Judaism:

> What is the meaning of the verse (Deut. 13:5) "Ye shall walk after the Lord your God?" Is it possible for a human being to walk after the *Shekhinah*; for has it not been said (Deut. 4:24) "For the Lord your God is a devouring fire?" But the verse means to walk after the attributes of the Holy One, blessed be He, as he clothes the naked, for it is written (Genesis, 3:2) "And the Lord God made for Adam and his wife coats of skin and clothed them," so do thou clothe the naked. The Holy one, blessed be He, visited the sick ... so do thou also visit the sick. The Holy One, blessed be He, comforted mourners ... so do thou comfort mourners. The Holy One, blessed be He, buried the dead ... so do thou also bury the dead.[36]

Similarly, we find that the second-century sage of the Mishnah Abba Shaul interprets the biblical song that Moses and all the people of Israel sang after they had passed through the sea: (Exodus 25:2) "This is my God and I will glorify Him" [*Zeh Eli ve-Anive-Hu*], to mean "This is my God and I will become like unto Him."[37] Rashi, the classic commentator on the Torah, provides a very beautiful interpretation of these words of Abba Shaul: "Abba Shaul resolved the word *ve-Anive-Hu* into its two components parts: *ani* [I], *veHu* [and Him], i.e. 'I will form myself after Him, I will cleave to His ways.'"[38]

In the history of Jewish philosophy the notion of *Imitatio Dei* occupies the thought of the principal Jewish thinkers. Maimonides determines in his *Guide for the Perplexed* that the Jewish historical event that exemplifies the way we are required to imitate God is when Moses asks God, "Show me now Thy ways, that I may know Thee." God answers Moses, "I will make all my goodness pass before thee."[39] But one must differentiate, says Maimonides, between two distinct attributes in God: His attributes of *essence* and His attributes of *actions*. His attributes of *essence* cannot be shown to a human being, not even to Moses; and thus God says to Moses, "Thou canst not see my face."[40] His attributes of actions are revealed to Moses, for, as Maimonides concludes, "the apprehension of these actions are the apprehension of His attributes ... with respect to which He is known ... what was made known to him were simply pure attributes of action: merciful and gracious, long-suffering ... [thus] the ways ... are the actions proceeding from God, may He be exalted."[41] Through this interpretation Maimonides solves the paradox of *Imitatio Dei*. To imitate God does not mean to become like Him, i.e. imitate His attributes of *essence*, but rather to walk in His ways and to follow His *actions* in the created world.

In Kabbalah and Hasidism, however, we find a very different interpretation of the *Mitzvah* of *Imitatio Dei*. After the *Tzimtzoom*, *Ein-Sof* begins to emanate the ten *Sefirot*, which manifest His revealed *Persona*, i.e. Its differentiated attributes. The ten *Sefirot* include the intrinsic qualities of the hidden *Ein-Sof*, whose Divine desire is to be imitated through Its *Sefirot*. Each and every *Sefirah* is a revealed aspect of the concealed substance of *Ein-Sof*, and, therefore, the imitation of the essence embodied in the *Sefirah*, is in itself the fulfillment of *Imitatio Dei*. Here we find an active chain of *Imitatio Dei*: the *Sefirot* imitate *Ein-Sof*, and man imitates the *Sefirot*. This is the main reason for the exhaustive search by every Kabbalist who strives to contemplate the esoteric knowledge, the "gnosis" that is mysteriously concealed behind each *Sefirah*. Once the Kabbalist begins to be enlightened by the secrets of the *Sefirot*, he aspires to imitate them and identify with them.

In the classic Kabbalistic composition *Tomer Devorah* (*The Palm Tree of Deborah*), the Kabbalist, Moses Cordovero of Safed teaches us how to imitate God:

> It behooves man to imitate His Creator, being like Him in both likeness and image in accordance with the secret of the Supernal Form. Because the foremost Supernal image and likeness is in actions, a human resemblance in bodily appearance only and not in actions degrades that Form. Of the man who resembles the Form in body alone it is said: "A handsome man whose deeds are ugly." For what value can there be in man's resemblance to the Supernal Form in bodily limbs if his actions have no resemblance to those of His Creator? As a result, it behooves man to imitate the acts of the Supernal Crown, which are the thirteen highest attributes of mercy implied in the following verse (Micah, 7:18–20):
>
> "Who is God like unto Thee, that beareth iniquity,
> And passeth by the transgression of the remnant of His heritage?
> He retaineth not His anger for ever,
> Because He delighteth in mercy.
> He will again have compassion upon us,
> He will subdue our iniquities:
> And Thou will cast all their sins into the depth of the sea.
> Thou will show faithfulness to Jacob,
> Mercy to Abraham.
> As Thou hast sworn unto our fathers from the days of old."
>
> Therefore it is appropriate that these thirteen attributes ... be found in man.[42]

Rabbi Moses Cordovero presents in *Tomer Devorah* a systematic connection between the ten Divine *Sefirot*, which are the attributes of God, and the ethical paths of the religious conduct that every person must fulfill. When one follows these norms, says Cordovero, one becomes identified with the ten emanations of *Ein-Sof*, and thus one becomes connected with *Ein-Sof* Itself. However, there is a special emphasis in Cordovero's system on the actions required from the person who wishes to imitate God: since God is the Lord of good deeds, every man should also perform good deeds. So we learn that the Kabbalistic *Mitzvah* of *Imitatio Dei* is not a theoretical *Mitzvah* but a practical one. Each chapter in *Tomer Devorah* specifies both the Kabbalistic theory and the practical deeds required for imitating a specific *Sefirah*, from the first one, *Keter*, to the last one, *Malkhut*. When Cordovero teaches, for example, how to imitate the fourth *Sefirah*, *Hesed*, he writes the following:

> How shall a man educate himself to acquire the *Sefirah* of *Hesed*? ... [by] loving God with perfect love ... for through the acts of Loving-kindness that man performs in the world below, he must have the intention of perfecting [also] the world above ... [this includes the following actions]: to carry out the *Mitzvah* of circumcision ... to visit the sick and to heal them ... to give charity to the poor ... to greet guests ... and give them a guest-house where they can rest ... to bring the bride under the marriage canopy ... [and], to create peace between man and his neighbor.[43]

This means that the Kabbalistic *Mitzvah* of *Imitatio Dei* requires the human being to develop a path of practical religious life in accordance with the sefirotical world of *Ein-Sof*. Through *Imitatio Dei*,[44] the religious behavior of man creates a direct linkage between the essence of the sefirotical world above and the nether world below. It is a process through which man copies the heavenly world, and, filled with the Divine flow, he becomes the micro-sefirotical world on earth. Cordovero's teachings were significant and influential, but the Kabbalistic concept of *Imitatio Dei* did not begin in Cordovero's time. We find this concept as early as the ecstatic schools of Kabbalah in thirteenth-century Spain. Rabbi Abraham Abulafia wrote extensively on the various techniques by which the Kabbalists, using combinations of the names of God, pronunciations, vocalizations, and meditations on the letters of the Hebrew alphabet, can capture the *Sefirot*. In his *Hasidism Between Ecstasy and Magic*, Moshe Idel presents prominent examples of these techniques.[45] When discussing selected texts from the ecstatic Kabbalah, Professor Idel examines the following words of Abulafia:

> Man can cleave to each and every *Sefirah* by [identifying] the essence of the influx expanding from its emanation on [to] the [rest of the] *Sefirot*, which are His attributes .... And it is necessary to concentrate [*le-hitboded*], [in order to attain] an apprehension, until the expert Kabbalist will attain from [the *Sefirot*] an influx of which he is aware.[46]

59

KABALLAH AND THE ART OF BEING

In *Sefer Gan Na'ul* Abulafia continues: "And he [the Kabbalist] should cleave to each and every *Sefirah* separately and he should integrate his cleaving with all the *Sefirot* together, and will not separate between the branches."[47] This concept of *Imitatio Dei* through cleaving to the *Sefirot* is also found in the school of Rabbi Joseph Ben Shalom Ashkenazi, who perceived the *Sefirot* not only as theosophical emanations but also as corresponding to powers and limbs within the physical structure of the human being.[48] This conception also penetrated into the spiritual world of Hasidism. According to the Hasidic master Rabbi Ya'akov Yosef of Polnoy (in the name of the Besht), man must follow God and imitate Him since the ten *Sefirot* of *Ein-Sof* are depicted in the spiritual and physical structure of the human being who was created in the image of God. Rabbi Ya'akov Yosef concludes: *There are ten Sefirot in man, who is called microcosmos.*[49]

The conclusion of this discussion is that the concept of *Imitatio Dei*, whose roots are to be found in the Bible and the ancient teachings of Rabbinic Midrash, has gained a prominent stature in Kabbalah and Hasidism. Although different Jewish thinkers and mystics mixed different flavors into it, this concept remains the chief *Mitzvah* in Jewish spirituality. The people of Israel are destined to walk in the way of their Creator, to imitate Him, and become like Him: They yearn to discover Him and to respond to Him. God, for His part, chooses His people and establishes an eternal covenant with those who in return vow to imitate Him and follow His ways. Thus, both God and His people are mutually required to keep that covenant. The Jewish concept of *Imitatio Dei* is, therefore, the mutual recognition between God and His people, the assurance of their partnership, and the unbreakable bond between them. This belief has shaped the spirituality of Jewish life and engendered within it an active imagination and dynamic psychology. The next chapter further examines the foundation of this psychology. It seeks to deepen our understanding of God's acts in the creation, followed by man's acts through *Imitatio Dei*. It further examines the urgency of God's yearning to grow, create, and individuate. I call this urgency God's *individuation*.

Tzimtzoom, God's Contraction in the Creation according to Lurianic Kabbalah

5

KABBALAH AND GOD'S INDIVIDUATION

God's shift from the Ayin to the Yesh

The analysis of the creation myth in Jewish mysticism, Kabbalah, and Hasidism in the previous chapters has clearly demonstrated that prominent Jewish thinkers and mystics have perceived the process that led to the creation, the creation itself, and the aftermath of the creation as the "stem cell" of the Jewish faith. From the creation myth everything stems, and thus every aspect associated with the creation determines the character of both God and the world, and the relationship between them. But the creation myth in Jewish spirituality has changed and evolved through the centuries. Although it was an immature concept in the ancient teachings of the Midrash and the Talmud, it reached its heights in the mystical works of Kabbalah and Hasidism. Here it became the core of the hidden mind of God, and the mystery behind the existence of man. In the major teachings of Kabbalah and Hasidism – the theosophical Kabbalah of Provence and Gerona, the Kabbalah's magnum opus, the *Zohar*, the ecstatic Kabbalah of Abraham Abulafia, the Safedian Kabbalah of Cordovero, the Lurianic Kabbalah of the Ari, and in the Hasidic schools of the Besht, Rabbi Schneur Zalman, Rabbi Ya'akov Yosef, and other masters of Hasidism – the perception of the creation was established as the esoteric seed of the human religious life, and became its *mysterium tremendum*.[1]

In the important works of the masters of Jewish mysticism and Kabbalah, the creation myth was understood as a reverent and mystical force of the religious life. The anthropomorphic approach that was adopted by the Jewish mystics enabled them to cross all barriers in their quest for God. They have perceived *Ein-Sof*, the God of Kabbalah, as a personal God despite His exaltedness and transcendentality: *Ein-Sof* is a responding God, a Divine partner who takes an active part in the dialogue with His people, accompanying His people through their days of happiness and days of sorrow. When we examine human history, as described in Jewish Scripture and in the treasury of the Jewish thinkers – claims a contemporary Jewish thinker – we necessarily arrive at the conclusion that God is "involved in our yearnings," to the extent that more than man is in search of God, "God is in search of man."[2] When examining the intent of God in creation through the prehistoric phases of His theogony and cosmogony, a clear, consistent pattern emerges; that is, the intent of God in creation involved an awakening in His mind, a Godly spark which required a shift from the *Ayin* to the *Yesh*. This, I believe, has been confirmed in the demonstration of the focal texts of the Kabbalists and Hasidic masters in the previous chapters. The mystery of the creation of the world arises from God's yearning to become the Creator. In order to become the King and the Almighty, to manifest His hidden inner life, to be revealed and actualized, to be realized and recognized by Himself and by His creatures, *Ein-Sof* shifts from the *Ayin* to the *Yesh* and brings the world into being. This central idea emphasizes and portrays God as an emotional and psychological entity, who is a living mind and spirit that develops, flourishes, and thrives. He is a Divine entity whose consciousness exists synchronically for Himself and for His creatures, since He yearns for and achieves recognition through human consciousness, and therefore the creation of humanity is an inseparable part of His essence and being. This God, who the Kabbalists call *Ein-Sof*, the Infinite, is not only Infinite through His primordiality and eternity, by being beyond good and evil, beyond space and time, He is also Infinite in His endless yearning to rise up, to create, and, like a fountain, to emanate His abundant flow. He is Infinite in being an active *Artisan* who unceasingly composes His thought and wisdom, word and sentence; an active *Artisan* who imagines and envisions. He is like a "chess virtuoso" who has played the game alone in His hidden life; or He is like a "student of Talmud" who has studied the Talmud alone; until an awakening arises in Him causing Him to step out of His loneliness and establish partnership with another player or another student. For God's aspiration for man, "It is not good that the man should be alone,"[3] is also true about God.

But since there is none other but God before the creation, He withdraws into Himself to create "the other" – the material world whose center is humanity – from Himself, although in truth He and "the other" are one and the same, since every created thing is composed of His essence. In our mundane life we tend to criticize those people around us who demand recognition. Sometimes we may even describe those who compulsively demand recognition as people who have a narcissistic personality disorder. We say about them that they have a grandiose sense of self importance; a preoccupation with fantasies of unlimited success, power, brilliance, beauty, or ideal love; exhibitionism; cool indifference or rage, inferiority, shame, emptiness, and lack of empathy. The recognition that the Kabbalists attribute to God, however, has nothing to do with these pathologies. For God's yearning for recognition is not, God forbid, a narcissistic perversion, but rather a stage of development on the way to the love of His creation. God's yearning for recognition is a positive, realistic feeling that He develops about Himself, which contains a built-in criterion for differentiating between healthy and unhealthy behavior. God's behavior derives from His dialectical desire to create and yet be recognized, for only by being recognized He sustains an ongoing dialogue between Himself and His creation.[4] Hence, God's desire is not the desire of the hedonist who desires only his own pleasure and happiness, but rather the desire of the Ultimate Giver, who spreads His goodness to His creatures, for He is the *summum bonum*, the Highest Good that contains all goodness, above and below.

On the notion of God's consciousness and His need to create a dialogue with another consciousness, Hegel claims that "Self-consciousness exists in and for itself when, and by the fact that it so exists for another,"[5] which means that every consciousness exists only in being acknowledged by another consciousness. This is for Hegel "the truth of self-certainty," for "consciousness in its activity is, in the first instance, a relationship of two extremes."[6] And thus, Hegel concludes: "The Lord is the consciousness that exists for itself, but ... it is a consciousness existing for itself which is mediated with itself through another consciousness."[7]

This notion of God's consciousness and His need for recognition has become the central theme in the creation myth of Jewish spirituality. Owing to the centrality of this Jewish mystical ideology, I would like to briefly present again the words of the focal texts from the worlds of Kabbalah and Hasidism that determine the purpose of the creation of the world and the relationship between God and His people. These texts establish the fundamental principle of God's conscious mind and His need to create the world in order to be known and recognized.

Sefer Ha-Yashar claimed that God created the world "in order to make His divinity acknowledged, and to show the honor of His greatness, and that [He] be happy in His acts ... the world was created for a great reason and this reason is the worship of the Creator ... in the creation of the world, *His perfection was augmented* .... so we know and acknowledge that the creation of the world is the perfection of God's name."

The *Zohar* asserted that "Since [*Ein-Sof*] is with these ten *Sefirot*, He created, designed, and formed everything within them. There He placed His unity so that they might *recognize Him*."

Rabbi Moses Cordovero wrote in his *Pardes Rimmonim* that "the emanation occurred so that the creatures *recognize* [the] power and exaltedness [of *Ein-Sof*]. ... The intent of the emanation was that through Him *His greatness will be revealed and the world will be ruled by Him*."

Sefer Etz Hayyim from the school of the Ari taught us that "The goal of the creation of the world ... the reason was because He ... *must be complete in all His actions and powers and names of greatness and exaltedness and honor*: And had He not made and actualized His actions and powers, it would be as if He could not be called complete, not in His action nor in His names and not [in His] attributes ... and if He did not have creatures, He could not be called a Master .... Only when the worlds are created, His actions and powers ... come into actuality and He is called *complete* ...."

Rabbi Nachman of Bratslav taught in *Likutei Moharan* that "[*Ein-Sof*] created the entire world only for the *glorification* that *He will be glorified* in Israel."

And similarly we found the declaration that summarizes centuries of Jewish teachings about the creation myth in the *Tanya* of Rabbi Schneur Zalman of Liadi : "It is known to all that the purpose of the creation of the world is *for the sake of the revelation of His kingdom*, may He be blessed, for 'There is no King without a nation,' Only 'In a multitude of people is the glory of the King'"(as said in Proverbs 14:28).

These classic sources are more than sufficient to validate the conclusion that some of the most influential Jewish mystics of the last millennium have treated the problem of the creation myth from a psychological point of departure. They have conceptualized the Creator through strictly anthropomorphic language; that is, as a Divine entity whose intention in the creation is to seek completion, augmentation, revelation, and recognition. Although Jewish mysticism teaches repeatedly that its anthropomorphic language is merely symbolic, historically the Jewish people understood this symbolism literally; they adhered to these classic texts of Jewish spirituality and internalized the concept of their Creator as an exalted and transcendental God who still remains personal and reachable. Their God came to be seen as the Divine entity who not only recognizes His people but also requires recognition; the God who not only actualizes the world but also is actualized Himself by becoming the Creator of His people. It was treatises such as the *Zohar, Etz Hayyim, Tanya* and other classics that were primarily responsible for this new concept of the Creator in Judaism. These treatises granted God with an invitation to dwell among His people on earth while still remaining as their exalted God in heaven. Thus, God's shift from the *Ayin* to the *Yesh* has been perceived by the Jewish people as God's personal penetration into every region of the human's life. Unlike in the intellectual Aristotelian philosophy, which preached about an emotionless and distant God, the God of the Kabbalists has become fraternal and present: Infinite but within reach, Eternal but yet accessible.

The worlds below and above: a chain of being

One of the most important beliefs that emerges from the Kabbalistic teachings is the belief in *Imitatio Dei*, which I have discussed above. Here I would like to deepen our understanding in regard to this profound *Mitzvah* in the context of Kabbalah. According to Kabbalah, the world below and the world above were created in a single instant, and thus the world below matches the world above. As a result, everything is linked with everything else, and the true meaning of all existence is that there is *a chain of being*. God, His world above, and His world below are all One, and, as the classic Kabbalist, Moses de-Leon teaches in his *Sefer Ha-Rimmon*, there is nothing that is not bound to the links of this *chain of being*:

> You should know that He, may He be blessed, is unique … and His true reality causes the true reality of all that exists. Indeed, the secret of His true reality is [hidden in] the notion of the supreme, eternal

beings [the *Sefirot*], and they are the secret of the chain that connects everything from His links to the lower links ... For indeed, there is nothing, and even the tiniest thing in the world, that is not connected to the links of the chain. And [thus] everything flows down in accordance with His secret and is linked with His unity, to teach [you] that He is One and is secret is One and all the worlds below and above are all one secret, and there is no separation in his true reality.[8]

But it is not only the world below that matches the world above. Man himself matches His Creator and is regarded in Kabbalah as the final culmination of the Godly creative process. Man is the pillar that sustains the existence of the world. When God created man He "breathed into his nostrils the breath of life,"[9] and man became a Divine creature. Kabbalah claims that from the first moment of man's creation he was not only destined to occupy the highest position in the world below, but, more importantly, he was destined to embody the image of the ten emanated Divine *Sefirot* on earth. "The image of God" in Kabbalah refers to a parallel between three things: the human body, the human soul, and God. The ancient Talmud had already taught that King David used to say five times "Blessed the Lord, O my soul."[10]

The Talmud asks:

> What caused David to say them ["Blessed the Lord, O my soul"]? He said them in honor of the Holy One, blessed be He, and in honor of the soul. Just as the Holy One, blessed be He, sees but cannot be seen, so the soul sees but cannot be seen. Just as the Holy One, blessed be He, upholds the entire world, so the soul upholds the entire body. Just as the Holy One, blessed be He, is pure, so the soul is pure. Just as the Holy One, blessed be He, lives in the deepest place, so the soul lives in the deepest place.[11]

In this Talmudic Aggadah the soul alone is compared to the Divine. In Kabbalah, however, both the soul and the body of man are compared to the Divine. Each and every part of the human body is constructed by the Divine wisdom, in accordance with the prototype of the upper world. Indeed, all five aspects of the human soul, which Kabbalah describes as *Nefesh*, *Rua'kh*, *Neshamah*, *Hayya*, and *Yekhidah*, descend from the world of the *Sefirot* to the physical human body. Hence, man constitutes the potential of the one single perfection of the worlds above and below.

The *Zohar* teaches:

> When the *Kadosh Baruch Hu* [the Holy one, blessed be He], created the world, He designed the world below on the form of the world above ... and He created man above everything ... for he upholds the world, so everything becomes one single perfection.[12]

KABBALAH AND GOD'S INDIVIDUATION

In central Kabbalistic works the human being's image is considered as the "perfect nature" that parallels the image of the supernal world. The great Talmudist and philosopher Rabbi Moshe Isserles of Cracow cites Rabbi Yehudah Hayyat (c. 1500), the author of *Minhat Yehudah* who wrote in his commentary to *Maa'rechet ha-Elohut* that the physical limbs of the "Lower Adam" are compared with the spiritual limbs of the "Supernal Adam," represented in the configuration of the ten Divine emanations. This is to say that the essence of Man is inherently connected to the Divine image.[13] Here we encounter the principal message of Kabbalah that is directed at the human being: God creates the world below as an image of the world above; God creates man below as an image of God above; and He requires that man imitate Him and follow His ways. The stages of God's development in the creation must be repeated and imitated by man in order that man becomes actualized and ready to fulfill his destiny as God's partner on earth. Every act of man on earth is nothing but an imitation of the Godly process of creation; man is a creative creature because God creates unceasingly.

The way of God in the creation is, for the Kabbalist, the greatest skillful process, representing the highest degree of the act of actualization. *Ein-Sof* is first and foremost the Creator. His creativity becomes the central precept of the Jewish religious belief and the core component of *Imitatio Dei*. Whenever man experiences the Divine breath of life; whenever he inhales or exhales, thinks or speaks, builds or destroys; whenever he senses the tension between the two eternal opposing forces of consciousness and unconsciousness that reside ontologically in the center of existence; whenever an idea emerges in his mind; whenever a thought erupts and rises up; whenever he desires, transforms, develops, and matures; whenever he senses the victory of his conscious mind over his unconsciousness; he links himself to the spirit of God and imitates Him. What is the nature behind this reality? In Kabbalah, everything that happens in the hidden life of God Himself is reflected in the unfolded life of every human being. Therefore, the Godly development of consciousness is our development of consciousness. Through the intensifying act of discovery of the mystery of the creation we learn that the human being resides in God as much as God resides in the human being, for the world above and the world below are one and inseparable.

Sefer Ha-Yashar teaches that the world above and the world below resemble one tree, whose roots emanate from heaven and whose branches spread to earth. All the secrets of the upper world can be learned from the lower world, if we only are aware, contemplative, and wise enough to understand and connect with the hidden Divine root by studying its revealed earthly branches:

> Every wise and contemplative man can understand the secrets of the upper world from the images of this lowly world. For we find that most matters of this lowly world are like the matters of the upper world, just as we know that the forms of this [lowly] world exist in the

core [the upper world] that contains them. And when we reason that the substance of the branches of the tree, its flowers and its blossoms exist [*in potentia*] under the earth; and even though they are not seen and they do not exist except through reason, we know that they exist. As for the root of a nut tree, an apple or an almond will not grow on it, since they do not exist *in potentia* in its root; only the thing that exists in the root *in potentia* is what comes out in the branches; therefore only the form of a nut will come forth [from a nut tree] ... Similarly we can understand that everything existing in this world comes forth from the power [that exists *in potentia*] in the upper world. For the upper world is like the root, and this [world] is like its branches. And therefore by contemplating the secrets of the lowly world we can understand the mysteries of the upper world.[14]

These words of *Sefer Ha-Yashar* have been rooted in the heart of Kabbalah as the *telos* of Jewish religious life: God must be imitated, the Kabbalists claimed, since He is the ultimate source and best example of creativity, wisdom, strength, compassion, and righteousness; and since He is like the root and we are like the branches of the same tree. Thus, learning all of God's characteristics teaches us both about His true essence and about our own destiny. The Kabbalists find God's characteristics, first and foremost, in the three major components of the creation myth: in His *intent* before the creation of the world, in His *involvement* in the creation during the process of the emanation of the *Sefirot*, and in His *relationship* with the creation and His chosen people after the world came into being. These are the cornerstones of the creation myth in the classic texts of Jewish mysticism. Indeed, these components result from the psychological transformation of God's shifting from the *Ayin* to the *Yesh* and establishing Kabbalah as the major force of Jewish spirituality throughout the last millennium. But what is the nature of this psychological transformation? To answer this question, I examine God's shifting from the *Ayin* to the *Yesh* through the lens of one central psychological term that will illuminate the creation myth in Jewish spirituality. This term is individuation.

God's individuation

Individuation in Jungian analytical psychology is a term applied to both human beings and God.[15] Although in the human being it is a personal individuation, in God it is the collective individuation. In both, however, it may be described as the development and fulfillment of their destiny and the manifestation of their inner *self*. I follow the Jewish mystics and Kabbalists who describe their God, particularly within the process of the creation myth, using purely anthropomorphic terminology and psychological denotations.

I use the term individuation in the context of Jewish mysticism and Kabbalah to denote the religious–psychological development and the gradual transformation and unfolding of the mind of God within the creation myth. I define individuation in Kabbalah to be God's *desire* to shift from the unconscious mind into the conscious mind, from silence to voice, from pre-thought to thought, and from thought to speech. It is God's will *yearning* to move from concealment to revelation, from the infinite state to the finite state, and from "nothingness" into "being." It is God's *aspiration* to manifest Himself through creation and to move from the realm of the *Ayin* to the *Yesh*. It is God's *ambition* to be in partnership with His creation and creatures. It is God's *urgency* to create the chosen people, to recognize them and be recognized by them. And it is, in my general definition, God's psychological transformation, beginning with His realization of His potentialities and ending with His self-actualization. Individuation as God's psychological transformation within Kabbalah is also the ongoing *confrontational dialogue* between the revealed Divine state, i.e. God's *desire*, and the concealed collective unconscious Divine state, i.e. God's collective unconsciousness. This "dialogue" sparks an awakening in the mind of the God who yearns to become the Creator. However, the spiritual growth that He realizes during the process of creation, is also the best ethical example that God sets for man. Thus, the concept of individuation represents God's spiritual growth through the act of creation, and man's spiritual growth through the practice of *Imitatio Dei*. It can be described as the subjective process of God's *integration*, during which He becomes acquainted with the wholeness of Himself, particularly with the aspects that were hidden in His inner *Self*. During this process He comes to realize that His wholeness can be achieved *only* through the manifestation of His *Sefirot*, the creation of the world, and the creation of humanity, since wholeness requires the necessary interaction with oneself and humanity. He, therefore, emanates His Divine *Sefirot*, creates the worlds of Emanation, Creation, Formation, and Making, creates His chosen people, gives them the Torah, trusts them with His commandments, becomes their King and Almighty, and guides them to walk in His ways and imitate Him.

Individuation in the context of Kabbalah is the process of God's becoming "individually" the Creator, of the Creation's becoming "individually" an alive world, and of the Jewish People's becoming "individually" the chosen people. It is the yearning of God, the Creation, and of the Jewish People to be complete, to become that which cannot be divided.

The term individuation was coined by Jung. In Jung's analytical psychology individuation signifies the central process of the spiritual and psychological development of the human being who strives toward fruition and self-actualization. Jungian individuation is a concept interconnected with the development of the individual's consciousness and with the establishing of the unity between the *ego*, which is the core of the individual's consciousness, and the *self*, which is the totality of the individual's general personality. But it also refers to the general unfolding and development of God's consciousness as He becomes crystallized as an individual. In fact, the terms "God" and "unconscious" are synonymous concepts in Jungian psychology and thought. Jungian scholars teach us that these are alternative terms for the "origin of the autonomous and irrational effects" to which creation is exposed. Basing this view on Jung's *Memories, Dreams, Reflections,* Aniela Jaffe' says that Jung would use the term "unconscious" when he wished to speak psychologically, and "God" when he wished to convey a mythical connotation.[16]

In his general definition of individuation Jung writes:

> I use the term "individuation" to denote the process by which a person becomes a psychological "individual", that is, a separate, indivisible unity or "whole."[17]

According to Jung, the unconscious part of the individual psyche must be understood along with the conscious part to fully comprehend that individual's behavior, because every individuation has two major principle aspects: one is the internal (the unconscious) and the other is the external (the conscious); and together they are subject to *integration*. This is what we mean by maturity. If this process is impaired, *integration* becomes the goal of therapy. When the unconscious and the conscious integrate, particularly in their emotional content, their experiences are shaped, and then they influence action and attitude.

Jung's analytical psychology was not received favorably by scholars of Jewish mysticism and Kabbalah.[18] Many of their criticisms were well taken, but their failure to acknowledge the many valid aspects of Jung's presentation was fundamentally in error. Jung did influence some of the leading scholars of Jewish mysticism and Kabbalah, although they never recognized or mentioned explicitly his influence in their work.[19]

As I have mentioned, Jung's definition of individuation relates explicitly to human transformation and growth. However, Jungian individuation also implicitly stands for the process of the psychological development of God Himself, who also strives toward fruition and self-actualization. God's individuation embodies the *collective* individuation, for it denotes the transformation of the collective spiritual history of the unconscious mind of God from before the creation shifting to reveal His conscious mind during and after the creation. And man, says Jung, "is the mirror which God holds up to Himself, or the sense organ with which he apprehends his being."[20] In psychological terms it means that the Godly *Self* is revealed in the human act of reflection.

If we examine the Kabbalistic process of the creation in light of the Jungian theory of individuation, we may say that the Godly concept of individuation begins in Kabbalah as a confrontational dialogue between God's inner opposites; that is, between His unconscious mind and conscious mind. Before God's awakening everything is included in Him: He is both "everythingness" and "nothingness"; He is both that which *can be* and that which *cannot be*. The confrontation between His opposites sparks in Him a process toward individuation, which is twofold: on the one hand it is a reaction to the strong sensation of the inner opposites residing in Him, and, on the other hand, it is a counter-reaction to that sensation, i.e. a desire to unite the opposites, which can be defined in Jungian terminology as *enantiodromia*. In order to individuate, God creates man and thus man becomes God's partner in the Godly process of His individuation, since "God is a contradiction in terms, [and] therefore He needs man in order to be made One ... God is an ailment which man has to cure," says Jung.[21]

These Jungian words sound like the Lurianic teachings of Kabbalah. And indeed, in a rare but very significant reference to Lurianic Kabbalah, Jung expresses his appreciation for the theurgical principle in Lurianic Kabbalah, according to which, after the *Tzimtzoom* and the *Shevirah*, man was destined to be in partnership with God in the restoration of the broken worlds. On this subject Jung writes as follows:

> The Jew has the advantage of having long since anticipated the development of consciousness in his spiritual history. By this I mean the Lurianic stage of the Kabbalah, the breaking of the vessels [*Shevirat ha-Kellim*], and man's help in restoring them {*Tikkun*}. Here, the thought emerges for the first time, that man must help God repair the damage wrought by the creation. For the first time, man's cosmic responsibility is acknowledged."[22]

These words of Jung not only praise the Lurianic concept of *Tikkun* but also acknowledge that the history of the world parallels the development of the collective spirit, which is the central Jungian myth. For Jung, the Lurianic Kabbalists reached the peak of spiritual comprehension of the development of consciousness when they considered themselves obliged to participate in the universal and collective *Tikkun*. The implication of Jung's statement is that through their own individuation the Kabbalists participate in God's individuation, which is done through the creation of the world on God's part, and through the restoration of the broken world on the human part. In the process of the transformation of God who creates the world and responds to humanity, His consciousness comes to fruition and opens the same opportunity for humanity.

One of the close associates of Jung, Aniela Jaffe', who is highly regarded both as an interpreter of Jung's psychology and as an important writer in her own right, who collaborated with Jung on his *Memories, Dreams, Reflections* and authored the classic work *The Myth of Meaning*, writes the following about Jung's approach to Lurianic Kabbalah:

> It was important for Jung to find the same thought in the Kabbalah of Isaac Luria, that the human being is to employ the forces he has, to participate in and aid the Divine life process, that the human is, in fact, indispensable in the work of redeeming the world, and that this redemption lies in uniting the opposites within the Godhead.[23]

KABALLAH AND THE ART OF BEING

The notion of unifying the opposites stands indeed at the center of the process of God's individuation, both in the Kabbalistic myth and in Jungian psychology. The process of individuation can be explained by the metaphor of a dream, says Jung, for a dream is an unconscious phenomenon that manifests itself in a chaotic and unsystematic form. Before the beginning of His individuation, God lacks any desire, for He is in a state of "unconsciousness," which resembles the state of a dream. There is, however, an element inherent in His "unconsciousness" which ignites His desire to "wake up," an element that can be defined as His ontological urgency of awakening: to rise up and immediately thereafter to be manifested and actualized. This urgency affirms that despite the chaotic state of God's unconscious mind, it still contains some consciousness *in potentia*, which is, in fact, the only element of autonomy in His unconscious mind. Within this urgency of awakening, early manifestations of individuation occur in the mind of God: emotions are generated and the will of God to create develops. But how does God rise up? According to Jung, in every process of individuation there is an ongoing confrontational dialogue between unconsciousness and the developing consciousness that ignites an awakening in the mind. If we apply this approach to the theosophical Kabbalah of the *Zohar*, to Lurianic Kabbalah, or to Hasidic thought, this would be the stage that I have called in the previous chapters *Hitore'rut*, formulated in the Kabbalistic texts by the phrase: *Ke-she-Alla Bi-re'tzono*, "when the Will [of God] emerged." This is the stage where God begins shifting from His unconsciousness to uncover His consciousness.

What do I mean by the expression "His consciousness"? Is it His *Ayin*, His "nothingness," or is it His *Yesh*, His "everythingness"? To answer these questions, we must recall the concept of *Tzimtzoom*. Here we are faced with two possibilities: if His consciousness is His *Ayin* and His unconsciousness is the *Yesh*, then in this stage God contracts His *Yesh*, as in the Catharsis myth in Lurianic Kabbalah discussed previously, which claims that the *Yesh* is the root of evil existing in the Divine reality, and thus *Tzimtzoom* suggests the purification of God from the impurity of evil.[24] According to this possibility, God's mind was enlightened during the process of individuation and He established His awareness by contracting His unconsciousness, which is darkness, chaos, and even evil. In other words, He took a step *forward*, and "gave up" His unconsciousness for the sake of gaining consciousness. He stepped from the *Ayin* to the *Yesh*. But if His consciousness is His *Yesh* and His unconsciousness is the *Ayin*, then in this stage God contracts His *Ayin* for the sake of the emanation of His *Sefirot*, His *Yesh*. According to this second possibility God was enlightened through the process of individuation and He established His awareness by the contraction of His consciousness. In other words, He took a step *backward* and "gave up" His consciousness for the sake of keeping His hidden unconsciousness. In both cases it is God's striving to contract one of His opposites in order to become One.

There is, however, a third possibility. It is both the Kabbalistic and the

KABBALAH AND GOD'S INDIVIDUATION

Jungian possibility. It suggests an *integration* of His opposites; that is, God integrates His opposites into one scheme of His new hyper-reality through His process of emanation, and *becomes united through His opposites*. Since God is the inclusion of all that exists, He represents all opposites and the unity of all opposites, and *every opposite is included in Him*. In Kabbalistic terms, the answer to the question whether His consciousness is the *Ayin* or the *Yesh* is that in the mind of God, consciousness and unconsciousness are both the *Ayin* and the *Yesh*. We must conclude, therefore, that the process of the creation of the world that involves God's individuation is not His separation from the *Ayin* to the *Yesh*, but rather His *integration* of the *Ayin* with the *Yesh*. This idea has been adopted and internalized by Kabbalah and Hasidism. The Hasidic Rebbe, Aaron ha-Levi, explains that the main purpose of God's creation and His emanation of all the worlds was to "reveal His completeness from the opposite" by creating all things and their opposites, for the sake of God's realization and perfection. By recognizing all opposites, God incorporates all aspects of reality, above and below, and becomes perfect, integrated and unified.[25]

Since according to Kabbalah, God is a duality of being – *Hokhmah* and *Binah*, Male and Female, the Supernal Father and the Supernal Mother, *Hesed* and *Deen* – He creates the world through the act of two opposing movements: contraction and expansion. This act of the two opposing movements is manifested through *Tzimtzoom*, for *Tzimtzoom* requires that at each stage there is both contraction and expansion: one force of limitation and one force of emanation. If one of these two forces is missing, there would be no creation: without limitation everything would immediately revert to God, and without emanation nothing would come into being. Thus, retreat and propagation together signify the dialectical process of the act called *Tzimtzoom* during the creation. After the *Tzimtzoom*, when God emanates His *Sefirot* couples, which are His revealed opposites, He manifests in them the differentiations of His inner *Self*. In each *Sefirah* He pours from both His conscious mind and His unconscious mind, and each *Sefirah* yearns to unite with its opposite in order to fully actualize: for *Hokhmah* is unconscious without *Binah*, and *Binah* is unconscious without *Hokhmah*; *Hesed* is unconscious without *Deen*, and *Deen* is unconscious without *Hesed*. Similarly, *Tife'ret* is unconscious without its opposite, *Malkhut*, and *Malkhut* is unconscious without *Tife'ret*. This is why the Kabbalist prays "for the sake of the unification of *Tife'ret* and *Malkhut* (*Leshem Yikhu'd Kudsha Be'rich-Hu u-Shekhinte'h*'), for only through unity are both unconsciousness and consciousness united in all of God's manifestations.

Furthermore, the process of the emanation of the *Sefirot* couples, which is the heart of God's individuation, allows Him not only to reveal His inner *Self* and opposites, but also to overcome the struggle between those opposites. The manifestation of *Hokhmah* and *Binah*, for example, allows Him to depart from His "bisexuality" for the sake of achieving Oneness. Thus, when *Ein-Sof* emanates Its male aspect, *Hokhmah*, and Its female aspect, *Binah*, *Ein-Sof* is elevated above masculinity and femininity, for *Ein Sof* purifies Itself from that which is partial and achieves Oneness. What is, then, the main purpose of God's Emanation? The main purpose of His emanating the *Sefirot* is not to divide Himself into ten *Sefirot*, but to unite Himself through the ten *Sefirot*.

At this stage of unity the human Kabbalist takes a crucial responsibility in helping God achieve His unity. Through the act of *Devekut*, in which the Kabbalist communes with God, he himself individuates. He unites the opposites within himself, and experiences the numinousness of oneness. When he performs *Devekut* in the nether world, he brings about harmony in the worlds above and below. Therefore, we may conclude that the struggle to overcome the opposites in the process of individuation is the struggle of both God and man.

There is a striking similarity between the theory of the union of the opposites in Kabbalah and the way in which this theory is explained in Jungian psychology. Jung perceived that most of the cosmogonic gods were bisexual by nature. He claimed that the prominent symbol of the "hermaphrodite," which appears in many faiths, combines powerful opposites. It is the strongest "uniting symbol," he asserted, for it epitomizes the unity of the opposites. At the same time Jung perceived that the unconscious substratum and the conscious mind are also opposites that yearn to unite, exemplifying the development of the collective spirit of humanity.[26] Elsewhere Jung claimed that the process of individuation is a result of inner conflicts including the conflict between the anima and the animus. In every man's unconscious, Jung suggested, is a hidden feminine personality, whereas in every woman's is a masculine personality. The feminine figure he called "anima," and the masculine, "animus."[27] These Jungian theories emphasize two important ideas: (a) God is "bisexual" by His nature, and (b) God's "bisexuality" derives from His "split" mind, i.e. His unconscious and conscious substrata, which are the opposites of His inner personality. The union of God's "bisexuality" into Oneness is, therefore, tantamount to the union of His two opposites: unconsciousness and consciousness. But what is the translation of this Godly union of opposites within the life of God Himself? Here we are faced with a crucial question in both Kabbalah and Jungian psychology, and as we shall see, both doctrines answer this question the same way. Kabbalah claims that the world is founded on intangible beings: Divine letters.[28] It is a world created and sustained by thought-transforming language. It is a world of *Logos* that pre-existed the creation of the world. This concept is the focal point in God's transformation from the *Ayin* to the *Yesh*. The *Ayin* is the prehistoric thought of God that subsequently transforms itself into letters, words, sentences, and other verbal forms of linguistic expression. God transforms Himself from the *Ayin*, from the non-verbalized phase, to the *Yesh*, to the verbalized phase. The genesis of God's revealed life as the Creator of the world, which occurs inside His mind, is dependent on His ability to transform His potential speech from pre-organized thought to organized words. When He speaks, He transforms, individuates, invents the language, emanates the *Sefirot*, creates the world, and becomes "individual." Thus, through His transformation from thought to speech God creates the world and integrates His opposites.

Similarly, we find in Jungian psychology that the act of speech that God performs in the creation allows Him to transform and integrate His opposites, which are for Jung the integration of unconsciousness with consciousness. Two great motifs, claims Jung, appear at the dawn of history: Darkness and Light. Darkness is the unconscious mind of God before He crystallizes His first verbalized speech, whereas Light is the conscious mind of God that is taken from within the unconsciousness of Darkness. But how is the Light taken out of Darkness? The biblical answer is – through speech! "Now the earth was unformed and void, and the darkness was upon the face of the deep; and the spirit of God hovered over the face of the waters. And God *said*: 'Let there be light!' And there was light."[29] Later on, we learn that God continues this process by separating the Light from Darkness: "And God saw the light that it was good, and God divided the light from the darkness. And God called the light Day, and the darkness He called Night."[30] Day and Light, Jung explains, are synonyms for consciousness, whereas Night and Dark represent unconsciousness. The Godly act of extracting the Light from the Darkness is the symbol of separating the conscious mind from the unconscious mind. However, at the same time it is also the symbol of integrating the two, since the main purpose of God is not to divide Himself to consciousness and unconsciousness, but to unite Himself through the two.[31]

From the point of view of Kabbalah, God's emanation of His Divine *Sefirot*, during the process of His individuation, is the act of God's manifestation of His revealed opposites. This process signifies two simultaneous Godly movements: *separation* and *integration*. On one hand, it is a movement of separation because God unfolds His inner wholeness into a divisible structure of ten differentiated *Sefirot*, i.e. He withdraws from His infinite being of Oneness and "breaks" that Oneness into ten *Sefirot*. On the other hand, it is a movement of integration because here God permits His opposites to dwell together in harmony, i.e. He creates a united world of ten *Sefirot*, a Godhead. The dialectics of these two simultaneous movements is inherent in the development and growth that characterizes God's individuation. During this active process, the only "change" that is generated in God is a "change" in His form, not a change in His essence. Before the process of the emanation of the *Sefirot*, the opposites "lived together" inside His divinity. After the emanation of the *Sefirot* they "live together" outside His divinity. The change in *Ein-Sof* is thus a *metamorphosis*, an external change of form, not an internal change of essence. There is, however, an important new transformation occurring now in God's mind: *before* the emanation He was unconscious, *after* the emanation He becomes conscious; that is, His mind has not changed, but His awareness has unfolded.

The duality of movements, separation and integration, allows God to become consciously acquainted with the *Sefirot*, His hidden aspects, to strive to make contact with them, and connect them to His self-image. However, since the process of individuation is not only a personal process but also an interpersonal one, God's separation and integration is an intersubjective process of relationship. It requires both a relationship with His individual *Self* and a relationship with "the other." The relationship with one's self is at the same time the relationship with one's fellow man, for one cannot relate to humanity unless one first relates to one's self. Individuation is one process of both integration of the opposites within the *self* and of creating relationships with others.[32] This perception is of great significance for our discussion as it illuminates that individuation is not only the unification of God's opposites, something internal in His Divine personality alone, but it also depends on His relationship with his creation interpersonally: one between God and Himself, the second between God and His people. God's yearning to unite all opposites, both His personal and His interpersonal, is the major reason for the creation of the world as clearly and vastly emphasized by the prominent Kabbalists and Hasidic masters.

Individuation as a Godly psychological transformation uncovers the inner aspect of the development of the mind of God. Its first stage is the theogonial stage, which manifests God's mind as an active mind, for God's mind is an everlasting dynamic energy that contracts and expands, runs and returns, *Ratzo va-Shov*. In this theogonial stage the unconscious part is a reality but yet in potentiality, similar to the Jungian theory where the human unconscious is referred to as "nothing" or as "a reality *in potentia*."[33] Kabbalah recognizes that the *Yesh* has always been hidden in God *in potentia*; that is, God has always had everything included in Him, both the *Ayin* and the *Yesh*. Therefore, we must return to our original conclusion and say: God does not develop Himself by "giving up" a part of Himself, but by integrating the various parts of Himself; that is, by uniting the *Ayin* with the *Yesh*.

God's shift from the *Ayin* to the *Yesh* has been perceived by the Jewish mystics as God's personal penetration into every region of the human's life. This perception elucidates the development and the gradual transformation and unfolding of the mind of God, who yearns to become the Creator of the world and the King of the chosen people. His individuation is the best ethical example that He sets for man, for inherent in the process of individuation is God's ultimate Art of Being. The next chapter introduces us to the four main components of this skillful Art.

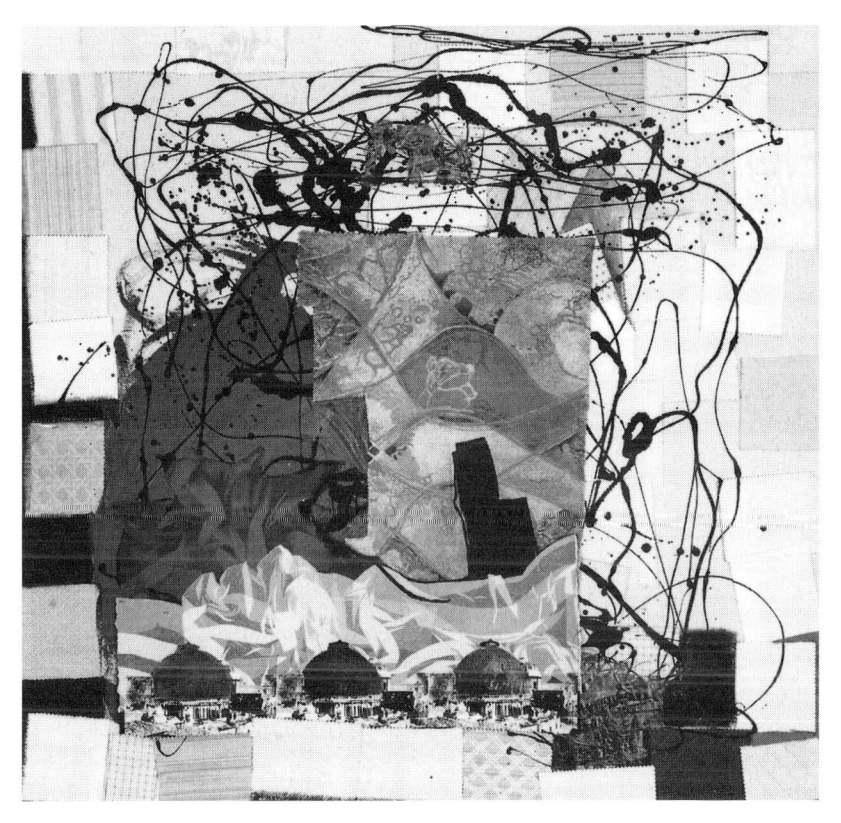

From Ayin to Yesh, God's Individuation

6

KABBALAH AND THE ART OF BEING

Awakening, courage, creativity, and loving

Imitating God according to Kabbalah and Jewish spirituality, as discussed in the previous two chapters, is the central human activity that endows the human being with self-affirmation and authenticity. *Imitating God is man's art of being which follows God's Art of Being.* It is the art underlying human self-realization. It combines the religious human experience with the essence of understanding, and yet it is above and beyond understanding. It is the human being's courageous self-actualization of the innermost potentialities – the *dynamis* of the human being's spiritual, emotional, and intellectual growth – that brings forth all hidden aspects of man and impels him toward fulfillment and fruition. In this chapter I would like to present a new perspective that analyzes what it means for man to imitate God's Art of Being in Kabbalah. I posit four prominent components of the Kabbalistic art of being and call them: Awakening, Courage, Creativity, and Loving. I will consider them in turn.

Awakening

The concept of awakening in Jewish spirituality is the single most complicated component of the Kabbalistic art of being, for there is no systematic explanation in the Kabbalistic teachings that defines it. Awakening signifies God's shift from the *Ayin* to the *Yesh*, from "nothingness" to "everythingness." As noted previously (p. 47), whenever the Kabbalists were required to describe this process, they merely stated the Hebrew words *Ke'-she'-Alla bi-Re'tzono*, "when [God's] Will emerged," (or other stoic statements, such as the *Zohar*'s words: "when the King received ordaining") without comment or clarification about what constitutes this mysterious statements. This lack of comment, however, was examined and challenged in the previous chapters and led to the conclusion that awakening (*Hitore'rut*) in Kabbalah emerges from God's ontological seed of potentiality, which dwells in the depth of His unconscious mind and yearns to pass to actuality in order to *become* and be an *individual*. Awakening is the natural urgency of the Divine and of every living thing, striving to bring something new into being, as the light breaks through the darkness in the dawn of a new day.

Aristotle begins his *Physics* II by claiming that existent things can be divided into those which exist *by nature* and those which exist from other causes. The task, for Aristotle, is to find the characteristic definition that distinguishes those things which exist by nature from anything else. Each of those natural things, he says, has within itself *the principle of motion and stationariness*, or *the principle of change and stillness*. Whereas things that are not *natural things*, such as "a bed and a coat and anything else of that sort" require an external cause in order to "rise up," those things that exist by nature have a creative force within them, and, thus, nature is a principle or cause of *change and stillness* in things that exist by nature.[1]

Aristotle's concept of the things that exist by nature may help clarify the notion of awakening in the two ultimate things that exist by nature: God and man. According to the teachings of Kabbalah, the existence of both God and man does not depend on an external cause: God (whom Aristotle would consider as the "First Cause" or the "Cause of causes") is the cause of Himself without any dependency on any external cause, for He Himself is the Cause of everything. And man, who carries the eternal soul of the Divine, also does not have an external cause, for he is a spiritual entity whose Divine soul is essentially a part of God Himself. Man, according to Kabbalah, is a micro-Deity, a fulfillment of God on earth. Therefore, the essence of both God and man belongs to the things that exist by nature, and, as Aristotle claims, those things that exist by nature and do not have an external cause, have within themselves the *principle of change and stillness*. Hence, the nature of God and man can be described in Aristotelian terms as *a source or cause of being moved and of being still … in virtue of itself, and not in virtue of an associated exterior attribute*.[2]

Both God and man have the internal principle of organism, which is a developmental principle that strives toward varying levels of potentiality and actuality. It is a principle that has *within itself* a force for future growth and development which yearns for self-realization. But here we are faced with a crucial paradox. If God and man rely on their internal principle of change in order to grow and develop, how can this growth and development, which did not exist in them in the first place, be identified with their nature? To ask this question in Kabbalistic terms, if God and man rely on their internal principle of growth in order to shift from the *Ayin* to the *Yesh*, how can they "rise up" and move from the *Ayin* to the *Yesh*, if the *Yesh* did not exist in them at the first place? Kabbalah's answer is that we should conceive of the *Yesh* as being within the *Ayin*. Since God is an entity that exists by nature, as a Natural Being and a Necessary Being, He exists in both *change* and *stillness*, constantly growing and developing. And thus He dwells in the infinity of the *Ayin* while the *Yesh* has also been with Him eternally; both co-exist within Him by His nature and both are the *internal* cause of His awakening.

God, therefore, dwells in the realm of change and stillness at once: He resides simultaneously in the domain of pregnancy and the domain of giving birth. His awakening is not characterized in Kabbalah as a single event that occurred at a certain point in time, since God is above time and beyond history. As "the Will emerges" in Him, He is continually transforming Himself *from stillness to change and from change to stillness* and continually "creating worlds and destroying them."[3] Awakening is built into the nature of God, and since man was created in His image and carries His eternal soul, awakening is built into the nature of man as well. In the Kabbalistic art of being, awakening is the foremost Divine quality that is implemented within man. When man "rises up" from his unconsciousness to his consciousness, when he perceives reality as a duality of meaning, and when he senses that his spirit resides in both *change* and *stillness*, he is on the path toward awakening.

But how can a man sense the advent of his awakening? In reference to this question, Kabbalah claims that the phenomenon of awakening is an involuntary and spontaneous state of existence. Here Kabbalah teaches its psychological meanings in an ontological denotation: the process of awakening within the human being refers to the natural state of existence of each man and woman. For every human being is a living organism, existing simultaneously in both change and stillness. This is not what the human being *does* but what the human being *is*, and therefore the activity of change and stillness together defines man's ontological nature.

The same holds for the notion of *will*. In Nietzsche's *Beyond Good and Evil* the term will refers to the basic aspect of the human being's existence. Will is potentially present in the human being at all times; without it the human being would not be a human being, for a man cannot realize his nature and existence except as he wills it in the journey of his life. And thus, bringing one's inner potentiality into actuality is the discovery of the inner power of man; it is the natural human actualized potency without which life would not exist. But at the same time it signifies a constant activity of change and stillness, since the discovery of every actualized will is instantaneously the discovery of another potential will that yearns to be actualized.

In the Kabbalistic art of being, awakening is the first theogonial phase imitated by the human being without any effort. It is the natural state of existence, the active process where the enlightened mind "rises up" from the darkened mind. At the very instant when awakening erupts, the conscious mind regains the awareness of change and stillness, which is in essence the duality of existence that constructs reality. It is sent forth from the depth of existence and it is immediately confronted with the dual meaning of life, since the first experience of every awakening is the breaking of the one into the two. In our lives, the duality of change and stillness could be translated into multiple existential conditions: it could be our success versus failure, health versus sickness, love versus hate, confidence versus fear, anima versus animus. When we perceive that our reality is a totality of opposites, we begin to experience the true meaning of being; first we acknowledge our opposites, and then we strive to integrate them.

When King Solomon, the wisest of all men and the poet of all poets, asserted that "there is a time for everything under heaven,"[4] he separated every existing thing into opposing components in essence and in time, saying:

> For everything there is a season,
> and a time for every matter under heaven:
> a time to be born, and a time to die;
> a time to plant, and a time to pluck up what is planted;
> a time to kill, and a time to heal;
> a time to weep, and a time to laugh;
> a time to mourn, and a time to dance;
> a time to cast away stones, and a time to gather stones together;
> a time to embrace, and a time to refrain from embracing;
> a time to seek, and a time to lose;
> a time to keep, and a time to cast away;
> a time to rend, and a time to sew;
> a time to keep silence, and a time to speak;
> a time to love, and a time to hate;
> a time for war, and a time for peace.[5]

Solomon, however, may not have intended to teach that there is literally a separate time for "everything under heaven," but rather that our diminished perception artificially separates the unity of existence into components, while in the true reality "the earth remains forever ... the sun rises and the sun goes down ... and there is nothing new under the sun." And still, when we look at creation, the duality of its essence manifests itself before our eyes. When man "rises up" and perceives reality as duality, while simultaneously yearning for the possibility of unifying that duality, he is awakening. In the Kabbalistic art of being, awakening is the foremost Divine quality that is implemented within man.

Courage

The concept of *courage* (in Hebrew *oz*) constitutes the second component of the Kabbalistic art of being. Why courage? Because courage signifies the *daring* to "rise up" from Darkness to Light, the *fortitude* to move from Thought to Speech in order to stand at the threshold of life. Here the human being imitates the first active phase of his Creator: like his God he awakens to a new dawn, yearning to strengthen his soul and searching for self-discovery. The sage of the Mishnah, Akavyah ben Mahalalel teaches: "Reflect upon three things and you will not come into the hand of sin: Know where you came from, where you are going to, and before whom you will have to render account and reckoning."[6] According to the Jewish faith every human being stands at the crossroads of Akavyah's expression: all human beings gaze into the past where they came from and look forward to the unknown future that awaits at the horizon of destiny. This indeed, requires courage. When standing at the crossroads of life, man's chain of actions begins: he "wakes up"; he discovers his motions; he reveals his emotions; he thinks; he speaks; he creates; he encounters opposing forces; he gets wounded; he heals himself; he matures; he individuates; he looks for a partner; he creates a covenant with his partner; he violates the covenant; his partner violates the covenant; he breaks; his partner breaks, he exiles himself, he exiles his partner; he teaches his partner about redemption; he goes to "sleep" again; and with the first light that breaks the dark of his "sleep" he will be "waking up" again to discover that "there is nothing new under the sun."

The courage that Kabbalah teaches is the courage to be. It is the courage to survive the cycle of life and to be nurtured and enhanced by its ascents and descents. But Kabbalistic courage does not embrace secular courage, whose existential meaning is that the courage to be is based on experiencing existence as a dreadful thought. Albert Camus once said on behalf of his secular philosophy of Existentialism: "I fear the fear of my existence." In Jewish spirituality there is no place for such fear. Instead, it suggests a concept of *awe*; a marvel inspired by the exaltedness of God; an affection that generates in the heart of the believer the feeling of immunity and protection. In Rabbenu Bachya Ibn Paquda's *The Duties of the Heart*, a Hebrew ethical work that greatly influenced Kabbalah and Hasidism, we read the following:

> The ... *awe* inspired by His elevated Glory and Almighty power ... does not depart from a person as long as he lives. It is the highest degree attained by the *awe* of God ... and serves as an introduction to the pure love of God and strong desire for Him ... a religious man once related concerning the *awe* of God a question to a person whom he found asleep in the desert. He asked that person "Are you not afraid of a lion, that you sleep here?" The person replied: "I would be abashed before God if He were to see that I fear any one but Him."[7]

The courage to be as represented by Jewish spirituality and Kabbalah is inspired by the sensation of awe that balances the fear of existence. This awe is not fear. The Hebrew language sharply distinguishes between *Yira'h* (awe) and *Pakhad* (fear). In fact, the latter is the opposite of the former: *Yira'h* means a religious sensation of exaltedness and courage, whereas *Pakhad* means a feeling of contemptible lowliness and fright. The ancient Jewish sages teach us that "everything is in the hands of heaven except for the *awe* of heaven,"[8] for the awe of heaven is solely in the hands of the human being. Once the human being discovers the grace of God in every fragment and measure of his reality – in the bread that he eats and in the water that he drinks, in the abundant Divine flow that he takes for granted, and in his wealth and health that he takes as a given – an exalted sensation of awe and courage originates in him.

However, while the discovery of the Divine flow within the mundane level of the human being requires the courage to be, the courage to be requires the courage to *risk*. The history of the Jewish people is saturated with examples of biblical fathers and mothers who have become monumental by taking a risk. Indeed, the covenant between God and Abraham, the father of Judaism, is based on a tremendous risk, since God tests Abraham's courage with the most solemn risk. He calls him: "Abraham," and Abraham answers: *Hinneni*! meaning "Here am I." Rashi comments on the term *Hinneni*: "So do the righteous answer, the phrase denoting both humility and readiness."[9] God then says to Abraham: "Take now thy son, thine only son, whom thou lovest, even Isaac, and get thee into the land of Moriah; and offer him there for a burnt offering upon one of the mountains that I will tell thee of."[10] Abraham obeys God without any hesitation, as it is written: "And Abraham rose early in the morning, and saddled his ass, and took two of his young men with him, and Isaac his son; and he cleaved the wood for the burnt offering, and rose up, and went unto the place which God had told him."[11] What kind of risk does Abraham take? What kind of religious movement does He make? Kierkegaard maintains that Abraham's obedience to God involves two movements: the movement of resignation and that of the absurd. Through his first movement, Abraham gives up Isaac in an act that Kierkegaard defines as Abraham's "private venture," which nobody could understand; through his second movement, Abraham creates a "leap of faith," which, according to Kierkegaard, could have been done only by the virtue of the absurd.[12]

The first movement of Abraham is the classic movement that the psychologists of religion would call *ineffability*, a term denoting the essential component of every mystical experience. It is reflected clearly in Abraham's mystical experience in the story of the binding of Isaac, the *Aqeddah*. Ineffability is the characteristic of a personal mystical experience that cannot be described, cannot be conveyed in words, and cannot be shared with "the other."[13] Since Abraham's mystical experience was his "private venture," as Kierkegaard suggests, and since the mystical experience is usually a state of feeling and not a state of the intellect, it is an experience that, by definition, has a quality that cannot be shared. But at the same time Abraham surely experienced some sort of knowledge or insight, a mystical quality, a *noetic quality*, i.e. an experience of illumination tinged with great significance.[14] And yet, Abraham in the *Aqeddah*, says Kierkegaard, enters into his mystical experience through the domain of the absurd. For Abraham is willing to take the "leap of faith," which is his courage to be, by virtue of a great risk. It is possible, indeed, that Abraham said to himself that God was testing him, and that He would not eventually take his son as a sacrifice on Mount Moriah (as Kierkegaard suggests); but his immediate submission, his *Hinneni*, only confirms the absurdity of his action. Here we are faced with the father of Judaism, who is willing to sacrifice his own son and fatherhood for the sake of keeping the partnership with God. Abraham, without any doubt, not only took the "leap of faith," he also established it as a risk that is required in man's relationship with God. In fact, he *created* that risk in the history of mankind and constituted it as an essential element in the heart of the believer who seeks God and must enter the domain of courage. Isaac could have been sacrificed as a burnt offering, but Abraham had the courage that allowed him to put his feelings above his intellect. At this historic point Abraham established the Jewish faith on unconditional trust in God. This is the Jewish people's peak whence they begin to understand that absolute belief in God requires *the courage to risk*, since *the power of true faith is beyond the power of reason*.

The courage to risk appears frequently in the classic teachings of Jewish mysticism, Kabbalah, and Hasidism. We find in the spiritual teachings of Hasidism that *the power of faith must always be higher than the power of reason*, and the *Tzaddik* who sacrifices his soul comes to his spiritual awareness by virtue of *faith, and without understanding*.[15] This concept is consistent with Kabbalistic symbolism, since according to the Kabbalistic hierarchy of the *Sefirot*, Faith is the second *Sefirah* called *Emunah* (also called *Hokhmah*) and is higher than the third *Sefirah*, Understanding, which is called *Binah*. In the teachings of Kabbalah, however, it is not only a notion of symbolism but an essential element of the praxis of the daily religious life. Faith is above Understanding; it is beyond rationalism; it is outside the realm of intellectualism; it is superior to logic; it is greater than the mundane wisdom of the human being. Faith denotes an absolute trust in God, and "trust in God is the tranquility of the soul" says Rabbenu Bachya Ibn Paquda.[16] Abraham trusted God. He was not only willing to bind and sacrifice his son, Isaac, but also to courageously bind and sacrifice his own mind, enact the word of God, and stand at the frontier of the absurd. This is the ultimate example of risk that had been set for eternity by the great forefather of Judaism.

The notion of taking a risk as a fundamental condition in the covenant between God and His chosen people was reinforced in the teachings of the sages of the Mishnah and the Talmud. The example is the mystical story of the four sages who entered the king's orchard (*Pardes*):

> Our rabbis taught: Four entered the *Pardes* and these are they: Ben Azzai, Ben Zoma, Akher (Elisha ben Abuyya), and Rabbi Akiva. Rabbi Akiva said to them: "When you reach the stones of pure marble, do not say 'Water Water.' for it is said: 'He that speaketh falsehood shall not be established before mine eyes'"(Psalms 101:7). Ben Azzai gazed and died. Of him Scripture says: "Precious in the sight of the Lord is the death of His righteous" (Psalms 116:1–5). Ben Zoma gazed and was stricken. Of him Scripture says: "Hast thou found honey? Eat as much as is sufficient for thee, lest thou be filled therewith, and vomit it." Akher cut down the shoots. Rabbi Akiva descended in peace.[17]

Almost 2,000 years have passed since this mystical story was written. It has been interpreted through the centuries by hundreds of Jewish mystics and scholars in different ways. In the last two decades this story has gained a new scholarly interest among prominent scholars of Jewish thought and psychologists of religion.[18] But the accepted scholarly interpretation is that "the four who entered the *Pardes*" story teaches about the mystical myth of the ascent of the soul in the Divine palaces (*Heichalot*) of the Chariot of God (*Merkabah*), stating that in the sixth palace there is an appearance of myriads of waves, but in its true reality there is not even a drop of water there. The interesting element in this story, relevant to our discussion, is depicted in the warning words of Rabbi Akiva: "Do not say 'Water Water.'" If we are to assume that the *Pardes* is the domain of the Divine *Heichalot* and *Merkabah*, then the four sages are standing indeed at the threshold of a tremendous risk; except for Rabbi Akiva, who seems to have been inside the *Pardes* before, the other three sages have never been inside, and they stand outside, at the frontier of the unknown. Rabbi Akiva warns them not to speak, and, in accordance with the story before us, they did not say a word. Why then was Rabbi Akiva the only one who descended in peace? Because the mystical curiosity, through which the conscious minds of the other sages are attracted to the journey, involves a risk, but for Rabbi Akiva, who was familiar with the *Pardes*, there was no risk. The other three sages are willing to take the risk, and then each in accordance with his personal mental capacity and righteousness pays a price. The Talmud teaches later on that all three sages except for Rabbi Akiva paid either with their lives or with their sanity.

There is another important element in the story of the *Pardes* that is relevant to our discussion. About Ben Azzai it says "*gazed* and died," and about Ben Zoma it says "*gazed* and was stricken." From here we learn that there are two forbidden conducts that cause immediate punishment: do not *speak* ("Rabbi Akiva said to them ... do not *say* 'Water Water'"), and do not *gaze*. Why does the Talmud set these two restrictions if the human being is required to have the courage to be? Is it possible to achieve any degree of courage without speaking and gazing? The answer to this question can be found in the concept of language in Kabbalah and in the mystical notion of sight in Jewish spirituality. First I will discuss the restriction I call "do not speak," and then the restriction "do not gaze."

As noted above, the Hebrew language according to Kabbalah is expressed as the most profound spiritual reality. All things exist by virtue of the Divine language, which is the thread that makes up the tapestry of God's essence. God uses language in the process of the creation of the world, and at the same time He *is* language; for when He shifts from the *Ayin* to the *Yesh* he transforms Himself into verbalized consciousness. And since God created the entire body of the Hebrew language, each and every word, even the simplest word is Divine. Hence, at the very instant that the human being expresses an internalized thought and says a word, he participates in the Divine process of creation and becomes attached to God. We find in different schools of Kabbalah varieties of linguistic techniques of Kabbalistic meditations and contemplations, which are based in their entirety on Hebrew letters. In the Kabbalah of Abraham

Abulafia and his school, *Devekut* is fundamentally rooted in the combinations and permutations of the names of God. In Abulafia's concept of language, we learn that language is perceived as the universe itself; it reveals the structure of the Divine names of God; it reveals the structure of the laws of reality; and each letter of the Hebrew alphabet is in itself an entire world.[19]

The Hebrew language is not a human creation but a Divine emanation and a result of Divine revelation. Thus, the Jewish people are identified as the people of the Torah, the people of the Book, for the Torah is the embodiment of the Divine letters that stand together as the *Shi'ur Komah* (the "measure of height") of the Deity.[20] The Torah is the essential ontology that has been handed down from God to the Jewish people. Every generation is required to study it, fulfill its commandments, and hand it down to the next generation.

The Mishnah teaches:

> Moses received the Torah from Sinai and gave it to Joshua; Joshua to the Elders, the Elders to the Prophets; the Prophets to the men of Great Assembly. The latter said three things: Be cautious in judgment, raise up many disciples, and make a fence for the Torah.[21]

Did the sages who wanted to enter the *Pardes* understand the Divine concept of the Hebrew language? Did they realize that when one enters into the Divine realm of the *Pardes* it is possible to mistakenly replace "Marble" with "Water?" Rabbi Akiva apparently was trying to warn them not to make the mistake of mis-speech, for when one sees "marble" and says that it is "water" one violates the realm of God's speech. The entrance into the *Pardes* is a profound example of the courage to be, for it represents the human being's yearning to act in a way that will change him thoroughly. But it is an act conditioned by previous experience and maturity. For whenever a human being wishes to enter the *Pardes*, he must know that his "entrance" is dependent on speaking the truth, being cautious in judgment, raising up many disciples, and making a fence for the Torah. At the heart of the religious experience, as represented by the story of the *Pardes*, the realm of speech demands silence, since it is a sublime domain beyond speech – it is the silent realm of experience. Anything that a man says in this hyper-territory would be a mistake, and thus the Psalmist teaches: "Commune with your own heart on your beds, and be *silent Selah*."[22] The courage to be necessarily involves risk, and its core is speechlessness. It is the domain of the heart, the abode of the experience, and not the property of the intellect. Abraham in the *Aqeddah* says nothing but *Hinneni*. For he is the great example of one who is willing to take the risk, to bind his son, his mind, and his speech; and thus he becomes the forefather of the Jewish people when at the end of his ordeal God says to him: "For *now* I know that thou art a God-fearing man."[23]

At this point I would like to say a few words about the second warning, "do not gaze."

Aristotle's *Metaphysics* begins:

> All men by nature desire to know. A proof of this is the joy we take in our senses; for in addition to their usefulness they are loved for themselves; *and above all others is the sense of sight.* For not only when inclined to action, but even when we are not going to act at all, *we prefer sight to almost everything else.* The reason is that this, most of all senses, makes us know and makes visible many differences between things.[24]

The desire to know, according to Aristotle, dwells in the natural curiosity of humanity. Man is not born with knowledge, but he is born with the inclination to desire the acquisition of knowledge. As one Aristotelian scholar properly remarks, we are living in the reality of *Epistemophilia* – love of *episteme*, which could be described as the love of the mind, the love of philosophy, the love of wisdom, and the love of being in love with wisdom.[25] We seek an explanation for the heavens and the earth, for the soul and the body, and we inevitably encounter difficulties. When a difficulty emerges we begin to examine it first by sight. In many languages the verb to "see" is synonymous with the verb to "know." When A speaks to B and asks "Do you *see* what I mean?" and B answers "I *see* what you mean," both A and B *see* indeed the meaning of their discussion, for seeing *is* knowing. Sometimes seeing is even an elevated kind of knowing that involves not only the capacity of the mind but also the capacity of the soul. The phrase that someone is "blind to the truth" speaks of one who will not understand. About Ben Azzai the story of the *Pardes* says "*gazed* and died," and about Ben Zoma it says "*gazed* and was stricken." The Hebrew word for *gazed* that appears in the original text is *Hitzitz*, meaning stared intensely. In Hebrew the word *Hitzitz* has a negative connotation; it clearly means invading the privacy of the subject by looking at it, despite the fact that the one who stares knows that his staring is not permitted.[26] In the Torah we find some profound examples that explicitly forbid impermissible looking. When God is determined to destroy the corrupt city of Sodom, He sends the angels to the city to help save Lot and his family. God was being merciful to Lot, and thus the angels say to him: "Escape for thy life; *look not* behind thee … But his wife *looked* back from behind him, and she became a pillar of salt."[27] When Moses wishes to see God he says to Him: "Show me, I pray thee, Thy glory," and God answers Moses: "Thou *canst not see* my face, for man shall not see Me and live."[28] Here we learn that although man has a natural curiosity to look at the hidden and the forbidden, to explore the unknown and to cross all limits, there is always a border that must not be crossed. This border varies, however, from one human being to another. All four sages, Ben Azzai, Ben Zoma, Akher, and Rabbi Akiva, entered into the same *Pardes*, but only one of them survived the journey. Thus, the intellectual and spiritual curiosity of each individual is shaped in accordance with the individual's capacity. While Rabbi Akiva could *see*, the other three sages could not. The Jewish commentators on the *Pardes* story teach that both Ben Azzai and Ben Zoma never achieved ordination, and Akher became an apostate.

The discussion before us links the two warnings, "do not *speak*," and "do not *gaze*" as two dialectical elements in the Kabbalistic art of being. On the one hand, every man must actualize his desire to know, for his intellectual and spiritual curiosity demands an ongoing search for self-discovery, and every man *speaks* and *sees* by his nature. On the other hand, every man must measure for himself the quality of his intellectual, ethical, and spiritual capacity, lest he is stricken, God forbid, like those sages who entered the *Pardes* but could not overcome the unknown challenge that the *Pardes* presented.

In the same way that the courage to be demands an encounter with the unknown, the Kabbalistic art of being demands great courage for self-affirmation and self-actualization. It demands active involvement in the Jewish commandments, in Jewish ethics, and in good deeds without foreknowledge of the results of those actions. For Kabbalah is a religious and spiritual way of life and not just a form of theoretical mysticism. But at the same time the Kabbalistic art of being demands from the human being a sensory awareness and a responsible mind. The life of the Kabbalist is the life that yearns to surpass life, and every life surpassing life is a courageous life. In order to live such a noble life, it is necessary to intimately sense the pulse of life and the heart rate of being. The Kabbalist finds the pulse of life and the heart rate of being in his active relationship with God, in *Devekut*, and in spiritual worship.

A central aspect of this relationship is submission – submission to *Mitzvot* and to the way of God. Submission emerges from the spiritual discovery of the Kabbalist, who finds God in every aspect of reality. There is no piece of reality – even in the mundane world – where God is absent. Absence of the Divine is merely an erroneous human perception, claims the Kabbalist. When he is embraced by the spirit of God, the Kabbalist becomes courageous through submissiveness. *Having courage and being submissive at the same time is the secret dialectical bravery of the Kabbalist.* Here he stands at the most vital core of life that combines the duality of these opposites: courage and submissiveness. He stands between non-being and being and he is reminded that God Himself had to overcome non-being in order to be. Thus, with courage and submission the Kabbalist conquers all of his anxieties, even his dreadful fear of death. Courage and submission necessarily include risk,[29] but once the Kabbalist conquers his fear, submits, and thereby overcomes the risk, he follows the way of Abraham in the *Aqeddah*; he self-actualizes, and, most importantly, he follows the way of God.

Creativity

Creativity in the Kabbalistic art of being is the human *telos*, since through creativity man strives to reach his highest goals by imitating his Creator and thus fulfills himself as a man created in the image of God. Creativity is a lifelong process in which the human being becomes gradually aware of himself; he learns to listen to his inner voice, to reach his genuine self, to discover his true potentialities, and to *bring something new into being*. The creative process explores all hidden dimensions of man's being: his physical, spiritual, psychological, emotional, and rational dimensions. Through the creative process all of these dimensions reach one another and become one, and man becomes authentic.

The Kabbalist's notion of creativity may be correlated with that of the existentialist. The feature of humane existence for the existentialist is that *he* is creative but other things are not. All other things are, without consciousness, simply what they are, whereas the existentialist, with consciousness, constantly evolves.[30] The Kabbalist, like the existentialist, awakens every day to a world of new opportunities and new choices. He must choose, and he must choose the principles by which he chooses. Unlike any other thing in the world, the Kabbalist is not determined and not complete: "Existence precedes Essence" means for him that as a human being he creates his essences as he goes along. In his creative acts he discovers the freedom to make a higher reality from his lesser world. Finally, the Kabbalist's journey of life becomes a creative expedition in hyper-reality.

The God of the Jewish people appears since the dawn of history as a creative Divine entity. In classic Kabbalah, God is compared to an artisan who creates the world like a skillful craftsman. In *Sefer Ha-Yashar* God is described as "The good *Artisan* whose one intent is to do lovely and good work, just as the good and wise *artisan* intends to create very beautiful vessels."[31] In the Lurianic Kabbalah we read how God fashions the world out of raw material:

> And this raw material was made in the manner employed by the Creator who fashioned out of matter one piece of matter, and afterwards in order to create everything, [He] inserted his hands into this piece of matter and thereby formed it into a vessel, and so it is said: *Ka-Khomer be'-Yad ha-Yotzer*: "as matter in the hands of the Maker."[32]

In Jewish spirituality and Kabbalah, unlike in some modern psychology, the human being's creativity is manifested through art, science, and other aspects of culture *not* to compensate for his own inadequacies, for creativity is *not* a compensatory theory, as understood, for example, in the psychology of Alfred Adler. Nor is it a regression in the service of the *ego*, as other psychologists suggest, but rather it is a healthy, active and vital process. It is the central module of man's individuation, and the pivotal spiritual action that empowers the human being to imitate his Creator, the ultimate Artisan. The creativity of the Kabbalist is not limited to the nether world. God provided within the process of His creation, through *Tzimtzoom* and *Shevirah*, a great opportunity for the human being to participate in the cosmic task of the creation. Every act of *Tikkun* is a creative act. The Kabbalists teach that the Torah is based primarily on an ongoing process of *Tikkunim*. The history of the Jewish people embodies the many acts of God and His miracles: His creation of the world; His creation of the Israelites as His chosen people; His creation of their Homeland, their

Temple, their Tribes, their Kingdom, their Law, and their Ethics. The history of God Himself is the history of creative *doing*: He thinks, speaks, acts, shapes, judges, rewards, and becomes the *Epitome Artisan* and Creator.

We find in the teachings of Aristotle that a subject cannot create that which is different from itself: a horse creates a horse, a bird creates a bird, a fish creates a fish, and a man creates a man. God, however, creates the horse, the bird, the fish, and the man. Does this mean that all four creatures are created in the image of God? The Torah teaches that although everything is created by God, only man is created in the image of God. What is it about man that is different from all other creatures? Kabbalah finds in every element of creation the hands of God, but in the human being it distinguishes a unique characteristic: man is the only creature whose image is the image of God because he is the only creature who is destined to understand the Godly process of creation and being, to develop a relationship with his Creator, to imitate His ways in the creation, and ultimately to be creative, like Him. Hence, man is the only creature who receives the immediate task of *Imitatio Dei*. Like God Himself, who created the world with speech, man is given the ability to speak and he immediately names the creatures of the world: "Man – teaches the Torah – gave names to all cattle, and to every beast of the field."[33]

At the center of the act of creation we find the encounter between God and man. In every creation there are two major phases: first, the subject creates an object; and, second, the subject and the object create a relationship between them. It is only when the relationship between the subject and the object is established that the creation can be declared as complete. In Judaism, the relationship between God and His people is implemented by submission and worship through the acts of the *Mitzvot*. However, the *Mitzvot* do not only fulfill the people's need but also fill the gap in God's created world. This world, created imperfectly, allows man, via a creative *Tikkun*, to participate as an equal partner in the *epos* of creation.

In his *Halakhic Man*, Rabbi Joseph Soloveitchik teaches that the Creator impaired reality so that humanity could repair its flaws. Man, for Rabbi Soloveitchik, is the one who continues the act of creation. Abraham inquired into the secret of creation and clearly grasped it when he arrived at the realization of monotheism: he studied the acts of God and understood the world, and thereby through his submission, he participated in the sublime nature of its creation. When man becomes a partner of God and repairs the defects of the cosmos, he approaches his true *telos*. Soloveitchik tells us that this act of creativity is the deepest desire of the Jewish people.[34]

But creativity has many faces: it is the process of the scientist or the artist who engulfs an abundance of information from a scientific observation of nature or from the depth of the spirit of humankind. The creative man always claims that there is a *law* governing all natural or spiritual phenomena. In physics, for example, there is a law of conservation of energy, stating that there is a quantity which we call energy that does not change in the manifold changes that nature undergoes. This is a mathematical principle; it determines that there is a numerical quantity which never changes; even when this energy is transformed into gravitational energy, kinetic energy, heat energy, elastic energy, electrical energy, chemical energy, radiant energy, nuclear energy or mass energy, it still remains unchangeable in quantity.[35] The law of conservation of energy may apply to the ten *Sefirot* in Kabbalah, and to the concept of creativity in Jewish spirituality. Because the ten *Sefirot* represent the Divine energy, it would be inconceivable for the Kabbalist to imagine that they diminish or increase in quantity. They are the Divine energy that conserves itself within itself. Thus, we find the emphasis in classic Jewish mysticism: "Ten *Sefirot* of Nothingness, ten and not nine, ten and not eleven."[36] But although the quantity of the *Sefirot* does not change, their quality might. The ten *Sefirot* are the manifestations of God, who reveals Himself through ten Divine attributes in order to become known to his creatures in the world and be enhanced by them. These ten *Sefirot* maintain a unique dynamism of opposites between themselves: Male versus Female, Loving kindness versus Judgment, Left versus Right, Above versus Below. Their quality may change in accordance with the eyes of the beholder. At times, Loving kindness, *Hesed*, will appear to increase or diminish, and at other times Judgment, *Deen*, will appear to increase or diminish. *The power to increase, enhance, or diminish the quality of the ten Sefirot is bestowed by God into the hands of man. It is this power that Kabbalah calls Creativity.* The enhancement or diminution of the sefirotical world of God was shifted in the creation from the Hands of the Divine Artisan to the hands of the human artisan. God placed the *Sefirot* between His world and man's world. Now, they stand as the "ladder" that is the bridge between divinity and humanity.

Jacob the Patriarch had a magnificent dream about the world of the *Sefirot*:

> And he dreamed, and behold a ladder set up on the earth, and the top of it reached to heaven; and behold angels of God ascending and descending on it. And, behold, the Lord stood beside him, and said: "I am the Lord, the God of Abraham thy father, and the God of Isaac" ... And Jacob awaked out of his sleep, and he said: "Surely the Lord is in this place; and I knew it not."[37]

Jacob surely had a mystical experience and a time of revelation. But he also experienced creativity. He saw the *Pleromatic* world of God as an active and dynamic world, with angels ascending and descending its "ladder." Although Jacob *did not invent* the "ladder" of the angels of God, *he did reveal* it in his dream, out of his belief in the existence of those angels of God. The energy that enabled his revelation emanated from his own creativity. The "ladder" of the angels of God is the ontology of the world of the Divine. It exists in the heavenly world with or without Jacob's dream. But Jacob *communicated* with the "ladder" by bringing his mind into a state of creativity, that is, he internalized his belief in God and His angels, he permitted his belief to become a part of his unconscious mind, and when his unconscious mind presented a yearning to be heard and become conscious he was ready to envision God in his dream. *Jacob epitomizes the man who is most awake when he is asleep*. His dream testifies to his creative activity. His creative act, however, did not change the internal essence of the world of God but only enhanced its quality. This is why "Jacob awakened out of his sleep, and he said: 'Surely the Lord is in this place; and I knew it not.'" For God was, is, and always will be present everywhere. But before he dreamed, Jacob could have not seen Him. Before he dreamed, he was awake but unconscious; when he dreamed, he became asleep but conscious. Jacob had to enter into a hyper-reality of sleep in order to discover God; his discovery manifests his creativity. Thus, the creative mind is associated with a deep sense of awe and astonishment; it is a sense of joy and ecstasy, a sense of delight and a rapture.

In Judaism man's creativity is not a new invention to the extent that man creates something which is decidedly new, *ex nihilo*.[38] The Talmud teaches us that "everything that even an experienced scholar may teach, already was said to Moses on Sinai."[39] Man's creativity is rather a psychological rediscovery and an enlightenment that allows him to connect with the collective wisdom of the Torah and thus become wise. The Torah is the collective core of the Divine creativity that nurtures every man's creativity. However, whereas the Torah is the revealed collective conscious of the Jewish people, the Kabbalah is the concealed collective unconscious of the Jewish people, yearning to become conscious.

At this point I would like to say a few words about the *collective unconscious*. The concept of the collective unconscious has become central to the psychology of religion in the last fifty years. I would like to briefly touch upon it and its affinity to Jewish spirituality. Jung describes his concept of the collective unconscious as a part of the psyche that is different from the personal unconscious. The latter is a property of personal experience, whereas the former is inherited certainly by cultural transmission in myth, legends, fairy tales, etc. The contents of the inheritance of the collective unconscious are collective because they aggregate the memories, reflections, and history of the people who have gone before. These aggregates are known in Jungian psychology as *archetypes*. According to Jungian analytical psychology, in addition to the personal unconscious, which mainly includes personal memories, wishes, and fantasies, there exists in every human being a collective unconscious, which includes archetypal national and universal memories. The collective unconscious is the deep reservoir of the psyche and can supply the raw material for change, transformation, and integration.[40] One should be cautious when comparing this Jungian concept with similar concepts in Kabbalah, since the consciousness of man and his creativity in Kabbalah is a complex concept. On the one hand, it would be untrue to say that Kabbalah does not identify itself as the Jewish collective hidden knowledge. Kabbalah claims to possess a definite form of wisdom that is present always and everywhere. The Jewish people share the teachings of Kabbalah, which are not only the esoteric holy books of Judaism but also are the core of the collective wisdom of God. On the other hand, Kabbalah puts a strong emphasis on the unique and single creative experience of each individual who gives birth to a new rediscovery and a new idea by means of his *individual* experience. Thus, the Kabbalist stands between the collective wisdom and his individual experience; indeed, the Kabbalist draws his creativity from both. Here we should emphasize that the esoteric creative discoveries of one who studies Kabbalah, as with many mystical studies, are likely to portray aspects of the collective unconsciousness more than the personal unconsciousness. For this reason the Kabbalistic notions tend to have the ring of archetypes and share many things in common with ideas from other mystical traditions that similarly grow out of forays into the collective unconscious.

The Kabbalists declare time and again that the secrets of the Kabbalah hold the absolute truth of being, which is hidden in the exalted life of *Ein-Sof*. And the secret of the secrets is concealed in God's name. God's most elevated name in the Torah is YHVH, a name which bears two meanings in Hebrew that are one: *Being*, and *Was-Is-Will Be*. The numerical value, *Gematria*, of the name YHVH, equates the numerical value of the most elevated name of man, ADaM.[41] This means for the Kabbalists that the perception of God that can be apprehended by man is that God Himself becomes *Adam Kadmon*, Primordial Man. And at the same time, the great name of God, YHVH, in His creative unfolding, is ADaM. The necessary conclusion is that God's hidden life and the absolute truth of being were depicted in man who was created in the image of God.[42]

The Kabbalistic art of being is thus not only the *Godly* Art of Being but also the human art of being. In an early book of Kabbalah, *Sefer Ha-Bahir*, we find the Kabbalistic teaching on *Sheva' ha-Tzurot ha-Ke'doshot* ("seven holy forms") of YHVH that parallel the physical forms of ADaM. Man is considered by the Kabbalists as *Adam Kadmon* and *Adam Elyon* ("Primordial and Exalted Adam"), as emphasized in the symbolical language of the *Zohar*. The *Zohar* indeed repeatedly presents its anthropological description of man, as being a creature constructed with the ten *Sefirot*. This theme is continued in the fundamental teachings of Hasidism. The Maggid of Mazheritch, for example, says that:

> man is a Godly part from above, and when his thought cleaves to the Exalted on high, he can know what is happening on high, because all the things that occur on high cross his thought, as was said by Rabbi Shimon bar Yohai ... "All virtues that rise up [*mito're'rim*] above, rise up below in the *Tzaddik*."[43]

This means that the intrinsic structure of both God and man is one and the same. When YHVH shares His Art of Being with ADaM, and ADaM imitates the art of YHVH, he becomes like Him; he escapes the solitude of his existence and enters into a dialogue with his Creator. Hence, the Kabbalist's creativity always results from an encounter with his Creator, and it takes place at the meeting point between the two,[44] for only when the Kabbalist arrives at his creativity through this encounter with God does he become "individual." Precisely at this meeting point the Kabbalist's awareness emerges; here he longs to discover his potentialities, and here he begins to bring them forth toward actualization.

Loving

Love is the single most subtle and necessary component in the Kabbalistic art of being. It is the skillful art of giving and receiving; it is the cause and the origin of the creation of the world, since God creates the world out of love. Before the creation of the world all that existed was God in infinity. When God's Will to create emerges, He gives a part of His Divine space and shares His wholeness with man; He withdraws into Himself through *Tzimtzoom*, and He prepares a new space for humanity to be created, so that He can develop a relationship with every man and every woman founded on love. Since the art of loving is the art of giving and receiving, and since God creates man in His image, man is endowed with the same potential for the art of loving that includes the ability to give and receive. God creates every human being not only as a receiver of love but also as a giver of love. God loves His beloved and His beloved responds to Him with love.[45] God creates Adam and pours into his body from His loving Divine spirit; this Divine spirit is transformed into the soul of man, and when the soul of man remembers whence she came, she yearns to return to Him through the same path of *loving*.

According to Kabbalah, the soul of man, while living in the body, is like a foreigner imprisoned in corporeality. The soul senses that her original abode, from which all souls are carved from and to which all souls cleave, is her mother's womb in the heavenly world. In the Kabbalistic world of the *Sefirot*, the mother's womb is *Binah*, the "Supernal Mother." The soul's deep yearning to return to her natural dwelling, her profound attraction to reunite with God and become one with Him, the uplifting sentiment of joy that occurs during her unification with her "Supernal Mother" in the act of *Devekut*, her eagerness to become an entity that gives and receives, all of these sensations are what Kabbalah calls *Ahava*, love.[46]

In Jewish spirituality there are three modes of love. The first is the love of God for the human being, the second is the love of the human being for God, and the third is the love of the human being for another human being. The first mode of love is an *unconditional* love. It is unconditional because God loves Israel without the condition of love in return. In order to maintain His love towards His creatures, God must first acknowledge Himself and love Himself. The creation of the world is the process of God's individuation, allowing Him to transform Himself from the state of aloneness to the state of partnership. It allows Him to reveal His inner opposites and manifest them among His emanated world, to step out of His singularity and create His people, and to sign a covenant of love with Abraham: a covenant that is the inception of His loving relationship with His people. The unconditional love of God is shown through the abundant flow that He unceasingly bestows upon His people. Even when the people of Israel violate the covenant and are cast out into exile, God demonstrates His continuing unconditional love by exiling Himself and dwelling among them through the exiled *Shekhinah*. God is the Epitome Lover. His generosity provides, endows, and sustains the world and its people *ad infinitum*. Without His generosity the world would not be sustained for one day, not even for one hour. The Jewish people acknowledge the endless love of God, and they praise Him since "through His goodness He renews every day the act of creation," as is said in the morning Jewish prayer.

The second mode of love is a *responsive* love. The Jewish people owe their entire life, both as individuals and as a nation, to God who created them and selected them to become His chosen people. They express their gratitude to Him and aspire to be like Him. In his *Sefer Ahava (Book of Love)*, Maimonides includes the Jewish laws that cover the religious obligations that a Jew must fulfill in order to respond to God with love. All of these *Mitzvot* signify the human art of responding with love to God. The first and the most important response of human love to God is the prayer of *Shema*, based on the words of the Torah: "Hear O Israel, The Lord Our God, The Lord is One: And thou shalt love the Lord thy God with all thy heart, and with all thy soul, and with all thy might."[47] Three times a day the Jew is obligated to recite the prayer of *Shema*.[48] While reciting the words, he meditates on the deepest ties that bond him to his Creator. After the *Shema* come the other laws of love: the blessings of the *Kohanim* (the Priests), the laws of *Tefillin* (Phylacteries) and *Mezuzah*, the law that obligates every Jew to write for himself a personal copy of the Torah, the laws of *Tzitzit* (Fringes), and the law of *B'rit Milah* (Circumcision). Through the actual implementation of all of these laws, the Jew confirms his responsive love for his Creator. In the Jewish faith these laws of love establish *Mitzvot Asse'* (the laws of actions), which the Jewish people are required to perform within the ritual of the love of God. The Jewish art of loving in its fundamental realm is the property of the spirit, for the Jew cannot love his Creator only through the prayer or blessing, or even in the ritual of circumcision; he must also realize his love of God through *Kavanah* and *Devekut*.

The concept of love of God in Jewish ethics and Jewish mysticism was first crystallized in the comprehensive eleventh-century Jewish classic *The Duties of the Heart*, by Rabbenu Bachya Ibn Paquda. The most important teaching of Bachya's work is the concept of love of God. Bachya defines man's love of God as follows: "[Love] is the *telos*, the final aim of all noble qualities and the highest degree which men who worship God may achieve ... Beyond it there is no further stage and above it there is no further rank."[49] "What is Love of God, and how does one love God?" Since the soul is a spiritual entity that recognizes other spiritual entities, it is only natural for her to be attracted to those who belong with her own nature, claims Bachya. Thus, the soul recognizes that she was carved from the heavenly world, her natural place, and by her nature she cleaves to that place and reunites with it. *Cleaving to her source is the soul's natural experience called love.* However, whenever the soul is lacking her natural sensation of "homesickness," whenever she is not tormented in the corporeal body, whenever she does not recognize other spiritual entities and is not attracted to them, she is a sick soul; because a man who does not love God is acting against his own natural spirit. Thus, if the corporeal body of man becomes a safe *haven* for the soul, it means that his soul has lost her natural connection with her safe *heaven*.

Bachya writes:

> What is Love of God? It is the soul's *longing* for the Creator, and *turning* to Him, so that she *communes* with His elevated Light, because the soul is a simple spiritual entity which in accordance with her *nature* communes with other spiritual entities that resemble her, and distances herself from those corporeal bodies that are against her ... and when the soul senses that [through this communion with the Creator] the Light [of God] empowers her essence and spirit, she will turn to Him and commune with Him in her thought, and contemplate Him through her ideas, and cleave to Him and desire Him. This is the ultimate pure love.[50]

In the Kabbalah of Provence and Gerona and in the *Zohar*, the Kabbalists endowed the notion of love of God with a special symbolism. Love of God became the principal form of the relationship between man and God. Among the *Sefirot*, Love is the *Sefirah* of *Hesed*, which literally means Loving kindness in Hebrew. Love of God, say the Kabbalists, is the root of the commandments; it denotes spiritual strength; it illumines every thought; and it is the bond that frees every human being from being alone, since with the love of God the human being is always in relationship with the Divine. The lover of God always feels secure and protected, powerful and guarded, and, therefore, his love for God facilitates his victory over his existential fright.[51]

Loving God also means knowing Him and having passion toward Him, for in the Hebrew language the verb to know denotes the same meaning as the verb to love. This is clearly illustrated in the Torah: "And the man *knew* Eve his wife; and she conceived and bore Cain .... And again she bore his brother Abel."[52] Since love of God is also knowing Him, man's love of God is connected with a knowledge that eventually leads to self-maturity and insightful growth.

Maimonides emphasized both the intellectual and even the passionate elements that must dwell within the man who loves God:

> And how and what is the proper love [of man for God]? It is to love God with a great exceeding love, to the extent that the soul will be

connected in the love of God, and he should be continually captivated by it, like those who are sick with love, whose minds are at no time free from the passion for a woman ... since the thought of her occupies the mind at all times ... as Solomon says (Song of Songs 2:5) "for I am sick with love ...." One can only love God through the *knowledge* with which one loves God. And in accordance with the knowledge will be the love. If [the knowledge of God is] little, [the love is] little. If [the knowledge of God is] much, [the love is] much.[53]

According to Maimonides, man's love of God is both a passionate and an intellectual process. It is a spiritual feeling, and yet it is an intellectual activity that emanates from the mind and signifies the curiosity and the willingness of the human being to explore the true essence of God. Once human beings enhance their knowledge of God, they enhance their knowledge of themselves. Therefore, the activity of love is the enhancement of the human being's awareness, for the act of love opens the creative paths of awareness in the mind and the heart of every human being.

The third mode of love is the love of a human being for another human being. It is a *social* love. The Torah teaches that in order for man to love his neighbor, he must first acknowledge himself and love himself, for love cannot be shared between two human beings unless they first love themselves. The Torah states: "Thou shalt love thy neighbor *as thyself.*"[54] On this notion the Kabbalists developed an entire code of behavior, known as *Hanhagot*. Moses Cordovero teaches in his *Hanhagot* that a person must learn to enjoy the company of his fellow men and treat them with a kindly spirit. He must never curse them, refrain from speaking derogatorily about them, respect them, and associate with them for the purpose of the study of the Torah.[55] The Ari emphasizes that a person must commune with his friend, because once he binds himself to his fellow man and creates fellowship with him, his mystical knowledge increases and his reverence of God is enhanced. He must restrain himself and not be angry but be humble and modest. He must honor his friends, honor and respect his wife, and always reside within the community.[56]

These three modes of love, the love of God for the human being, the love of the human being for God, and the love of the human being for another human being, illustrate the existential dialogue in the Kabbalistic art of being, since by means of love God and man give and receive, and relate to one another. Hence, the art of loving in the Kabbalistic art of being teaches us to step out of our lonesomeness and live in society; it guides us how to create a dialogue with that society, to respect and honor "the other" and to be in relationship with "the other", to love ourselves and our fellow men, and to commune with God not only as individuals but also as members of the human family. Most importantly, the Kabbalistic art of loving is the art of the healthy and pure soul. When the soul is immaculate in accordance with her nature, she seeks to unite with other spiritual entities in order to become whole. For every action that promotes the soul's unification on earth individuates the soul through the art of loving; her attraction to beauty and esthetics, her attraction to knowledge and discovery, and her attraction to other human souls and to the spirit of God are all manifestations of love. For love is the inner voice that unceasingly reminds the soul of her need to grow and develop and become whole and complete. All souls are carved from love and to a love they yearn to return.

Kabbalah and self-discovery

The four components of the Kabbalistic art of being, Awakening, Courage, Creativity, and Loving are the major milestones on the path of individuation. They guide the human being in following God's actions, in imitating His ways in the creation, refining the soul, and elevating her from the mundane earthly world to the spiritual realm of the Divine. When a man realizes that all four of these ingredients reside in his spirit in potentiality, he begins to craft and develop them in his actual life. The Kabbalistic art of being uncovers the true reality and the ultimate end of every man and every woman who follows the word of the Torah, who fulfills the *Mitzvot* and studies the Kabbalistic symbolic meanings of every layer of existence. The Kabbalistic art of being is the discovery of the purpose of being. However, this art is not a simple art. It requires a curious mind and an inquiring heart; it demands a sincere will to explore the true substance of life; it needs a profound aspiration to probe and master the hidden life of God, the destiny of humanity, and the chain of being that links God and humanity. Existentially, the Kabbalistic art of being is a master skill of living that allows the human being to emerge and become complete and fulfilled.

When Rollo May writes about the term *Existentialism*, he accurately states that it comes from the Latin root *exsistere*, meaning literally "to stand out, [and] emerge."[57] Rollo May, like other existentialists, correctly stresses that while the emphasis on the notion of *essence* was the main domain of Western thought (such as in the philosophies of Socrates, Augustine, Pascal, and others), in *Existentialism* (such as in the philosophy of Kierkegaard, Nietzsche, and others) the emphasis is first and foremost on *existence*, since for the existentialist, as Sartre eloquently determines, "Existence precedes Essence." Although the philosophers of *Existentialism* are as distant from the Kabbalist as east is from west, we may say that at this crucial point the Kabbalist parallels the existentialist thinker. The Kabbalist follows the classic biblical answer of the Jewish people, who agreed to *do* first and only afterwards to examine what they had agreed to do, as formulated in the Torah: *Na'ase' ve-Nishma'*, "[All that the Lord hath spoken] we will do, and listen."[58] The Kabbalist permits himself to be activated by the power of *Ein-Sof*, to enter into the mystical experience, and to take the leap of faith beyond essence and reason, because he puts his full trust in God, his eternal partner. We may metaphorically claim that the existentialist's formula, "Existence precedes Essence," is translated by the Kabbalist into "Experience precedes Essence," since the Kabbalist leads a purposeful life by entering into relationship with God only when he is ready to enter the *Pardes* without precondition. This is the fundamental ingredient that installs the life of the Kabbalist not on the roots of his intellect and rational thinking, but rather on his spiritual and mystical experience. The Kabbalist's leap of faith is indeed an emotional experience; he surrenders himself to the Divine power, and only then does he discover the power of his own spirit. This art of surrender is a difficult art, since society teaches us to be suspicious and untrusting, to dispute and disagree, to command and control, and to protect ourselves at all costs. But the Kabbalist realizes that only through surrender does he empower himself. He surrenders to God and becomes even more secure and safe; he enters into the mystical experience not only because he has a curious mind and an inquiring heart, but also because he seeks to emerge and to be. He realizes that he must enter into the *Pardes* and take the journey of life, for the layer of his revealed self must encounter with the layer of his concealed self. When he enters into the *Pardes*, he expands and grows and brings his opposing forces into a complete integration; that is, he brings forth his potentialities into fulfilled actuality. Here is where the Kabbalist discovers himself. Through his mystical experience and acts of *Imitatio Dei* he finds the central vigorous center of his life. When he is at the core of his experience, he does not ask and does not inquire, he does not speak and does not gaze, he does not fear and does not tremble, but he strides into his experience. He becomes ecstatic with life, since he has reached life that surpasses life, reality that surpasses reality. Here he increasingly senses that the human being who lacks the courage to enter into the *Pardes* in order to become himself will eventually lose himself. Therefore, he surrenders his rationality in favor of his experiences, and he puts his trust unconditionally in God's hands and communes with Him without boundaries. Like Abraham in the *Aqeddah*, the Kabbalist says *Hinneni*!

The Kabbalist's awakening is his encounter with his inner and true world. His creativity is his rediscovery of God's spirit in him. His courage urges him to actively participate in the struggle between his conscious and unconscious mind, between his good inclination and his evil inclination. This struggle reveals to him that in every act of creation there is an element of destruction. Now he educates himself to face every crisis in life with optimism; for if in every act of creation there is an element of destruction, it follows that in every element of destruction there must reside the seed of a new creation. That seed he finds in loving God and humanity. With these acts he becomes bright and brave, aware and enlightened.

The Kabbalistic art of being also teaches the Kabbalist about God and the world. The mystical and spiritual path of the Kabbalist protects him from the fragility and the artificiality of the world. His epistemological perspective of the world permits him to relate to the central ingredients of his existence with a symbolic outlook. Through his personal experiences he discovers the dialectical nature of the nether world. He unfolds the reflection of God within the nether world and realizes that the source and origin of everything is in *Ein-Sof*. His mystical goal is directed not toward the lower world, for the lower world is ephemeral, but toward ascending to the upper world, where the Divine *Sefirot* will be revealed to him and he will finally commune with his authenticity. In the world of the Divine *Sefirot* he learns that the Godly emanations are constructed dialectically by means of duality and opposites; and he also learns that *he* is constructed by means of duality and opposites. Here he realizes that each person is only half a person, always dependent on the missing half for his or her very existence, but God alone is the undivided, eternal entity who completes every soul that yearns to unite with Him. Since he realizes that his soul is emanated from Divine elements, he cleaves to God and yearns to return his soul to her place on high.

We read in *Sefer Ha-Yashar*:

> The soul is emanated and taken from high forces, since the Creator, blessed be He, made her out of four [Divine] elements: from the power of his Reality, His Vitality, His Wisdom, and His Oneness. Of all these four [Divine elements] the soul was composed. And when the soul departs from the body ... all four [Divine] elements return, each one to its place ....
>
> If the soul was not [emanated] from heaven, she would not have known Him and recognized Him .... But as she understands the exaltedness of the Creator, we know that she is emanated from heaven, and therefore yearns to return on high.[59]

In conclusion, I would like to briefly review and summarize the following ten principles that constitute the Kabbalistic art of being:

1. God is the sole Creator; He is awakened, creative, courageous, and loving.
2. The Kabbalistic creation myth symbolizes God's individuation.
3. The process of the creation necessarily involves *a risk* and *a crisis*. Only by taking the risk and by overcoming the crisis can the Creator and His creatures become.
4. Creation is an activity of the mind and the heart. It is the awakening of every thought, the birth of language, and the genesis of speech.
5. Creation expresses a shift from potentiality to actuality, from darkness to light, from unconsciousness to consciousness, from the *Ayin* to the *Yesh*.
6. All worlds, above and below, are created simultaneously, and thus everything that exists, above and below, constitutes one chain of being.
7. Existence is an ongoing and never-ending creativity, and thus creation is the ontology of eternal recurrence.
8. Every existing thing is a result of God's creativity, and thus all creativity is the breaking of the One into the two and the many.
9. All things come from the One, depend on the One, wish to imitate the

One, and yearn to return to the One.

10 The Kabbalistic art of being is God's Art of Being, and therefore when men and women study the Kabbalistic teachings of God's relationship with the world and its creatures, when they follow His ways and imitate His actions, they enhance their lives, affirm their destiny, achieve fulfilled and actualized life, and while still on earth they enter the *Pardes*, the Divine realm of life, the one and only true life.

These ten principles, which constitute the Kabbalistic art of being, put the Kabbalist on the threshold of redemption. The fulfillment of these principles elevates his consciousness from mundane reality to hyper-reality. Now he begins to explore not only his life on earth but also the destiny of his soul in eternity. That eternity dwells, for the Kabbalist, in the Messianic days and eventually in the redemption of the world. Thus, while the Kabbalist is trying to live by his Kabbalistic principles, they are not ends in themselves; they are the means that prepare him to wait for the Messiah. Therefore, he waits and he fills his heart with eschatological yearnings. The Kabbalist's eschatology and his mystical sensation of waiting for the Messiah are the subject of the next chapter.

SHEKHINAH, the Kabbalistic Divine Presence

7

WAITING FOR GODOT AND THE JEWISH ART OF WAITING

The myth of Godot

Samuel Beckett's *Waiting for Godot* describes the following experience. One evening, an evening like any other evening, two elderly men who could be any men, like you and me, on a country road by a lonely tree, in the middle of nowhere, are waiting for someone by the name of Godot to appear. Their names are Estragon (Gogo) and Vladimir (Didi), and they have an essential existential task: they must wait together for Godot to arrive!

Gogo and Didi are waiting; they occupy their time speaking about their waiting, until an unidentified "boy" comes to share with them the news that "Mr. Godot won't come this evening but surely to-morrow." When the small boy departs, Gogo and Didi discuss the possibility of suicide by hanging themselves from the naked tree (the only prop on the stage). But then they decide that hanging themselves would be a meaningless act. Suicide would have been their preferred solution, but they are incompetent to carry it out, for even the idea of killing themselves is simply too boring for them. So they decide not to do it. And thus, they continue to wait for Godot who "won't come this evening but surely to-morrow."[1]

Waiting for Godot opens with the absurd statement "Nothing to be done," since for Gogo and Didi there is "nothing" to do except wait for Godot. It is a play of "nothingness," for it lacks a plot. It has neither beginning nor end, no literary development or structural progress. And yet, it is an opus in which "everything" is happening in the co-existential life of Gogo and Didi. Their shared activity of waiting transforms them from a world of "nothingness," of *Ayin*, to a world of "waiting," of *Yesh*. And although in their world the *Ayin* is the *Yesh* and the *Yesh* is the *Ayin* – for it is a world of no time, no order, and no program – their waiting experience creates an illusory world where they can live and may even be saved.

Gogo and Didi's world, however, is not a simple world of waiting; it is a world *about* and *while* waiting. One of Beckett's scholars[2] accurately translates the play's original French title *En attendant Godot* not as *Waiting for Godot* but as *While Waiting for Godot*. The orderly world of Gogo and Didi is a world without tangible fundamental principles and without boundaries; and therefore it is a world of no universal ontology. It is a world of their own, a world of their thought only, a world of their frame of mind, a world of their mind-reality, a world of waiting. Even their shift from one "activity" of waiting to another "activity" of waiting, a shift that could have signified a small change in their existence, is of their mind-reality only; for Gogo and Didi live inside their minds.

Gogo and Didi's life is an ongoing journey of waiting *while* speaking. The only thing that sustains the existence of their life is their intentional dialogue: they *speak* about their waiting and verbally create for themselves a dialogical world of speech; they are *waiting while speaking*. Their intentional dialogue while waiting is a conscious activity of speech. I call this intentional dialogue talking. It provides them with an illusion of existence and a delusion of protection. Their dialogue is the only thing that they own. Their endless voyage of talking is what breaks their dread of silence and saves them from their fear of annihilation; it is their own verbal invention. What do Gogo and Didi speak about while waiting for Godot? Since they wait, they speak; but because the point of their speech is that there is no point, their speech is pointless; and yet, their pointless speech is the point of their speech. Soon after the start of Act 2 Estragon says: "In the meantime let us try to converse calmly, since we are incapable of keeping silent." And immediately thereafter they have the following self-referential dialogue, which describes their existential condition:

Vladimir: What do they say?
Estragon: They talk about their lives.
Vladimir: To have lived is not enough for them.
Estragon: They have to talk about it.

This is the only place in the play where Beckett reveals almost explicitly his philosophical point of view about the human activity that I call talking. Beckett's sarcastic criticism is directed toward the human need to talk, which he perceives as a pathetic anachronism in the human race, an inferior urgency in human lives. The act of talking, he implies, is an act that embodies human ridicule; it creates for the human animal an illusion that pretends to conquer mortality; but at the same time it evades the true problem of life: death! And thus by talking, the human animal creates a broken shield: a denial of death. Talking allows one to be a member of a community, to be a part of a "religion," and even to be heroic. Talking is a mainspring of human activity that overcomes the fear of death by denying it.[3] For Samuel Beckett talking is an activity of the utmost irony by its very nature, and therefore Vladimir and Estragon are satirized as they ridicule other people who "talk about their lives."

Estragon and Vladimir criticize others but they have no sense of "the other." Since they live inside their minds they have no topography; they have no location or sense of direction. Their position is faulty and they lack a program. In short, they live in their minds and are lost in their minds. However, they do understand the absurdity of their world. They know that they are nowhere, that they have no point of return, and that they have no place to go to. Despite the repeated appearances of the boy who fails to recognize them and whose repetitive message to them is: "Mr. Godot told me to tell you he won't come this evening but surely to-morrow," they do realize that Godot will never come. Indeed, this realization is the key to the entire Beckettian philosophy of the absurd, for once Gogo and Didi understand and realize their pointless point in life, their conscious dialogue becomes their only life saver. Therefore they create an intentional non-conventional program: they wait for Godot, speak about their waiting while waiting for Godot, and realize that Godot will never come.

Thus, Gogo and Didi speak to one another and they speak to themselves at the same time. Since their world is a world of no order, their dialogue is also a monologue. Since waiting is the only thing that has been left for them to do, they wait and allow us to share with them their experience of waiting. But what is "waiting" in *Waiting for Godot*? *Waiting*, for Gogo and Didi, could be the search for the self, but it could also be the experience of losing the self. It could be their single most religious experience or their most heretical one. It could be their spiritual yearning to return and commune with God, or their atrocious experience of separation from God. It could be their conscious marveling at the fullness and enlightenment of the celestial *Pleroma*, or their conscious painful awareness of the ultimate abyss. It could be a great hope that they desire to fulfill, or an unendurable despair that they dreadfully fear. Beckett's waiting could also be looked at as a Gnostic image; that is, waiting, whose binding element is not what *does* take place, but rather what *does not* take place; and thus, Gogo and Didi's existential direction would be a downfall, or as Harold Bloom puts it, a "Descent."[4] The only unambiguous wish that is shared by Gogo and Didi is their aspiration to remain together; for they must stay together while waiting for Godot, who "won't come this evening but surely to morrow."

Why are Gogo and Didi waiting for Godot *together*? Because they lost their individuality and have no distinctiveness. Except for their existential condition that obliges them to be linked together in a symbiosis, their presence on the stage is meaningless. But they are meaningless together, and for them that is meaningful. They are two, and yet they are one; they are in partnership for life, under the natural law that "man cannot live alone," a law that can be phrased as "two-getherness." They cannot be separated one from the other, for they share the same deserted destiny; the destiny of waiting "two-gether" for Godot. They are linked "two-gether" by something incomprehensible, but yet their incomprehensible linkage is their lucid nexus; they are different in character, different in temper, different in rage, and yet they are the "identical twins" of the human condition.[5] At the same time Gogo and Didi's partnership determines the core of their mission; they consciously realize "two-gether" that one never waits alone for Godot, since waiting – what I call eschatological waiting – is an activity that is always performed in partnerships. Their coupling unit exemplifies, therefore, their mutual dependency. It is their necessity to belong as one and their urgency to be linked as one; like two lost souls who find comfort in the arms of one another. Hence, Estragon asks: "How long have we been *together* all the time now"? And Vladimir answers: "I don't know. Fifty years maybe."

Waiting for Godot can be perceived as a messianic play. Some scholars saw the theological seed of Godot in Luke's account of the crucifixion, as summarized by St Augustine: "Do not despair: one of the thieves was saved. Do not presume: one of the thieves was damned." Gogo and Didi indeed refer to those thieves after the beginning of the first act when Didi says: "Two thieves, crucified at the same time as our Savior."[6] But the messianism of *Waiting for Godot* is far beyond the realm of a particular religion, for the play embodies universal and existential principles of messianism. I call the first messianic principle in the play *the absence of Godot*, the second principle *the leader character versus the follower character and their two-getherness*, and the third principle *speech versus immobility*.

The first messianic principle in the play portrays the absurd human hope for some entity to arrive, an entity that has in its power to make a difference; for "making a difference" is in essence the infrastructure of every salvation. However, it is the absence of this mysterious entity, the absence of Godot, that sustains the messianic reality of Gogo and Didi. Without Godot in their minds, they would have nothing to wait for; with the appearance of Godot – if God forbid Godot would appear – they would also have nothing to wait for. Their only solution is to wait for the absent Godot, for his absence allows them to create a reality of waiting "en attendant." Thus, the first paradoxical, unbreakable rule of messianism is established in the play; that is, the human condition exists in such a way that the human animal always anticipates the hidden and concealed Messiah of the "other world" to appear, on condition that the Messiah for his part never reveals himself; for had he revealed himself, he would not be the Messiah.

The second messianic principle in the play is symbolically depicted in the names Didi and Gogo. Didi, as implied by his name (French "dis"), is the more speaking persona, the philosophical, the reflective and the *leader character*. He is the aware persona of the two heroes; the one who initiates the activity of waiting and induces his friend to wait with him. Gogo, as implied by his name (English "go"), is the more mobile persona of the two heroes; he is the character who moves and shifts and changes and reverses. He is the *follower character* who is perpetually controlled by his leader. He is the one who does not initiate the activity of waiting but rather the one who is dragged into it. The two characters complement each other: the first introduces leadership and speech ("di[s]" "di[s]"), and the second introduces loyalty and mobility ("go" "go").[7] Indeed, when one examines carefully the words of the dialogical interplay between the two heroes, one discovers that Didi is far more messianic than Gogo. While Didi is portrayed as the leader character who is *actively* waiting, Gogo is portrayed as the follower character who is *passively* waiting. The latter repeatedly forgets the subject and the reason of his waiting, and therefore he is frequently reminded by the former to join the venture of waiting. Hence we hear the following repeated formula:

Didi: Let's wait and see what he says.
Gogo [forgets and asks]: Who?
Didi [reminds him]: Godot.
Gogo: Good idea.

(*Later on*)

Didi: I thought it was he.
Gogo [forgetting again]: Who?
Didi [reminding him again]: Godot.

This exemplary dialogue reflects one of the peak meeting points in the play between awareness and unawareness, between the one who actively waits, and the one who passively waits and must be constantly reminded to join the quest of waiting. It is a dialogue based on mutual dependency: Didi must remind Gogo to be waiting, and Gogo must agree with Didi to be following him and to be waiting "two-gether" with him as his follower. This mutual dependency and shared covenant is the essence of their state of "two-getherness"; for in every messianic program there is a leader factor and a follower factor, an active force and a passive force. Every messianic plan requires a leader character who persuades a follower character to comply with the leader; for the glorious meeting with every kind of Godot is too great to be carried out by one person alone. After all, meeting with Godot is an encounter with the unknown; for Godot is the hidden and concealed entity, the "other worldly" figure who could be an angel of God, the Messiah, or even God Himself. Thus, the leader character, who is always the aware persona, is the one who constantly reminds the follower character, who is always the unaware persona, that both of them share the same fate and hence must wait together. In our play, Didi personifies the leader, the prophet, whereas Gogo personifies the follower, the people. Didi exemplifies the head of the herd, Gogo exemplifies the sheep, and both Didi and Gogo share the same fate of waiting "en attendant."

The third messianic principle in the play is symbolically depicted in the conflicting tension between Gogo and Didi's *speech* and *immobility*, a principle that ascends to peak dramatic moments at the very end of both acts in the play, when Beckett uses the exact same text and "participates" in the play through a single significant theatrical direction:

Estragon: Well, shall we go?
Vladimir: Yes, let's go.

They do not move.
Curtain.

This text reflects the dialectical tension between *speech* and *immobility* that occurs throughout the entire play. It reveals Gogo and Didi's motion expressed in speech versus their motionlessness expressed by their immobility, and it eventually frames the two characters in a picture of void and chaos. Thus, speech versus immobility is the theme in the play that delineates Gogo and Didi's ambiguous condition of life and the ambiguous life of every human being who is torn between the essential need to express the spoken word and the incompetence to implement it, between the natural need to act and the inability to act, between the existential urgency to move and the incapability to do so. This tension is the focal point of the play's messianism, for it portrays in strong colors the conflict between hope and despair, between the yearning of the spirit to be redeemed and the inability of the body to act accordingly. It is a tension resembling the point of clinical death, when the mind consciously realizes that the body no longer responds to the brain, for the two are in total separation. Gogo and Didi are waiting together for Godot and they say, indeed, "let's go," but as in a dream where the dreamer is consciously aware that his body betrays him, they are paralyzed together and "they do not move." In fact, at the core of their discussion we learn that their reality, like our reality, could be just a dream:

Estragon: I was asleep. Why will you never let me sleep?
Vladimir: I felt lonely.
Estragon: I had a dream.
Vladimir: Don't tell me!
Estragon: I dreamt that–
Vladimir: DON'T TELL ME!

Vladimir does not wish to hear Estragon's dream. He does not wish to know if he lives in a reality or a dream; if he discovers that his life is a dream it would be a dreadful thought, and if he discovers that his life is a reality it would be even worse. In both cases he will not be able to endure the consequences. "DON'T TELL ME," he says to Estragon. Instead, he prefers to wait for Godot.

Finally, when Gogo and Didi speak about waiting for Godot their dialogue leads to no result; it freezes the time and creates an ontology of waiting. Thus, Godot is born in their minds. But Godot never arrives, for the ontological core of their messianism is only in the experience of their waiting. Furthermore, since the heart of Beckett's play is not Godot himself but the act of waiting for him, and since the act of waiting embraces Didi and Gogo's existential condition, their reality is a reality of absurdity. Their act of waiting is their single most authentic element of existence, and yet it is the single most absurd element of existence; for it illustrates their miserable condition in which they yearn to bring their dream to realization while that realization might be the dreaming itself. The act of waiting is their natural element of existence, for it embodies their hunger and thirst to actualize their desire and hope, if those aspirations are even conceivable for them. However, if Godot, God forbid, arrives, Didi and Gogo's act of waiting becomes the end of their desire and hope. If Godot arrives they will have nothing to wait for, and the voice of the "boy" who repeatedly says: "Mr. Godot won't come this evening but surely to-morrow," will be silent forever. The act of waiting dwells between their absurd speech "let's go," and their paradoxical immobility "they do not move." It resides between the expression "let's wait," and its counter-expression "Godot won't come this evening." The act of waiting is the preposterous promise that "reassures" Didi and Gogo that whenever they come back to the stage of life they have something to do, contrary to the opening statement in the play, "Nothing to be done."[8]

The three messianic principles that underline the existential life of Beckett's heroes in *Waiting for Godot* can also be found as central principles in Jewish messianism. Before I introduce them in the framework of Judaism, I present a brief conceptual and historical description of the major messianic trends in Jewish mysticism.

Messianic trends in Jewish mysticism

The origin of the Jewish concept of *waiting* emerges from the Jewish biblical messianic belief, although the term *Messiah* in the Bible is never used to connote the eschatological figure of the Messiah. The term *Messiah*, meaning "anointed" or "consecrated" is found thirty-nine times in the Bible; it mainly refers to the kings of Israel and Judea and occasionally to the High Priest. Only after Israel rebelled against God and was driven out of their homeland did the term *Messiah* begin to signify eschatology and waiting. What is eschatology in the context of Jewish spirituality? In general terms eschatology is the doctrine of the End of the Days and of the "renovation" of the world. It involves the destiny of the individual and the fate of the collective. The Oxford Dictionary defines it as "the department of theological science concerned with 'the four last things'; death, judgment, heaven, and hell." In the context of Jewish spirituality, however, it is a term used to connote the Hebrew expression *A'kha'rit ha-Yamim*, which literally means "the last [or the end] of the days." The expression *A'kha'rit ha-Yamim* appears for the first time in the Torah in the blessing of Jacob,[9] and it also occurs more than thirty times in the ancient texts of the Dead Sea scrolls.[10] In Jewish spirituality the concept of eschatology is a complex one, for it encompasses numerous schools of thought and an endless quest. It develops along with the intellectual, spiritual, moral, and social experiences of the Jewish people, and it takes place on the stage of human history. It is marked with a vision of a better humanity at the End of the Days; with continuity and paradoxicality, particularly in reference to the figure of the Messiah, with the terminal wars between Israel and the Gentiles; with the belief in judging individuals after death; and with the faith in the resurrection of the dead and the eternal life of the righteous people.[11] At the center of Jewish eschatology stand the beliefs in *Yemot ha-Mashi'akh* (days of the Messiah), in *Bi'at ha-Mashi'akh* (coming of the Messiah), and in *Ge'ullah* (redemption). Jewish eschatology is marked with the reinstitution of the kingdom of David; with the revelation of God's hidden knowledge of the End; and with apocalyptic changes in the cosmos – some of which will be catastrophic in nature – that will eventually lead to the "Light of the Messiah." According to many of the classic texts of Judaism, everything would culminate in the End of the Days in the perfection of the Jewish law. The Messiah would enhance and spread the word of the Torah, enlighten the minds of the people, and bring a deeper understanding of God.

Since the belief in the Messiah is an essential and inseparable part of every Jewish eschatology, messianism and eschatology are frequently used interchangeably in the context of Judaism. It should be emphasized, however, that while Jewish eschatology is the comprehensive doctrine of the belief in the End of the Days, and while every aspect of Jewish eschatology is at once messianic, not every trend in Jewish messianism is eschatological. In fact, some of the prominent Jewish messianic experiences can be defined as apocalyptic and eschatological, whereas others are non-apocalyptic and non-eschatological, and may even be entirely ahistorical.[12] Jewish eschatology is born with the rebellion of the people of Israel against God. It comes about with the destruction of the Jewish kingdom and with the exile of the Jews from the Promised Land. This new reality creates two opposing poles in the spiritual and religious life of the Jewish people: on one hand they struggle to keep their faith while far away from their homeland, on the other hand they long to return to that homeland. Hence, the Jewish people of the last 2,000 years can be generally described as the paradigmatic messianic nation that has unceasingly nourished a yearning spirit to be redeemed. It is a nation that has sought to restore its home and renew its language; to reconstruct its culture and to rebuild its temple; and ultimately to resume its national, political, and spiritual independence under the renewed kingdom of David. Thus, Jewish messianism stems from the long historical exile of Israel and its hope to be redeemed and returned to its land.

There are four essential components in the spiritual history of the Jewish people: sin, exile, repentance, and redemption. The Jewish sages claim: "Because of our sins were we driven from our land." Rabbi Eliezer teaches that the redemption of the people of Israel is directly and unquestionably dependent upon repentance: "If Israel repent they are redeemed; and if not, they will not be redeemed." But Rabbi Joshua makes the issue hard on Rabbi Eliezer and asks: "If they do not repent, will they not be redeemed? [and he answers] The Holy One, blessed be He, will place over them a king whose decrees will be harsh ... and Israel will repent and return to good deeds."[13] Indeed, in the minds of the Jewish sages, philosophers, and mystics, the ultimate redemption of Israel was indisputable. The only aspects in question surrounded the nature of the redemption, the vision of the End of the Days, the figure of the Messiah himself, and the time of his coming.

The Messiah himself does not appear in the Jewish sources in the form of one particular person, but rather in the figures of various redeemers and saviors. Moses is considered the first Jewish Messiah. He redeemed the people of Israel from slavery in Egypt and led them on the road to freedom; he is the master of all prophets; the magical figure who performed miracles in Egypt and Sinai, and the man of God who handed down the Torah to the stiff-necked people of Israel. Moses, the Midrash says, is the first Messiah, "the first redeemer," in contrast to the later Messiah, who is "the last redeemer."[14] He is recognized as the biblical messianic figure for whom the world was created, as taught by the sages of the Talmud: "Rab said: The world was created only on David's account. Samuel said: On Moses account; Rabbi Yochanan said: For the sake of the Messiah."[15]

King David is the second prototype of the Jewish Messiah. His great political power and wisdom allowed him to unify all of the tribes of Israel and establish the first powerful Jewish nation by means of struggle, courage, and heroism. He led the Israelites in extensive wars against their neighbors and succeeded to become the greatest Jewish king of glorious victories. He is the Jewish messianic figure who portrays the royal savior of the newly born nation of Israel; he is the wise soldier, the brave warrior, the mindful strategist, and the heroic king, but above all he is the man chosen by God to crystallize the kingdom of Israel and unite the Jewish nation in the Promised Land.[16]

Another incomparable biblical figure of the Messiah is Elijah, the loyal prophet of God who fought the war against Canaanite idolatry in Israel, defeated the false prophets of Ba'al on Mount Carmel, and proved the power of God to the people of Israel and to their hostile neighbors. The Bible's description of Elijah's ascent to heaven in a chariot of fire[17] gave rise to the Jewish myth that Elijah's return is expected before the coming of "the great and terrible day of the Lord."[18] The Midrash tells us that when the time for the redemption arrives, it is Elijah who will announce the Messiah to the Jewish people; he will rebuke Israel and will open the gates of repentance for them; he will settle all of their disputes; he will advocate Israel's rights and plead for Israel's redemption before God; and he will predict the coming of the Messiah and comfort him. According to Jewish popular belief based on Midrashic teachings, Elijah is the source of the blessings and good fortunes of the Jewish people. At the Passover Seder meal he is welcomed in every Jewish home with a special cup of wine placed specifically for him; and at the Jewish circumcision ceremony, the *Sandaq*, the godfather of the newly born child, is honored with *Kisse' Eliyahu*, the chair of Elijah, which symbolizes the promised redemption. Because of his eminent and miraculous personality Elijah has achieved the rank of the redeemer of the Jewish people. We read in the Midrash: "Two prophets emerged for Israel from the tribe of Levi: The first was Moses and the last was Elijah. And both of them redeem Israel on [God's] assignment. Moses redeemed them from Egypt ... and Elijah will redeem them in the Future to Come."[19]

One of the central themes in the messianic idea in Judaism is bound up with the myth of the "two Messiahs": Messiah son of Joseph and Messiah son of David. Messiah son of Joseph is portrayed as the warrior Messiah who comes forth from the seed of Joseph son of Rachel. The Midrash teaches that when Rachel bore her son, Joseph, "it was prophesied to her that the Messiah would come forth of her."[20] According to this belief, Messiah son of Joseph is the first of the two Messiahs: he is described as the legendary army warrior who leads the military legions of Israel in the messianic wars and wins great victories, but finally he dies at the hand of a Satanic creature called *Armilus* in a battle in which the army of Israel is defeated by *Gog* and *Magog*.[21] After the death of Messiah son of Joseph, his body is left unburied in the streets of Jerusalem for forty days, a number which symbolically parallels the forty years in which Moses led the Jewish people in the Sinai desert. Like Moses, Messiah son of Joseph portrays the example of the Jewish redeemer who himself cannot escape tragedy. Both Moses and Messiah son of Joseph must pay with their lives in order to redeem the entire community of Israel. But unlike Moses, whose place of burial is unknown, Messiah son of Joseph comes to life again. Forty days after his death the second Messiah, Messiah son of David resuscitates him and effectively replaces him. Messiah son of David is portrayed as the ultimate Messiah in Judaism. He defeats *Armilus* and all forces of evil; he is present at the resurrection of the dead; he opens a new era for the study of the Torah; and he puts an end to sufferings and horrors. Whereas Messiah son of Joseph is the dying Messiah who perishes in the messianic catastrophe, Messiah son of David is the living Messiah who prospers and reinstitutes the idealic Davidic kingdom.[22]

The development of the messianic idea in Jewish mysticism and Kabbalah is complex, for it comprises a wide spectrum of different Jewish figures and trends who have appeared throughout the centuries. I would like to briefly specify in chronological order six prominent Jewish messianic trends of the last millennium:

Ecstatic spiritual messianism of Abraham Abulafia

This unique messianic trend was created by the influential ecstatic Kabbalist, Rabbi Abraham Abulafia, in the last quarter of the thirteenth century, when Abulafia was active mainly in Sicily, Palermo, Messina, and other places in Italy. Abulafia was the first Kabbalist to see himself publicly and explicitly as a Messiah, a notion that created a great tension and controversy, since the *Halachic* authority at that time, Rabbi Shlomo ben Abraham ibn Adret (Rashba) denied Abulafia's messianism. Nevertheless, Abulafia's messianic teachings flourished and became a powerful messianic doctrine that combined spiritual experiences with messianic aspirations. His messianic mystical teachings incorporated techniques of prophetic eschatology, ecstasy, and *unio mystica*. Abulafia exemplifies the personal mystical Messiah in Judaism. His messianic aspirations and teachings influenced some of the prominent messianic mystics of Kabbalah and Hasidism.[23]

Kabbalistic theosophical and theurgical messianism in Spain

This trend flourished in the thirteenth century, following the twelfth-century early Kabbalistic school of Rabbi Isaac the Blind in Provence. It subsequently included the major teachings of the Kabbalah in Gerona headed by Rabbi Moses ben Nachman (Nachmanides), Rabbi Ezra and Rabbi Azriel of Gerona, Rabbi Jacob ben Sheshet and the Kabbalist brothers Rabbis Jacob and Isaac Cohen. It culminated in the thirteenth century with the magnum opus of Kabbalah, the *Zohar*.[24] The early Kabbalists of Provence and Gerona and the author of the *Zohar* believed that the secret of the nature of creation is directly connected to the Messiah: whereas the creation marks the way of the descent from the Godly *Ayin* to the *Yesh*, the Messiah marks the way of the ascent from the *Yesh* to the *Ayin*. The Messiah, they claim, will show us the way back to "our Divine home," for the messianic path is the way of return to the origin of creation and not to its end.

According to the *Zohar*, the Messiah dwells in a hidden abode called *ken tzippor* (the "Bird's Nest"), and he will be revealed at first in upper Galilee. The messianic era will begin with the revelation of the "Light of the Messiah," which will be unfolded in our world; however, the redemption itself will not signify a new world but a restoration of the original world. At the time of the redemption the creation will be dressed with the original robes that were formed in the mind of God "when the will to create emerged," and the original nature of the creation will be finally revealed. The exile of the *Shekhinah* will come to an end, and harmony will be reinstated in the world of God. At "that day" the hidden secrets of the Torah will be revealed, and the esoteric gnosis of Kabbalah will be known to all. "At that day God will be One and His name One."

In the *Zohar* the mystical Kabbalistic approach treats the Messiah through the theosophical symbolism of the ten Divine *Sefirot*, and thus the Messiah himself becomes *Hypostasis* and a symbol associated with various *Sefirot* that emanate from *Ein-Sof*. According to the *Zohar* the Messiah is the symbol of the tenth *Sefirah*, *Malkhut*, which is associated with the *Shekhinah*; at times he is the symbol of the ninth *Sefirah*, *Yesod*, which manifests righteousness; and at other times he even symbolizes the first *Sefirah*, *Keter*, which is related to the "Supreme Will" of *Ein-Sof*. A special status and recognition is given in the *Zohar* to Rabbi Simeon bar Yohai, the chief Kabbalist hero of this book, and his *Have'rim*, his comrade Kabbalists and disciples. Rabbi Simeon and the *Have'rim* resemble in their mystical proficiency and exemplary ethical conduct, a dress rehearsal of the messianic era. In the eyes of the *Have'rim*, Simeon is the living symbol of the Messiah who is the *Tzaddik*, an attribute associated with the Kabbalistic *Sefirah* of righteousness, *Yesod*. However, Simeon not only symbolizes righteousness; he epitomizes righteousness. He is defined as *Tzaddik Yesod Olam*, "the righteous man who is the foundation of the world," and "the pillar of the world." He is portrayed as the chief *Zoharic* Kabbalist who teaches the *Have'rim* the innermost esoteric secrets of Kabbalah; he teaches them about the four hidden levels of the soul, about the world to come, and about the eternal existence in the afterlife. He reveals to them the true destiny of the Jewish people by showing them the mysterious meaning of the Hebrew letters and words in the Torah. And most importantly, he personifies the human unification with the Divine by his union with the *Shekhinah*, and thus he theurgically brings harmony in the upper world of God. In light of his eminent stature as the greatest Kabbalistic persona, Simeon bar Yohai becomes the *Zoharic* Messiah hero who is both *the redeemer* and *the redeemed*. Through his dedication to the Torah, his proficiency in the Kabbalistic symbolism, and his superior ethical deeds he brings redemption to the entire cosmos, to the Jewish people, and to himself.[25]

Pre-Lurianic messianism in the fourteenth and fifteenth centuries

This trend marks, for the first time, the Kabbalistic messianic movement that created magical and talismatic procedures which intend to cause radical changes in the order of nature. At the center of this trend stands *Sefer Ha-Mal'ach ha-Meshiv* (*The Book of the Responding Angel*), and the main messianic Kabbalists of this circle are Rabbi Abraham ben Eliezer ha-Levi, Rabbi Yehudah Hayyat, Rabbi Asher Lemelin Reutlingen, and Rabbi Shlomo Molcho.[26]

Lurianic messianism in sixteenth-century Safed

This extremely complex and influential movement of Kabbalah combined, for the first time, Kabbalah, ethics, and messianism. The leading figures of Lurianic messianism are Rabbi Isaac Luria (the Ari) and his disciple Rabbi Hayyim Vital. Both Luria and Vital were acknowledged by their disciples as Messiahs. Luria's major Kabbalistic work is *Sefer Etz Hayyim* (*The Book of Tree of Life*), and Vital's major messianic work is *Sefer Ha-Hezyonot* (*The Book of Visions*). In Lurianic Kabbalah the figure of the individual Messiah was diminished. As discussed in previous chapters, according to Lurianic Kabbalah the creation was bound up with a Divine crisis termed "the breaking of the vessels," a crisis that caused the Divine sparks to fall within *Olam ha-Assiyya*, "The World of the Making." Now it is the responsibility of the Jewish people to free these Divine sparks from the abyss and cause their return to their pristine position. Lurianic Kabbalah calls this theurgical act, *Tikkun*; it is the mending of the "broken vessels" and it is placed in the hands of every person among the people of Israel. Here the myth of the Messiah is no longer a myth of a particular figure but rather of the collective body of Israel, and thus the Messiah becomes the whole of the nation of Israel rather than the individual redeemer.[27]

Sabbateanism in the seventeenth century

This is the most important messianic phenomenon in pre-modern Judaism, for it portrays a wide messianic influence on tens of thousands of Jewish people who wholeheartedly believed in the messianism of Sabbatai Sevi and followed him. At the center of this messianic trend stand Sabbatai Sevi and his prophet Nathan of Gaza.[28] Sabbateanism is the largest messianic movement in the history of Judaism. I will limit my discussion to noting that Sabbateanism based itself on Kabbalistic interpretations of the idea of the Messiah, with extensive paradoxical and antinomean ideologies. Eventually Sabbatai Sevi and thousands of his followers converted to Islam.

Hasidic messianism of the eighteenth, nineteenth, and twentieth centuries

Hasidic messianism is the last Jewish messianic trend. It began with the emergence of Hasidism in eastern Europe almost 300 years ago and is alive and well today. It has combined mystical and spiritual messianic elements and has drawn its ideas from all Jewish messianic schools that preceded it. At the center of this trend stand the founder of Hasidism in the eighteenth century, Rabbi Yisrael Ba'al Shem Tov (the Besht) and other Hasidic masters, such as Rabbi Menakhem Nakhum of Chernobyl, Rabbi Yitzhak Aitzik Yehudah Safrin of Komarno, Rabbi Menakhem Schneerson of Lubavitch, and others.[29]

These messianic trends had a powerful impact on the Jewish people. They provided crucial theological answers to the exiled Jews who have sought salvation for many centuries. They also suggested apocalyptic, catastrophic, and utopian models of redemption, followed by golden messianic eras fulfilled with great knowledge of the Torah, with worldly peace and tranquility. The spiritual and religious fabrics of these messianic trends have become the essentials of Jewish identity.

The Jewish concept of waiting

The most intense element that the above-mentioned messianic trends contributed to Jewish life is the acute psycho-religious element of messianic expectation. Both the individual Jew and the collective nation of Israel gradually entered into a sphere of anticipation and developed an impetus toward a mystical mentality of waiting. In fact, the tendency to wait for the Messiah has become so central in Jewish religious life that it has even surpassed the significance of the Messiah himself. Although the centrality of the idea of waiting for the Messiah has ancient roots in Jewish Rabbinic Midrash and Aggadah, it was Maimonides who established it as one of the *Thirteen Principles of the Jewish Faith*. Ever since, the psycho-religious notion of waiting has claimed supreme importance in messianic Judaism. Maimonides' teaching, "I believe with complete faith in the coming of the Messiah, and even though he should tarry, nevertheless *I shall wait for his coming every day*," penetrated into the daily prayer of every Jew[30] and shaped the Jewish psychology of waiting. The belief in the coming of the Messiah sustained the Jewish people throughout the centuries in exile: it comforted and empowered the Jews, allowing them to hope for their Savior who would promptly arrive and bring with him salvation and redemption.

While describing the days of the Messiah, Maimonides uses a political approach and determines that "there is no difference between this world and the days of the Messiah except for the [absence of] suppression by the nations." According to Maimonides' teaching, the national freedom of the people of Israel is what will signify the days of the Messiah. It will be a time when the people of Israel will no longer be ruled by other nations, the kingdom of David will be restored, and Israel will finally enjoy national independence once again.[31] However, despite his political approach, in his *Introduction to the Mishnah* Maimonides forcefully emphasizes that waiting for the Messiah is the important ingredient of the Jewish law. It is the human act of waiting for the Messiah, he stresses, which is one of the thirteen principles of Judaism:

> And the Twelfth Principle [of the Faith of Judaism, among the Thirteen Principles] is the Days of the Messiah; that is, to believe and accept that he [the Messiah] will come, and not to think that he will tarry. *If he tarry – wait for him*! And do not limit him with time, and do not make speculations and calculations to determine the time of his coming. Thus, the sages say:[32] "may the soul of those who calculate the End, perish."[33]

These words of Maimonides, the greatest Jewish *Halachic* authority of all time, establish two components of the messianic *Mitzvah* required of the believers in the faith of Judaism: *believing in the coming of the Messiah unconditionally* and *waiting for him unceasingly.* For Maimonides, the core of the Jewish law concerning the Messiah is not to be found in trying to understand the messianic figure, nor in calculating the time of his coming, which in itself is prohibited by the Jewish law. In fact, believing in the Messiah and waiting for him are so important for Maimonides, that the figure of the Messiah himself becomes secondary in his thought. The heart of the Jewish *Halachah* concerning the Messiah dwells in the depth of the human belief and in the act of waiting. In daily Jewish religious life this belief translates itself into a continuing frame of mind of anticipation. The Jewish people pray for his coming and will wait for him even if his arrival is delayed, or, better put, especially when his arrival is delayed.

The notion of waiting has its roots in the ancient Midrash and Aggadah. In one Midrash we learn that as much as the people of Israel yearn for the coming of the Messiah, the Messiah also yearns for the people of Israel who wait for him. Rabbi Yehoshua' ben Levi describes his meeting with the Messiah as follows: "When I came to the Messiah, he questioned me and said: 'What are the people of Israel doing in the world whence you came?' I said to him: 'They are waiting for you every day.' Immediately he lifted up his voice and cried."[34] In this Midrash it is clear that the Messiah is the Redeemer who feels for the people of Israel and who shares their pain of waiting. However, the notion of Jewish waiting is more complex than is represented by this literal interpretation. While the Messiah can be seen as having been sent by God, he can also be seen as God Himself, as taught by another Midrash that tells about a king who married a lady and then left her to travel overseas. He tarried there many years until the lady's friends began saying to her: "The king has left you … How long are you going to keep on waiting [for him]?" But the lady went in the house and took out her marriage contract, read it, and found comfort in it. Finally, one day the king returned home. He said to her: "I am astonished that you have waited for me all these years." She answered him: "Were it not for my marriage contract … my friends would have caused me to be lost." This parable teaches that the nations of the world look at the despised, and exiled people of Israel and say to them, you have vanished from the stage of history for your God has left you and your Messiah has betrayed you, "come and be like one of us." But the people of Israel have an eternal and unbreakable contract signed with their God that requires them to keep waiting. So they enter into their synagogues and houses of study, they read the Torah, and they find in it comfort and hope. When the time arrives, this Midrash teaches, God will say to the Jewish people: "I am astonished, how were you able to wait for such a long time?" And Israel will reply to Him: "Were it not for the Torah which you gave to us, the nations of the world would have caused us to be lost."[35] This parable was understood by the Jewish people as a metaphor for the relationship between Israel and God, which represents the relationship between Israel and the Messiah. Although God had left the midst of the Jewish people, He left them with the Torah that maintains the eternal assurance of His return to their midst and for their return to their homeland. The separation of the Jewish people from their God and homeland is therefore temporary. Thus, because the Jewish people accepted the Torah, they share an unbreakable contract with God; and because they commit themselves to unceasingly waiting to be reunited with Him, God will unquestionably return to their midst and bring them back to their homeland. All is conditioned on the ability of Israel to wait, even though the waiting might last for an extremely long time; a time so long that it would even astonish God.

In Jewish mysticism, Kabbalah, and Hasidism the notion of waiting for the Messiah became a matter of primary religious value and of foremost religious concentration. As indicated above, in Kabbalah the messianic figure was portrayed as a symbol of the Divine *Sefirot*. Thus, for example, Rabbi Moses de-Leon portrayed the Messiah as the last *Sefirah*, called *Malkhut*, and Rabbi Abraham Abulafia portrayed the Messiah as the first elevated *Sefirah*, called *Keter*.[36] The question is, what is the meaning of this symbolism in Kabbalah, and how does the *Sefirotic* symbolism shape the ideology of Kabbalistic messianism? To answer this question we must return to the Rabbinic teachings on the Messiah. The Talmud maintains the tradition that the Messiah pre-existed the creation of the world: "Seven things were created before the creation of the world: they are, Torah, Repentance, the Garden of Eden, Gehenna, the

Throne of Glory, the Temple, and the Name of the Messiah."[37] The Kabbalists accepted this Talmudic approach; however, they believed that the pre-existence of the Messiah stems directly from the Godly process of the emanations of the *Sefirot*, and therefore the Messiah does not only pre-exist the creation of the world, but also belongs to the sefirotical world of *Ein-Sof*, for he is an emanated *Hypostasis*. Thus, when the day comes the Messiah will appear as an actualized *Sefirah* with the ability to bring down the Godly influx, known in Hebrew as *She'fa*. He will quench the thirst of the world and nourish it. His goodness will flow unceasingly, like an eternal fountain who quenches the thirsty world and sustains its life and welfare. He will constitute the renewed kingdom of the house of David and redeem the exiled *Shekhinah*.

Rabbi Moses de-Leon teaches in his Kabbalistic classic work, *Sheqel Ha-Kodesh*, that the ten emanated *Sefirot* are the hidden secrets of existence, corresponding to the Ten Sayings by which the world was created, and matching the Ten Commandments that hold the purity of the Divine wisdom. Regarding the second *Sefirah*, *Hokhmah*, Rabbi de-Leon says:

> When the emanation was emanated out of *Ayin*, all things and all *Sefirot* were dependent on thought. God's secret existence emerged from this single point. That which abides in thought yet cannot be grasped is called *Hokhmah* [Wisdom]. What is the meaning of *Hokhmah*? *Hakkeh mah* [wait for *mah*]. Since you can never grasp it, *hakkeh*, "wait," for *mah*, "what" will come and what will be. This is the sublime primordial wisdom emerging out of *Ayin*.[38]

These words of Moses de-Leon do not seem to be directly connected with messianism, but they imply a significant Kabbalistic symbolism relevant to our discussion on waiting. According to de-Leon's Kabbalistic explanation, the first thing that comes forth from *Ayin*, i.e. from the first *Sefirah* called *Keter*, is the second *Sefirah*, Wisdom, that is called *Hokhmah*, which is the *Yesh*. The esoteric yearning of every human being is to grasp the Divine emanation of *Hokhma*h, i.e. to understand the wisdom of God and cleave to it. However, there is a secret that is hidden in the Hebrew name *Hokhmah*. If you break the word *Hokhmah* into two words, it reads: *Hakkeh mah*. The Hebrew word *hakkeh* literally means "wait," and *mah* means "what."[39] According to Moses de-Leon, "That which abides in thought yet cannot be grasped is called *Hokhmah*." This means that the transition from the *Ayin* to the *Yesh* requires that we learn the art of waiting, for the essence of Wisdom is based on waiting. Furthermore, since *Hokhmah* is the beginning of existence (and indeed it is called *Reshit*, beginning), it signifies the starting point and the nature of existence, which is founded on waiting. The encounter with the Divine wisdom is thus an existential encounter, which requires waiting for that which is unknown. Thus, Moses de-Leon taught the Jewish people a great lesson in life; that is, the discovery of the Divine wisdom, and therefore the discovery of every wisdom, requires patience, perseverance, persistence, and waiting. For wisdom itself, *Hokhmah*, is the ontology of waiting.

Godot and the Jewish Messiah

While discussing Samuel Beckett's *Waiting for Godot*, I presented three main principles that underline the messianism in this masterpiece. I called these principles (1) *the absence of Godot*, (2) *the leader character versus the follower character and their two-getherness*, and (3) *speech versus immobility*. I would like to examine these principles in light of Jewish messianism.

The absence of Godot

The first messianic principle in *Waiting for Godot* portrayed the absurd hope of the two heroes in the play for some entity to appear. This entity, they believed, had the power to make a difference in their lives. They called him "Godot." But despite the fact that he constantly failed to arrive, his *absence* sustained their messianic reality. Without Godot in their minds they would have nothing to wait for; with the appearance of Godot – had he appeared – they would also have had nothing to wait for, for had he appeared, he would have ended their waiting. Their only solution, therefore, was to wait for an entity who was absent; for his absence allowed them to create a reality of waiting "en attendant."

Does this rule apply to Jewish messianism? Do the Jewish people reflect a paradoxical collective human condition that perpetually anticipates the coming of a Messiah whose ontology is *in absentia*? Does the Jewish Messiah reveal himself, or does he remain *in absentia ad infinitum*? Here we are confronted with one of the central perplexities in Jewish messianism. The Jewish people pray for the coming of the Messiah; they long for him; they devote their utmost sincere and inward intentions to welcome his arrival; and they believe in his redemptive power even if he delays his coming, as taught by Maimonides: "even if he tarry – wait for him!" However, through the entire history of Judaism every single entity who claimed to be the Messiah failed. Although in the history of Judaism many figures were declared to be the Messiah, they were all finally disputed and rejected. Some of these figures were regarded as misleading, deceptive, or simply false Messiahs. Such was the case with prominent messianic figures as Abraham Abulafia,[40] or Sabbatai Sevi. The latter was even considered to be mentally ill.[41]

One of the amazing messianic emergences in our generation is that of the Lubavitcher Rebbe of Habad Hasidism. About ten years before the passing of the admired Habad Lubavitcher Rebbe, Menakhem Mendel Schneerson, some of his *Hasidim* declared that he was the Messiah. On June 12, 1994 the Rebbe passed away. This came as a terrible shock to his Hasidic community in Crown Heights in New York and *K'far Habad* in Israel. A year after the Rebbe died, Rabbi Simon Jacobson, one of the dedicated students of the Rebbe and a talented writer in his own right, published a marvelous book on Habad Hasidism.[42] The book is indeed a jewel, for it portrays with a sensitive pen the major religious and existential fabrics of the contemporary life of Habad Hasidism, written by a Habadnik *hasid*. It deals with Habad's concepts of Love, Marriage, Charity, Anxiety, Responsibility, Unity, Miracles, Redemption, God and other central issues of Hasidic religious life. At the end of this book under the title "The Rebbe as the Messiah?" Rabbi Jacobson asks: "How would the Rebbe have answered the question of whether or not he is the Messiah?"[43] However, Rabbi Jacobson's short epilogue does not address this question directly. On one hand he claims that "The Rebbe clearly stated that we have now reached the threshold of redemption, and we must all do our part in anticipating and preparing ourselves for this era, through study and good deeds." On the other hand, to answer his main question he states: "No person can dictate who the Messiah is; only by studying and understanding God's words in the Torah about the Messiah can we realize who meets these criteria."[44]

This example remarkably illustrates the messianic tension within the Jewish belief. Obviously the question whether the Lubavitcher Rebbe is the Messiah remains here unanswered. Rabbi Jacobson does not deny that his Rebbe is the Messiah, nor does he explicitly confirm that he is the Messiah. Instead, he refers the answer to the individual *hasid* who studies the Torah. He also reminds us that since the Rebbe taught that we have now reached the threshold of redemption, "we must all do our part in *anticipating* and preparing ourselves for this era." There are significant differences between Rabbi Jacobson's formula of messianism and that of *Waiting for Godot*. Whereas in the latter the hope for the coming of Godot illustrates absurdity and hopeless reality, in the former the hope for the coming of the Messiah portrays an affirmative and hopeful reality. While in the latter it is implicit that Godot will never arrive, in the former it is obvious to the *hasid* that the Messiah will ultimately arrive; in fact, the Rebbe was already believed to be the Messiah before he passed away. However, in both formulae it is the *absence* of the Messiah that empowers the messianic reality. For the absence of the Messiah is the primary force that creates the reality of waiting "en attendant." If the Messiah arrives or if he is alive and among us, the believers might adhere to him and follow him for a while; sometimes they may even continue to believe in him for many years after his disappearance, as in the case of Sabbatai Sevi. But eventually when the thought of a new Messiah appears, the belief in the old Messiah fades away. The only thing that will surely remain forever is the act of waiting for him, whoever the Messiah will be.

Furthermore, this example illustrates that the physical passing of the messianic figure does not erase from the hearts of the believers the urge to continue to believe in his messianism. Three years after the passing of the Lubavitcher Rebbe, a full page advertisement appeared in the *New York Times*[45] commemorating the third anniversary of the Rebbe's passing. The advertisement quotes the words of the Kabbalist Hayyim Vital (who himself was held as a

Messiah in sixteenth-century Safed) and reads as follows: "*Moshiach* [the Hebrew for Messiah] will thereupon rise up to Heaven just as Moses ascended to the firmament, and will subsequently return and be revealed completely for all to see."[46] The page quotes the Talmudical words of Rabbi Judan as saying that one of the names of the Messiah is Menakhem ("comforter"), implying that since the first name of Rabbi Schneerson is Menakhem, he is the true Messiah: "R. Judan son of R. Avio says [about the Messiah], his name is Menakhem ...."[47] But even more significant is the title of this page, which appears in large letters under the picture of the Rebbe and reads: **"The third of Tamuz is not the Rebbe's yahrzeit."** The third of Tamuz is the Hebrew date that commemorates the passing of the Rebbe. The writer emphasizes that this date should not be considered as a *yahrzeit*; that is, as the anniversary day for the passing of the Rebbe. The direct implication of this statement is clear: since the Rebbe is the Messiah, it is inconceivable that he has died.

Next, the body of the text reads as follows:

> Three years ago today (3 Tamuz 5754), the Lubavitcher Rebbe, Rabbi Menakhem Schneerson was liberated from the limitation of corporeal existence. It was the commencement of a new era ... The Rebbe, the scion to the Royal House of David, was absolutely clear when he prophesied *"The time of your redemption has arrived."* As part of the Redemption process, the Rebbe so presciently foresaw the formidable Communist empire crumbling into a footnote to history ... that Israel would emerge unscathed from beneath a fusillade of deadly Iraqi missiles ... that the world's swords would be beaten into plowshares ... In its final manifestation, Redemption will mean a world perfected. A world characterized by peace, harmony prosperity, health, spiritual awareness, and a profound understanding of man's purpose on earth. **The Rebbe is among us. His presence is more profoundly felt than ever before.** The idea of redemption is on the front burner. Men, women and children have had their consciousness raised in anticipation of Moshiach. The Rebbe, no longer bound by physical limitations, is accessible to all of us, everywhere and at any time ... Amazing stories keep pouring in from all corners of the globe. People are experiencing miracles large and small ... *We believe with complete and uncompromising faith in Moshiach and the resurrection of the dead. The Rebbe continues to inspire and direct the drive towards Redemption in ways beyond our limited human vision. We are absolutely certain the Rebbe* will *lead us to our ultimate and eternal Redemption.*[48]

This page ends with the Hebrew *Yekhi adonenu morenu ve-rabenu Melekh ha-Moshiach le-olam va-ed* [meaning, May our master, teacher, and Rebbe, King Messiah live for ever and ever]. The page is signed by Rabbi Yitzchok Springer, Shofar Association of America, and concludes with the words: "We encourage newspapers, organizations and individuals to reprint the above for distribution." This text teaches that messianism has not been neutralized from the world of Hasidism, and is alive and well in today's Jewish spiritual world. It reflects the human condition that anticipates the return of the Messiah who once lived within the limitations of corporeality, who was later "liberated from the limitation of corporeal existence," and who will finally return as the ultimate redeemer. In the eyes of his *Hasidim*, even if the Rebbe's material presence is no longer among them, he nevertheless did not die, and now "his [spiritual] presence is more profoundly felt than ever before." Thus, because the Rebbe remains *in absentia*, "he continues to inspire and direct the drive towards Redemption."

Unlike Didi and Gogo, whose waiting is existentially hopeless, the Rebbe's *Hasidim* remain in the spirit of faith and expectation; they continue to wait for him, feeling assured of his return, and they prepare themselves for his coming. However, in both cases, it is the *absence* of the Messiah that empowers the waiting.

The leader character versus the follower character and their two-getherness

The second messianic principle in *Waiting for Godot* that was discussed (pp. 106–107), emphasizes the unbreakable partnership between the two heroes in Beckett's play, a partnership that is essential in every messianic pattern. I called it *the leader character versus the follower character and their two-getherness.* According to this principle there is always a leader who reminds the follower that both of them must wait two-gether for the Messiah. In the history of Jewish messianism this pattern appears time and again in the relationships between the prophets and the people of Israel. The prophet rebukes and calls upon the people of Israel to wait for the Messiah and prepare for the End of the Days; and the people respond to the prophet and create partnership of two-getherness with him. According to this formula we may state that behind every Messiah there is a leader character who provokes, induces, and sometimes even instigates a follower character to join him in his belief in the Messiah. The leader is usually an individual who can be described as an intellectual, a man of great charisma, a scholar, a great speaker, a politician, a person who claims that he is a man of God; in short, a convincing influential persona. The follower usually belongs in a group of people; he lacks individuality; he is in constant search of his own identity; he feels inferior, unworthy, and miserable; he is persecuted either physically or psychologically or both; and, thus, he is mentally ready to belong in a group of followers, for he yearns to be redeemed. The most profound example for a leader character in the history of messianic Judaism is that of the prophet Nathan of Gaza, who in the seventeenth century became the living force behind the false Messiah Sabbatai Sevi.[49] Nathan of Gaza is the best example of the leader whose systematic audacity, sharp intellect, and charisma made him the first great theologian of heretical Kabbalah. Gershom

THE JEWISH ART OF WAITING

Scholem describes him as a "brilliant scholar," as an active persona who was an "ascetic sinner and saint," who made himself the "herald" of the Messiah. Sabbatai Sevi, on the other hand, was a "poor leader." He was "devoid of will power and without a program of action." Scholem accurately concludes: "The two men complemented each other in a remarkable fashion, and without that combination the Sabbatian movement would never have developed."[50] But who is the follower character in this drama? Nathan's followers were the Jewish European communities of Venice, Amsterdam, Hamburg, Izmir, and other Jewish centers that believed wholeheartedly in his prophesies and in the prophesies of other leaders who followed him.[51] These were Jewish communities that suffered persecutions and expulsions and were filled with messianic expectations. They embraced the messianic prophesies that came from the school of Nathan of Gaza, and even when Sabbatai Sevi left the Jewish faith and converted to Islam in the year 1666, his Jewish followers continued to believe in his messianism, and thousands of them followed his conversion and became Muslims like him; for when the power of messianism strikes, it is a power with no limit.[52] Thus, Nathan as the leader character and these Jewish communities as the follower character created a perfect combination for a startling messianic agenda. Two-gether they created a Sabbatian movement that long outlasted its founders.

Speech versus immobility

The third messianic principle in *Waiting for Godot* which we discussed above (pp. 107–109) is depicted in the tension between speech and immobility. This principle reflects the dialectical tension that accompanies every messianic drama. On the one hand, the people who wait for the Messiah believe in him and speak about him; on the other hand, to use Beckett's words, "they do not move," for the power that is responsible for bringing the Messiah is not in their hands, but rather in an otherworldly entity. Speech versus immobility is the ambiguous Jewish human condition of every Jew who is torn between the essential need to express the spoken word; that is, to speak about the *Mitzvah* of waiting for the Messiah versus his limited ability to bring the Messiah. It is the mystifying human condition that stands between activity and inactivity; the nebulous human element that dwells between the natural need to act and the inability to act, between the existential urgency to move and the lack of power to do so, between the essential exigency to be articulate and the human lack of compassion that makes us inarticulate. This portrays in the Jewish spiritual world the tension between hope and despair, between the yearning of the spirit to be redeemed and the inability of the body to act accordingly. It is the antagonism between Beckett's "Let's Go," and, "They do not move."

According to a well-known Midrash, God demanded that the Jewish people take upon themselves four oaths: "*not* to rebel against the kingdoms [of the nations who rule Israel], *not* to expedite the End [through prayer and acts of compassion]; *not* to reveal the secrets [of the Jewish heritage]; and *not* to climb up the walls [i.e. to avoid wars with their hostile neighbors]: Since this is the case, why will the Messiah come? To bring together the exiled communities of Israel."[53]

This Midrash has greatly influenced the passivity and the immobility of the Jewish people in the context of their messianic waiting.[54] It has taught the Jewish people that although they are under the obligation to purify themselves and the world through *Tikkun*, the end to their suppression by the nations, the ultimate coming of the Messiah, and the date of his coming are all unequivocally in the hands of God and God alone. This belief required of the Jewish people that they pray, hope, and wait for the coming of the Messiah, but refrain from participating in acts that may expedite his arrival. This indeed fits perfectly the formula of speech versus immobility. On the one hand, the messianic *Mitzvah* is to enhance the activity of waiting for the Messiah, and, on the other hand, the Jewish messianic oaths demand passivity toward any mystical, spiritual, religious, or political action that may hasten his coming. No wonder that many ultra-orthodox (including Hasidic) Jews have refused to recognize the new Zionist State of Israel. Obviously they have perceived the creation of the new state as a heretical act that has freed the Jewish people from the suppression of the nations *not* by the hand of God, but by the hand of man. This act, they say, is a severe violation of the religious oaths that the Jewish people vowed to keep. And thus, they claim, the idea and the existence of the Zionist State stand in contrast to the essence of the Jewish Messiah and the Jewish fate. A classic example of the anti-Zionist Hasidic approach was written by Rabbi Yoel Teitelbaum, in his *Va-Yoel Moshe*, emphasizing that the "emigration [*Alliyah*] to the land of Israel before the Messiah arrives, against God's oath, [is an act which] delays the redemption."[55] In other words, messianic waiting is so significant for these ultra-orthodox Jews that it supersedes even acts that bring important earthly benefits to the Jewish people.

To conclude this chapter I would like to emphasize the following fundamental ideas within the context of Jewish messianism.

1   The uniqueness of Jewish messianism stems from the Jewish historical reality of 2,000 years of exile. However, the messianic element is inherent in the Jewish faith. It pre-existed the creation of the world, as taught in the Midrash,[56] and it continues to exist even after the return of the Jewish people to their homeland. The belief of waiting for the Messiah is therefore an element inherent in the Jewish *Pneuma*; a messianic ingredient that exists in the psycho-religious life of the Jewish people, beyond time and history.

2   The Jewish messianic element can be seen in Jewish spirituality from three different expressions: it can be seen as a *national activity*, as a *Divine activity*, or as a *personal activity*. In the central messianic texts of Jewish philosophy and Kabbalah, the Jewish messianic element appears as the reaction of the Jewish people to their exile. Although the central texts of Jewish philosophy differ sharply from those of the Kabbalah in regard to their perception of

the Messiah and the messianic days, such as in the case of Maimonides versus the *Zohar*, both of them describe the messianic element as a national activity of waiting. In Lurianic Kabbalah, however, the messianic element was refined in the myth of *Tzimtzoom*; i.e. in God's "exile" into the depth of His hidden self. Here too the Jewish people are required to wait for the Messiah unceasingly. However, God's withdrawal during the act of *Tzimtzoom* portrays a different messianic element; that is, a purely Divine activity that leads to the creation of the world. In the act of the *Tzimtzoom* God "exiles" into Himself, and then He progresses to create the world. This messianic element of Divine activity has evolved and been reshaped. It was cultivated in the messianic teachings of Hasidism as the *hasid*'s personal exile into his psychic reality. Thus, whereas in sixteenth-century Lurianic Kabbalah the expression of the exile is bound up with the myth of the Godly *Tzimtzoom*, where God shifts into the depth of His hidden self, in eighteenth-century Hasidism the expression of the exile is bound up with the myth of human *Tzimtzoom*, where the individual *hasid* withdraws into the depth of his psyche. In Hasidism, the messianic element was psychologized and personalized. Here it has become an individual activity remote from national activity, cultivated as a profound, personal activity; that is, a human existential act of *Imitatio Dei*.[57]

3   Waiting for the Messiah is the profound religious Jewish activity that sustains the spiritual goals, aspirations, and desires of the Jewish people, and upholds the affirmative reality in the hearts of those who will never lose their hope and who will always keep the faith. The notion of waiting for the Messiah has not declined, and the *Mitzvah* of waiting has only been reshaped and crystallized as the primary living force in Jewish life. Thus, the Jewish people wait for the Messiah "even if he tarry," and believe in his coming unequivocally while he is *in absentia* and because he is *in absentia*. For the Messiah is the entity that always dwells beyond time and history. Judaism has seen different messianic figures and movements that appeared over the centuries on the stage of its history. However, in all of these forms the essential messianic element has been bound up in the hearts of the people of Israel with the existential urgency to return to the pristine, utopian way of life. The Jewish concept of waiting can be perceived, therefore, as a psycho-religious yearning to bring every existing thing back to its starting point of purity and perfection, a yearning of the creatures of God to return and rest in the abode of their Creator. Thus, the art of Jewish waiting for the Messiah is a reflection of the Jewish frame of mind that anticipates physical and spiritual redemption.

As for the Messiah himself, we do not know when he will arrive. Franz Kafka suggested that "the Messiah will come only when he is no longer necessary, he will come only on the day after his arrival; he will come, not on the last day, but on the very last."[58]

Waiting for the Messiah

8

TESHUVAH

The conclusive return to God

Sin, repentance, exile, and redemption

The history of the Jews as the chosen people mirrors the dialectics between their waiting for the Messiah and the idea of the coming of the Messiah, between Exile and Redemption, and between Sin and Repentance. Our first questions in this concluding chapter emerge from the complex relationship between sin, repentance, exile, and redemption. Were the Jewish people rooted out from their homeland and exiled because of their sins? Is it in their power to redeem themselves from the exile and bring the Messiah and the redemption if they only repent? These essential problems are already in controversy among the Jewish sages of the Talmud:

> Rav said, all the ends have come to an end, and the thing [the redemption] is conditioned by repentance and good deeds ... Rabbi Eli'ezer says, if [the people of] Israel do repentance, they are redeemed; if not, [they are] not redeemed! Rabbi Ye'hoshua' said to him: if [the people of] Israel do not do repentance, are they not redeemed? The Holy One, blessed be He, will present them with a king of harsh decrees, and thus He will bring them back to the righteous way.[1]

According to the first opinion presented here by Rabbi Eli'ezer, the redemption is indubitably conditioned by repentance. But the second opinion presented by Rabbi Ye'hoshua' stresses that both redemption and repentance play a necessary part in the life and the history of the Jewish people, a history that is dictated by God Himself. Therefore we may claim, as formulated in the words of the great Jewish thinker, the Maharal of Prague, that:

> The opinion of Rabbi Eli'ezer; that is, that if the people of Israel do repentance, they are redeemed, if not, this thing [redemption] is doubtful, is wrong! For there is no doubt in regard to the redemption of Israel ... Because the exile is [merely] an accident [*mikre'*]; for the exile in itself is a thing that is contrary to the [Godly] order of the world; since, in accordance with the order of the world, it is proper

that the Jewish nation will be under the authority of God, may He be blessed. And thus if indeed [Rabbi Eli'ezer means] that the exile is conditioned by the sin [of Israel], [we should answer him] that the sin also is not substantial [*ba-e'tze'm*], but rather an accidental thing. And a thing that is accidental does not have [a permanent] life. And, undoubtedly, it is inconceivable that the [people of Israel] will not do repentance; unquestionably they will do repentance.[2]

The Maharal's commentary on the above Talmudical controversy is nurtured by his belief that the Godly order of the universe (*Seder ha-Olam*) was premeditated by God, and thus the world was specifically structured to match the destiny of the chosen people to whom the world to come was promised. Although both repentance and redemption are inherent in the fate of the Jewish people, and, therefore, are substantial to their life and destiny, sin and exile are merely accidental to them. Furthermore, although redemption is indeed the *telos* of the Jewish people, it is not, by any means, conditioned by their repentance. Since their sin is not the direct reason for their exile, their repentance cannot be the direct reason for their redemption. What is, then, the cause for the exile of the Jewish people? The Maharal's answer to this question is: "The cause for the exile is ... the sin [of the Jewish people], but the cause for the cause [*Sibbat ha-Sibbah*] is concealed from us."[3] Maharal's commentary on the relationship between sin and repentance demonstrates an exemplary position in the extensive Jewish spiritual literature on *Teshuvah*.

Since the birth of Judaism, Jewish religious life has wrestled with the problem of sin and repentance. Hundreds of Jewish tractates on repentance give testimony to the fact that this problem lies at the center of Jewish thought and ethics. But it is not only the hundreds of treatises written on the subject of repentance that make it so central in Judaism, but rather the incomparable influence that these have had on Jewish religious life. The continuously changing and evolving theme of repentance has shaped and reshaped Jewish ethics and spirituality. Repentance, as confronted by Jewish spirituality, is characterized by three separate and distinct stages. The first stage, to be found in the Bible, and the second stage, to be found in the works of the Jewish sages of the Mishnah and the Talmud (*HaZaL*), are not within the purview of this chapter. Although biblical verses and *Hazalic* dicta are noted, my focus in this chapter rests almost exclusively on the third stage – the selected works of the Jewish philosophers, Kabbalists, and Hasidic masters of the last millennium.

From the tenth-century eminent composition of Rav Saadia Gaon, *The Book of Beliefs and Opinions*, to the twentieth-century classic work of Rav Avraham Yitzkhak Ha-Cohen Kook, *The Book of the Lights of Return*, the concept of repentance has been confronted with numerous movements in Jewish thought. Indeed, in the last ten centuries, it is difficult to find a theological path of repentance that has not been explored by Hebrew authors. Repentance has been conceptualized as the return of man from sin, the return of the soul to her primordial Divine source, the spiritual and even intellectual cleaving to God, the mystical enlightenment according to Kabbalistic symbolism, the cosmic return of the world to its utopian beginning, the freedom of man from the chains of his own being, the religious *unio mystica* with God, and even as the secular Zionistic return of the people of Israel to their homeland.

The hundreds of texts that were written on repentance in the framework of Jewish thought in the last ten centuries have established an ideological typology in the *Teshuvah* literature. Some part of this typology is what I intend to examine in the following analysis.[4]

Typology of Teshuvah in Hebrew ethical literature

Rav Saadia Gaon was the first Jewish thinker to bridge the religious literature of the ancient Jewish sages of the Mishnah, Talmud, Midrash, and Aggadah, with the philosophical thought of his own time. In his *Sefer Ha-Emunot ve-ha-De'ot (Book of Beliefs and Opinions)*, Saadia introduces, for the first time in the history of Jewish thought, four basic principles of repentance that have shaped the literature of *Teshuvah* for generations: *Azivat ha-Khet* (Detachment from the Sin), *Kharatah* (Remorse), *Vidduy* (Confession), and *Hakhlata she-Lo Lakhazor la-Khet* (Determination Not to Return to the Sin).[5]

Following Rav Saadia, it was Rabbenu Bachya Ibn Paquda, at the turn of the twelfth century, who transformed the theme of repentance into its next phase. Bachya is the extraordinary Jewish philosopher and mystic who was highly influenced by Islamic Sufism, and who is regarded as one of the important sources for profound concepts of morality that later appear in the classic texts of Kabbalah and Hasidism. In his *Hovot ha-Levavot (Duties of the Heart)*, he devoted the seventh chapter of his book to the *Mitzvah* of repentance, determining that repentance should be based in its entirety on *Kavanat ha-Lev*, i.e. on the inwardness of the heart. Bachya teaches that repentance is an inner performance or "spiritual duty of the heart" rather than an external, physical, or "practical duty of the limbs." His pneumatic work established a new concept of repentance in Judaism, based on contemplation and spiritual worship. He is the first Hebrew writer to institute and introduce the religious ideological type of *Spiritual Repentance* in Jewish thought.[6]

Rabbi Jonah Gerondi followed the path that was paved by Bachya. In the middle of the thirteenth century he composed his famed comprehensive work, *Sha'arey Teshuvah (The Gates of Repentance)*, under a Judeo-Spanish influence. Rabbi Jonah expanded the four basic principles of repentance that were established by Rav Saadia, and assigned instead twenty spiritual principles of repentance. They are regret, forsaking sin, suffering in deed, worry, shame, humbling oneself with all one's heart and lowering oneself, humility in deed, breaking of physical desire, improving one's deeds in the area of his offense, searching for one's way, investigation of the magnitude of the punishment, regarding the lesser sins as severe transgressions, confession, prayer, mending the misdeed as far as possible, pursuing loving kindness and truth, confronting the sin and struggling against it constantly in the penitent's mind, forsaking the sin when desire is still within the capacity of the penitent to sin again, and, finally, turning as many sinners as possible from transgression and helping them return to the way of God.

These twenty principles illustrate in *Sha'arey Teshuvah* an emotional and individual experience, which begins with a deep sensation of guilt and remorse, and is nurtured by urgent psychological feeling of distress and agony. It is a psychological religious conception which emphasizes that man's mental pain and suffering result from his sinning, which is eventually a healthy feeling; for it is a feeling that brings the sinner forth to revisit and re-examine his inner world. Rabbi Jonah, even more than Bachya, puts the penitent on a psychological progressive search that leads him toward an inner exploration, where he is confronted with his hidden self. Here the penitent discovers that his transgressed soul has experienced a wound and a downfall; and from here he rises up in search of mending and healing. Rabbi Jonah's program of repentance empowers the penitent to bring himself into an intimate, spiritual, and inner inquiry, beginning with a profound transition of his consciousness and ending with a compelling mental determination not to return to his iniquities. At each and every step in the way of the penitent he looks for the inner signs that show him the proper path of return. For while the sinner is the one who has lost his way, the penitent is the one who rediscovers it; and the principles of repentance are the signs that direct him on his path of return. If Bachya is the first Hebrew moralist who instituted and introduced the ideological type of Spiritual Repentance in Jewish ethics, Rabbi Jonah Gerondi is, without a doubt, the Hebrew moralist who elevated Spiritual Repentance to its greatest heights.[7]

About two generations after Bachya's time, the first comprehensive work on the Jewish laws of repentance appeared by Maimonides, in his *Halakhic* work *Laws of Repentance*, which he included in his classic *Book of Knowledge*, the first of the fourteen volumes of *Mishneh Torah*. In this magnum opus of *Halachah*, Maimonides argues, although implicitly, that the ideal penitent should be identical to the ideal *Hakham*, the wise and intellectual man, that he portrayed in his philosophical work, *The Guide for the Perplexed*.

In his *Laws of Repentance* Maimonides writes:

> Permission[8] is given to every man ... so that he, by himself, on account of his own intellect [*da'ato*] and thought, knows the good and the bad and everything that he desires; and there is none that hinders him from doing the good or the bad ... but he, on account of himself and his own intellect tends to the way that he desires ... Since our permission is in our hands, and, prompted by our mind [*da'atenu*] we have committed all the transgressions, it is proper for us to return in *Teshuvah* and depart [from] our wickedness ... In a time when one

person or the persons of the land sin, and the sinner does sin prompted by the reason of his intellect and his will [*me-da'ato u-bi-re'tzono*] ... it is proper to punish him ... and *since man sins due to his intellect and his will, he likewise does repentance based on his intellect and* will ... Since permission is granted to man ... he must zealously try to do repentance and to confess his sins in his mouth, and cleanse his hands from his sins, so that when he dies, he is *Baal Teshuvah* [literally, an "owner" of Repentance], and he will gain the right of the life in the world to come ... and what our sages said [about the righteous in the world to come]: "their crowns in their heads,"[9] this means intellect [*da'at*] that they have intellectualized; Since they have gained the life in the world to come <u>because</u> of [their intellect]. The "crown" that our sages referred to here, is the intellect [*de'ah*]. And what is the meaning of their saying: "And they enjoy the brightness of the *Shekhinah*"?[10] That they know and intellectualize [*yodde'im u-massigim*] the truth of the Holy One, blessed be He ... every soul that is discussed in this matter is not the soul that needs the body, but the spiritual form of the soul [*tzu'rat ha-nefesh*],[11] which is the intellect [*de'ah*] that has been intellectualized from the Creator in accordance with its power ... And there is no reward that is greater than this reward, and there is no bliss [*tovah*] that is above it; and this is what all the prophets desired.[12]

Maimonides' hidden agenda and his true opinion on the matter of repentance are gradually revealed in his teachings. His point of view perceives repentance as an intellectual process that is more complete in accordance with the intellectual level of each person who seeks a way of return to God. According to Maimonides' thought, every man must constantly strive toward the peak of intellectual life, for eternity resides on the summit of the intellectual Heaven, called "The World to Come." This intellectual palace awaits only those penitents who succeed in conquering their evil inclination and become *Tzaddikim*; eventually their heads will be crowned forever with the brightness of the *Shekhinah*, which is the glory of the Divine intellect. Maimonides' ideal penitent is no different, therefore, from his ideal wise and intellectual man, the *Hakham*, who aspires to unite his intellect with the Divine Active Intellect, as portrayed in his *Guide*. Repentance, claims Maimonides, is thus the meeting point between the ethical and the intellectual religious activities of every man, since the ethical life is inseparable from the intellectual life. Every sin signifies a twofold descent in the life of the sinner: his ethical descent and his intellectual descent. And likewise, every act of repentance signifies a twofold ascent in the life of the penitent: his ethical ascent and his intellectual ascent. However, claims Maimonides, the nature of the good deeds versus the evil transgressions of each individual are determined first and foremost in accordance with the individual's intellectual capacity. In his words: "Since man sins due to his intellect and his will, he likewise does repentance based on his intellect and will." Man's ongoing journey of study, in particular the study of the Torah and the Aristotelian teachings of the sciences as they were understood in the Middle Ages, prepare him to the study of studies, which is *Yediat HaShem*, the Knowledge of God, a knowledge that substantiates the quality of his moral life. Thus, the power and the merit of the penitent can emerge only from his continuing practice of study, which enhances his intellect and eventually leads him to the way of God. Hence, repentance is an inseparable part of man's intellectual growth. Repentance elevates the human being toward his ultimate destiny; that is, his intellectual unification with the Active Intellect while he lives in this world, and his intellectual unification with the crown of the brightness of the *Shekhinah*, when he will be living a perfect life in the world to come. Furthermore, the penitent who worships God *out of* love achieves the final and highest human rank and becomes "The Lover of God," a rank that was given to Abraham our father who was called by God: "My Beloved."[13] Thus, Maimonides concludes his *Laws of Repentance* with a dramatic manifesto concerning the theme of "Love of God," and he writes: "One does not love the Holy One, blessed be He, but only in accordance with his intellect [*de'ah*] through which he knows Him. And in accordance with the [rank of his] intellect, the love will exist. If little, little; if much, much."[14] For Maimonides, worshiping God *out of* love is the highest degree of devotion, and it signifies the highest religious domain: *Repentance out of Love*. For every level of repentance is an integral part of the worship of God, and the end of every repentance is aimed at the bliss that is waiting for the penitent in the world to come. When man enriches his intellect through the study of the Torah, as well as through the study of physics and metaphysics, then he rediscovers that he was created in *Tzelem Elohim*, in the image of God.[15] His *Teshuvah* is thus a twofold return: he returns to God and at the same time he returns to his *Tzelem Elohim*, that is his own authenticity. I call this incomparable teaching of Maimonides on Jewish repentance *Intellectual Repentance*.[16]

Another unequaled concept of Jewish repentance, although very different from that of Maimonides', appeared in the second half of the twelfth century among the circle of the pious people of the German Jews, known as the *Ashkenazi Hasidim*. The two influential works that were composed by the leading Rabbis of this religious circle are *Sefer Hasidim* (*The Book of the Pious People*) and *Sefer Ha-Roke'akh* (*The Book of the Maker*). Here we find profound ascetic elements together with a demand that gives rise to the need for a repentance in which the punishment must be as intense as the sin. These ascetic features, which presumably are the result of an influence of medieval Christianity on *Ashkenazi Hasidism*, demand that the sinner punish his body even more than his soul. The sinner is required to torture himself by starvation for forty days of fasting, by sitting in the freezing snow during the frosty days of winter, or by sitting in the steamy ground among the fleas during the burning days of the summer. This exceptional view of Jewish repentance may be defined as *Ascetic Repentance*. Although the *Ashkenazi Hasidim* meant that the torture of the body will eventually lead to the purification of the soul, their ascetic practice in repentance stands contrary to the teachings of repentance according to the Sepharadic Jewish thinkers, such as Saadia, Bachya, and Maimonides, who viewed repentance as entirely an internal practice, occurring in the mind and the heart of man, rather than in the ascetic affliction of the external body.[17]

The controversy over the religious status of the penitent (*Baal Teshuvah*) compared with that of the righteous men (*Tzaddik*) enraptured the foremost Hebrew ethical writers of the Middle Ages. The basis of this controversy is already to be found in the Talmud, presenting the well-known argument in Tractate *Berachot* (34b) concerning the religious levels of the *Baal Teshuvah* and the *Tzaddik*. Thus, we read in the Talmud: "In the place where penitents stand, even the complete righteous cannot stand." Here the two speakers are Rav Abbahu and Rav Yokhanan. Their controversy is rooted in the understanding of the biblical verse: "Peace, peace to him that was far and to him that is near."[18] In Rav Abbahu's opinion, the penitent stands on a higher rung than that of the righteous man, for the verse opens with the *Baal Teshuvah*, who is hinted at in the word "far," and ends with the *Tzaddik*, alluded to in the word "near." Rav Yokhanan, on the other hand, differs from Rav Abbahu's opinion and claims that the *Tzaddik* is the one who stands on a higher rung than that of the penitent. The conclusion of this Talmudic debate hints at a possibility of siding with Rav Yokhanan; that is, that the one who was "far" is really the *Tzaddik*, since he is far removed from sin and consequently he is on a higher level than the *Baal Teshuvah*. This dispute is not decided in the Talmud, and the two views remain unresolved beside each other.

The dispute over the penitent's status received a vigorous emphasis in *The Book of the Righteous*, known in Hebrew as *Sefer Ha-Yashar* attributed to Rabbenu Tam.[19] The anonymous author of this work devoted the entire tenth chapter of his book to the theme of repentance; yet, beyond his concern with the actual nature of repentance, he deals with the problem of the status of the penitent, *Baal Teshuvah*, compared with that of the righteous man, *Tzaddik*. At the very beginning of the chapter, the author determines that the complete *Teshuvah* does indeed eradicate the sinner of all his sins and delivers him from punishment by God, "yet – says the author – he has no merits, and he cannot aspire to the religious level of the complete righteous men who never in all their days committed a sin."[20] Thus, the author explains the words of the Rabbis in the Talmud in an opposite sense to that of its original intent:

> What our Rabbis, of blessed memory, said (*Berachot* 34b): "In a place where the penitents stand, even the complete righteous men cannot stand," they spoke the truth. For it is known of the righteous (*Tzaddikim*) and the intermediate (*Benoniyim*) that each has a level of his own with the Creator, blessed be He, the one higher than the other; and that is why our Rabbis, of blessed memory, said that the righteous do not stand on the level of the penitent, for it is not their

proper place and they do not belong in the class of the penitents, but in another place.[21]

Thus, the conclusion from the words of *Sefer Ha-Yashar* is that every man has a religious level with God: the penitents in their own place, and the righteous men on their own place. But the penitents, as against the righteous ones, are only *Benoniyim*, that is of lesser stature than the religious stature of the righteous.

Would it be correct to assume that the problem before us was a central religious issue to the studies in medieval *Teshuvah* literature? Was the author of this classic book aware of the fact that the portrayal of the *Baal Teshuvah* on a lower level than that of the *Tzaddik* has something unattractive about it? Was he aware of the fact that his position on this matter might result in leaving the sinner in his sin and impurity since he will never be able to reach the level of the *Tzaddik*? It seems that the words of the author of *Sefer Ha-Yashar* on the subject of our discussion were written as a reaction to another position and in an atmosphere of controversy. Indeed, the discussion before us reflects an important ideological struggle in the classic teachings of Jewish repentance. In the focal medieval Hebrew works that were composed by the philosophical writers between the tenth and the twelfth centuries, such as in Saadia's *Book of Beliefs and Opinions*, in Bachya's *Duties of the Heart*, and in Maimonides' *Laws of Repentance*, the righteousness of the *Tzaddik* represents the highest religious stature. Therefore, in their teachings, the status of the *Tzaddik* is always superior to that of the *Baal Teshuvah*. However, a major ideological turning point occurs with the emergence of Kabbalah in the thirteenth century, a turning point that was sharpened more and more until it was established in the central book of Kabbalah, the *Zohar*. The Kabbalistic approach taught, in complete opposition to what was said by the philosophical moralists, that since repentance pre-existed the creation of the world, as taught in the Midrash,[22] it should be seen as a religious activity that restores the damaged world to its original perfect condition. Hence, say the Kabbalists, the act of *Teshuvah* should not be perceived merely as a psychological, educational, or religious process by means of which the wicked man repents of his sins and returns to the ordered path, but rather as a return to a supreme *Sefirah* in the world of God. Repentance itself, the Kabbalists claim, is the third *Sefirah*, the "Supernal Mother" called *Binah*. From *Binah*, as formulated by the Kabbalist Rabbi Azriel of Gerona, there has been set aside "a light of Repentance that illumines the thought of the penitent."[23]

The author of the central work of Kabbalah in the Middle Ages, the *Zohar*, established the Kabbalistic basis of repentance even more deeply than did the first Kabbalists of Gerona. He elevated the *Baal Teshuvah* from his lowliness and from the defilement in which he had been immersed to the point of giving him a lofty importance, for the penitent has a short path to God. Therefore the level of the *Baal Teshuvah*, says the *Zohar*, is higher even than that of the *Tzaddik*:

> Happy are the penitents, for behold, in one hour, in one day, in one

minute, they are near to the Holy One, blessed be He, something that does not happen even to the completely righteous men who draws close to the Holy One, blessed be He, in the course of several years ... We have learned: "In the place where the penitents stand, the completely righteous are not permitted to stand," because they, [the penitents], are nearer to the King than all of them, and they draw others unto themselves with great willingness of heart, and with great force, to get them to approach the King.[24]

The controversy over the status of the *Baal Teshuvah* compared with that of the *Tzaddik* is thus revealed as not just a dispute over their spiritual status. This is the key point for understanding the chronological and ideological boundary between the Hebrew ethical writers of the Rabbinic-philosophic group and the Hebrew ethical writers of Kabbalah. Whereas for the philosophical sages repentance represents a return from the sin, for the Kabbalists it represents a mystical return to the Divine *Sefirah* of *Binah*. The *Zohar*, like many other Kabbalistic works, supports this ideology with an original Kabbalistic symbolism: the "Hall" of the *Tzaddik* is the ninth *Sefirah*, *Yesod*, whereas the "Hall" of the *Baal Teshuvah* is the third *Sefirah*, *Binah*. Thus, since *Binah* is higher than *Yesod*, the *Baal Teshuvah* is necessarily higher than the *Tzaddik*.

Here we must return to *Sefer Ha-Yashar*. Should we proclaim, according to the above conclusions, that the anonymous author of *Sefer Ha-Yashar* was then a philosophical writer and not a Kabbalist? The answer to this question is indeed complex and problematic. This anonymous author presents a Kabbalistic approach in almost every theme of his book. His treatment of theosophy and cosmogony, his concepts of creation and evil, his concepts of love and fear of God, prayer and asceticism, are all very close to those of the Kabbalistic works of Gerona, although he refrains from using the Kabbalistic terminology explicitly.[25] On the other hand, this author seems to disagree with the Kabbalists on the issue of repentance. According to his view, repentance should be looked at as a religious and psychological process that brings the transgressor back to the straight and narrow, but it must not be perceived as a religious activity that elevates the *Baal Teshuvah* above the *Tzaddik*. We may see *Sefer Ha-Yashar* as an important document that implicitly authenticates the religious ideological struggles emerging in the Jewish spiritual world of the Middle Ages.

The Kabbalistic symbolism of Teshuvah

Two cardinal elements stand at the heart of the Kabbalistic literature on repentance in the magnum opus of the Kabbalah, the *Zohar*. The first is the Midrashic motif regarding the pre-existent status of *Teshuvah*, and the second is the *Zoharic* conception of mystical symbolism. The *Zohar* emphatically stresses the ancient Midrashic ideas that "Repentance preexisted the Creation of the world,"[26] and that "God engraved the world only after He had created Repentance."[27] At the center of the *Zoharic* teachings we read:

> When the Holy One blessed be He wished to create the world, He looked in Thought [*Histakel ba-Makhashavah*], the Secret of Torah, and engraved engravings, but it could not exist until He [first] created *Teshuvah* ... And there [in *Teshuvah*], all [the Hebrew] letters were engraved and formed ... He looked at this Palace [the *Sefirah* of *Binah*, which is *Teshuvah*], and engraved forms of the entire world before Him.[28]

Since repentance pre-existed the creation of the world, says the *Zohar*, it is a Divine archaic entity. Repentance has an ontic status; it is a "Palace," *Heichal*, in the world of God on high; it is the high third *Sefirah* in the world of emanation of *Ein-Sof*, the *Sefirah* that the Kabbalists call *Binah*.[29] *Binah* is the heavenly *Sefirah* of "Femininity" in the world of *Ein-Sof*. She symbolizes the Divine Motherhood and the Godly Womb; She emanates the lower seven *Sefirot*, from *Hesed* to *Malkhut*; She is the source of birth and the origin of every soul; She is the core of everything that exists and of everything that has life; and She is the exalted *Sefirah* that substantiates the "Family" in the realm of God.

According to a central thirteenth century Kabbalistic doctrine called *She'mitot* from the school of *Sefer Ha-Temmuna*, the complete cosmic cycle of life occurs in the lower seven *Sefirot*, from *Hesed* to *Malkhut*, and lasts for forty-nine thousand years. Each *Sefirah* among the lower seven *Sefirot* sustains and governs the universe for 6,000 years, followed by an additional 1,000 years, the seventh thousand, in which everything rests.[30] After 49,000 years, when all of the seven *Sefirot* – *Hesed*, *Deen*, *Tife'ret*, *Netzakh*, *Hod*, *Yesod*, and *Malkhut* – conclude their cosmic life cycle, they ascend to the bosom of the "Supernal Mother," *Binah*, and return to her Womb. Now, after 49,000 years, all of the worlds come to complete rest, above and below. *Binah*, the Kabbalists teach, is *Sha'ar ha-Nun*, the "Gate of Fifty."[31] *Binah* is *Sefirat ha-Yovel*, the conclusive anniversary *Sefirah* of the Jubilee.[32] *Binah* is the "Age of Understanding," for the Hebrew word *Binah* literally means understanding. *Binah* is the complete and final redemption for all of the *Sefirot* and for all of the souls of humanity who come to rest in her abode. She is the domain of the complete redemption for the entire creation, since She absorbs all "seven days of the week," which, according to the *Zohar*, correspond to the seven lower *Sefirot*. Most importantly, *Binah*, says the *Zohar*, is called *Teshuvah*, since She is the source of return, as depicted in Her name – TESHUVAH – which literally means in Hebrew "Return." For everything comes from the Womb of *Binah* and everything returns to the Womb of *Binah*.[33]

One of the greatest Kabbalists of thirteenth-century Spain, Joseph Gikatila, teaches the following Kabbalistic symbolism in his *Sha'arey Orah* (*The Gates of Light*) concerning *Binah*:

> And this *Sefirah* [*Binah*] also *Melabenet*, whitens the sins of Israel and

is called *Kippurim* [*atonement*]; since She is the secret of *Lebanon* [*LaBaN* in *Hebrew* means white], and She is grasped in the world of mercy, which is all white. And She whitens the sins of Israel ... And this *Sefirah* is called in the language of our sages, may their memory be blessed, *Ha-Olam ha-Ba*, the world to come, and since She is called *Kippurim* ... She is *Sod ha-Hayyim*, the secret of life ... [thus] we pray in *Yom ha-Kippurim* "inscribe us for life in the book of life," meaning, {inscribe us} in this exact *Sefirah* [in *Binah*] ... And because this *Sefirah* is *Olam ha-Hayyim*, the world of life, She is called *Olam ha-Ba*, the world to come ... for she always springs Her blessings and comes every day and every time and every hour, and emanates blessings to the world; as it is written "And a river emerges from Eden."[34] "Emerges?" That is, it does not ever cease [to emanate] ... and it is called *Olam ha-Ba*, for it goes and returns forever.[35]

Thus, *Binah* is the Sabbath of Sabbaths, *Shabat Shabaton*, which is *Yom ha Kippurim*, the great Day of Atonement; She is the source of life, and therefore, the secret of life, *Sod ha-Hayyim*; and She is the ultimate place of return, the world to come, *Olam ha-Ba*. All of the above Kabbalistic symbols are reflected in *Binah*'s Divine life, and all of them symbolize for the Kabbalist the profound esoteric meaning of repentance. Hence, repentance in the classic medieval teachings of Kabbalah is the mystical path of return that signifies the Kabbalist's yearning to ascend to the exalted world of God, to return his soul to her origin, to the Womb of the "Supernal Mother," and thus to experience *Devekut*. Within the mystical practice of communion with *Binah* through ethical deeds, prayer, meditation, and contemplation, the Kabbalist expresses his spiritual and ecstatic passion to return his soul to her primordial state. Only in *Binah* will his soul be resting in ideal delight and perfection, a perfection that the soul had experienced *before* she had been imprisoned in the corporeal body. And since he is built according to the construction of the *Sefirot*, for "The Icon [*de'yocan*] of Adam is the Icon of above and below,"[36] the Kabbalist knows that the power of his repentance will influence and mend both his earthly life and the heavenly world: he knows that his repentance performs a profound theurgical act; for he not only mends his lower *Icon*, but he also mends the upper *Icon* of God on high. Thus, when the Kabbalist repents he repairs himself by returning to his own originality and authenticity; and at the same time he even repairs the world of God.

The Kabbalistic symbolism of the early Kabbalists of Provence and Gerona, paved the way not only for the *Zohar* but also for the Kabbalists of Safed and for the masters of Hasidism. However, not all Jewish mystics looked at repentance as theurgy. In the teachings of the sixteenth-century Jewish mystic, the Maharal of Prague, repentance is understood as the return of the material, disorderly world into its immaculate, spiritual order. Repentance is thus a cosmic act, says the Maharal, but it is not a theurgical act. When a man or a woman repent through the practice of good deeds and the study of the Torah, their repentance prepares for the return of the world to its pure world of origin, to *Seder ha-Olam*. This pure world is the spiritual world that pre-existed our material world, and returning to it means complete cosmic restoration. Through the religious process of repentance, man becomes free from the material world, liberated from the slavery of the nations, redeemed from the burden of exile, and unshackled from the chains of evil.

In his classic ethical composition, *Netivot Olam* (*The Paths of the World*), the Maharal writes:

> The main interpretation of [repentance] is that the penitent returns to the blessed God with all of his heart and all of his soul, *since it is the order of the world*, [*Seder ha-Olam*], that the world returns to the blessed God. And it [the world], does not have an existence of its own; but only through returning to God whence it came and to where all that exists return ... For this is the root of the Torah; that She [the Torah] is the order of the world that the blessed God arranged ... When the sinner returns to the blessed God, his iniquities become his rights, since here there is an act of return to the blessed God, which is [an act] of return to the order of the world.[37]

The Maharal's interpretation of repentance empowers every human being with a cosmic skill and a world responsibility, and thus man is required to do repentance since only through repentance can he restore the flaws of the world and bring it back to *Seder ha-Olam*, which is the original Divine cosmic order that has been set by God since the dawn of history. However, the Maharal's philosophy on repentance is directed only to the flaws in our earthly reality, i.e. the reality that is *outside* the realm of God. This unique interpretation represents a *Cosmic Repentance*, but strongly rejects the *Theurgical Repentance*. While in cosmic repentance man repairs the earthly world alone, in theurgical repentance he repairs both the earthly world and the world of God.

Although the Maharal's powerful teaching on repentance has held great respect among Jewish scholars, it has not been perceived as the primary belief in the Hebrew literature of *Teshuvah*. As mentioned, the roots of the theory of Theurgical Repentance that already appeared in the Kabbalah of Provence, Gerona, and the *Zohar* developed the Jewish mystical belief that mending the discord in our earthly world below has direct influence on repairing the disorder of the Divine world above. This theory reached an even greater heights three centuries after the *Zohar* in the Safedian Kabbalistic school of the Ari, known as Lurianic Kabbalah. Here it was established as the major force of Jewish spirituality. Here repentance was perceived not only as a return of man from sin, but also as the profound cosmic religious act that mends the world of man *and* the world of God.

According to the Ari, and as discussed in previous chapters,[38] when an "awakening" occurred in the mind of *Ein-Sof* and His Will to create emerged, *Ein-Sof* contracted Himself in the act called *Tzimtzoom*, and thereafter He sent His lights to create the world. But the "vessels" of the world could not withhold the strength of the Divine lights, and thus the world that was supposed to be created in perfection was shattered. The Lurianic creation myth that involved the "awakening" of God, His *Tzimtzoom*, and the "breaking of the vessels" (*Shevirat ha-Kellim*) concluded in the teachings of Lurianic Kabbalah with one powerful answer to the problem of the shattered world: *Tikkun*!

What is the essence of the concept of *Tikkun* in Lurianic Kabbalah? *Tikkun* means that every man and every woman must dedicate their religious, spiritual, and moral life to mending the shattered worlds above and below. It means that the repentance of every human being does not purify the human being's sins alone in the lower cosmos but also the sins in the upper cosmos. It means that sin is not limited anymore to the specific transgression of man, but is linked to the universal sin of the cosmos that dared to be materialized through the emanation of the Divine lights. And it means that the ultimate task of humanity is in taking the heavy responsibility of mending the worlds, since the human beings are partners with God. Ever since man was created in God's image, he was assigned by God to mend that which had been broken by God in creation. Hence, through each individual act of repentance, the penitent must direct his intention not to mending himself alone, but also to mending the broken worlds. In Lurianic Kabbalah man does not stand in the center of the universe for the sake of himself, but rather for the sake of the universe and for the sake of Heaven. Thus, Lurianic Kabbalah in its essence does not propose an anthropocentric belief, but rather a theo-cosmocentric belief. For the mission of every man and woman is to bring salvation to the world, to redeem the *Shekhinah* from exile and to restore the harmony in the world of God, as formulated by the Ari: *Le-Shem Yikhud Kudshah Brich Hu u-Shekhinte'h*, "For the sake of the unification of the Holy One, blessed be He, and His *Shekhinah*." Even the exile itself is not only the result of historical events; it is rather the existential ordeal of every member in the congregation of Israel. It is a test for the chosen people, who were destined to complete the ultimate task in the history of humankind: to fulfill *Tikkun Olam in the Kingdom of Shaddai*, namely to repair the world in the Kingdom of God. And thus, repentance is both the cosmic and the meta-cosmic *Tikkun*. It is the human's ultimate yearning to repair all that exists, to restore existence to its pristine purity.

In *Reshit Hokhmah* of Rabbi Eliyahu de-Vidas from the school of Lurianic Kabbalah we read the following:

> The soul is the daughter of the King of kings, the Holy One blessed be He; and God gave her to man in this world, contrary to her will … and her descent to this world was for the sake of the *Tikkun* of the Torah and the *Mitzvot* … Man should rise up to return through repentance; he must think that the *Shekhinah* is in exile because of

[our sins] ... and that [the *Shekhinah*'s] redemption from exile is dependent upon our repentance ... And the inward intention in the word *Teshuvah* ["return"], is the return of the *Madregot* [*Sefirot*] to their pristine core and their mending [there] ... And the way of repentance is by mending *Ha-Tzinorot ha-Nishbarim* [the *Broken Vessels*] and by returning the [Divine] flow to its place, to each place as it was [before the vessels broke].[39]

Tikkun is thus the *telos* that the Lurianic and post-Lurianic Kabbalists assigned to human repentance. It is an ongoing process and a way of life, which man constantly practices, regardless of his personal sins or virtues. *Tikkun* is achieved by the daily study of the Torah and by the continual fulfillment of the *Mitzvot*. When a men or a women participate in *Tikkun*, their deeds not only mend the world below and the world above, but also heal their souls in their current life and in other *Gilgulim*, i.e. in other lives.[40] However, the exalted purpose of *Tikkun* resides in the mending of the disharmony in the world of God, which was damaged during the cosmogonial era. Hence, *Tikkun* is the human's and the world's recovery; it is the individual's and society's resurrection; it is the earthly and the heavenly renewal; and it is the conscious recognition that everything comes from the One and yearns to return to the One. Furthermore, Lurianic Kabbalah endowed the Jewish people with a new messianic emphasis: the Messiah is no longer the one who brings the redemption, but rather the one who symbolizes it. In Lurianic Kabbalah the secret and the power of redemption have been taken from the hands of the Messiah himself and placed into the hands of every man. Therefore, every *Mitzvah* is *Tikkun*, and every *Tikkun* is a messianic act; thus, repentance is the differentiation of the good from the bad, as formulated by the disciple of the Ari, Rabbi Hayyim Vital:

Every deed of the *Mitzvot* that we do all the days of our lives, including [even] our death, is for the sake of the differentiations [*Be'rrurim*, i.e. differentiations of the good from the bad]; and when the differentiating [*Be'rrur*] is completed, the Messiah will come.[41]

Teshuvah in Hasidism: the Tzaddik, the Devekut, and the Simkhah

There are three focal points from which Hasidism conceives its exclusive approach concerning repentance: the first is its belief in the stature of the *Tzaddik*, the second is its theory of *Devekut*, and the third is its psychology of *Simkhah*, namely *Religious Happiness*. I will consider these points in turn.

The Hasidic belief in the stature of the *Tzaddik* emerges with the inception of Hasidism in the first half of the eighteenth century.[42] According to this belief, in every generation there are select and peerless individuals who live among us, whose spiritual, intellectual, and leadership qualities ascend to the highest realm in the exalted world of the Divine. These men are crowned in the Hasidic world with the title "Rebbe"[43] or *Tzaddik*. The Hebrew word *Tzaddik* means literally a "righteous man." However, the term *Tzaddik* in Hasidism does not denote an ordinary righteous man as understood by the ancient Midrash or by the classical Jewish thinkers. Here the *Tzaddik* represents an exceptional, dazzling, and brilliant human being; he is exceptional in his proficiency in the Torah and the *Mitzvot*; he is dazzling in his understanding of the art of Kabbalah; and he is brilliant in his personal abilities as a social and spiritual leader. He is called by his *Hasidim*, his followers, *Tzaddik ha-Dor*, the *Tzaddik* of the generation, and he is described by them as a man of great stature and a spiritual leader with unequaled charisma.

Through his spiritual strength and meditative concentration, the *Tzaddik* ascends to the celestial *Sefirot* in order to commune with the Divine, for his ultimate goal is to achieve a lasting *Devekut* with *Ein-Sof*. However, he is compelled to descend from the heights of the supreme world down to the earthly world in order to redeem the "broken world." His societal duty coerces him to sustain an ongoing encounter with his *Hasidim* for the purpose of repentance. The *Tzaddik*'s primary duty is to repair the souls of his *Hasidim*. Thus, he realizes that he must descend from his elevated realm to dwell among his *Hasidim* in order to help them mend their broken souls. The *Tzaddik*'s descent is known in the Hasidic terminology as *Nefilat ha-Tzaddik*, the downfall of the *Tzaddik*, and it means that he is forced to go down to the people so that he participates as the people's spiritual leader in their penitential process.

In the Hasidic text, *Ben Porat Yoseph*, we read the following:

> The soul of the *Tzaddik* is composed of the souls of the people of his generation, so that he will be able to uplift them, when his soul communes with God, may He be blessed, through [the study of the] Torah and through prayer, and uplift the sparks of their souls, so that they ascend with him. And if the people of the generation are wicked, and he is a *Tzaddik* – and he is not at all at their level to the extent that he can not bring them up – then sometimes it is necessary that the *Tzaddik* descend from his level, through a sin that is reflected on him by the [acts of the] people of his generation ... and after he lowers himself to their level, he is able to uplift them when he returns to his [lofty] level.[44]

This paragraph demonstrates the concept of *Nefilat ha-Tzaddik*, which involves the role of the *Tzaddik* as the savior, the rescuer, and the liberator of the entire community of his *Hasidim* from their own transgressions. The *Tzaddik* is portrayed as an elevated figure, whose task is to commune with God, to bring the message of God to his *Hasidim*, even to "sin" by falling down to their material and lowly level. Most importantly, the *Tzaddik* must make an extraordinary spiritual effort in lifting his *Hasidim* up to a higher level. The *Tzaddik* stands as an intermediary between God and his *Hasidim*, in a way that resembles the biblical doctrine of atonement, when the High Priest would make the sacrifice and the confession for all the people of Israel, as stated in the Torah: "And Aaron shall lay both his hands upon the head of the live goat, and confess over him all the iniquities of the children of Israel, and all their transgressions, even all their sins."[45] In Hasidism, the biblical sacrifice of the "live goat" has been replaced with Hasidic prayer and devotion. However, the core of the biblical formula has not been changed; that is, although each individual in the community is required to repent, the main task of repentance is given into the hands of one elevated human being who carries the heavy responsibility for the purification of the entire community. Whereas in the Torah this human being is the High Priest, in Hasidism it is the *Tzaddik*.

The second focal point, which is unique to the Hasidic theory of repentance, is *Devekut*. First we must emphasize that the conception of *Devekut* is not an invention of Hasidism.[46] *Devekut* is discussed extensively in Kabbalistic literature as an exalted ideal of the mystical life of the Kabbalist. In Kabbalah *Devekut* is a contemplative quality: it is bound up with the individual's mystical experience, and it could also be the peak of the Kabbalist's ecstasy, who yearns to unite his soul with *Ein-Sof*, as in the Kabbalah of Abraham Abulafia. However, in Hasidism, the concept of *Devekut* is not a remote model of spirituality that can be achieved only by the elite, i.e. the *Tzaddik*, but rather a spiritual way of life that can be fulfilled by every simple *hasid*.[47] The father and founder of Hasidism, Rabbi Israel Baal Shem Tov, known as the Besht, was the first of the Hasidic masters to speak about the Hasidic theory of Divine immanence, according to which there is no place on earth that is void of God's presence.[48] His theory of pantheism determined for the Hasidic spiritual world that when the soul of the *hasid* is not utterly unified with God through contemplation, the *hasid* is like one who worships *Elohim Akherim*, a worshiper of idols. The Besht clearly established this idea when he wrote: "Whenever man separates himself from God, may He be blessed, instantaneously he worships other gods [*Oved Avoda Zarra*]."[49]

Thus, the religious state that signifies the basic and most natural sin of every man is described in Hasidism as the *hasid*'s separation from God. At the very moment when the *hasid* halts his concentration on God, even for an instant, he stands on the threshold of sin. However, there are two directions to his spiritual detachment from the Divine: although he recognizes, at the instant of his separation, that he stands on the frontier of sin, his sense of separation signals to him to commence *Teshuvah*. The *hasid* "experiences his destruction, every minute of it, when his thought departs from God," says the Besht. Each destruction is a sin, and every construction is *Teshuvah*; each sin is *Yeridah*, a descent, and every repentance is *Alliyah*, an ascent; each sin is *Katnut*, smallness, and every repentance is *Gadlut*, greatness. All dimensions of reality – time, space, and thought – abide by this rule in the Hasidic world of spirituality.

TESHUVAH

What, then, is the *hasid*'s essential state of mind? Where is his *existentia*? The *hasid* seems to constantly dwell in one of the following states. He is either in *Devekut* with God or in separation from God. He is either in sin or in repentance. From here we understand that sin, like repentance, has a paradoxical positive status in Hasidism, since its ontic constituent serves as a requirement for repentance. Hasidism has given the ancient Talmudical formula: *Yeridah Tzorech Alliyah*,[50] ("descent for the sake of ascent,") a new meaning: that the need to ascend and repent necessarily requires a descent and a sin, because "*Yeridah* – says the Maggid of Mazheritch – is for the sake of *Alliyah* in order to come to an even higher stage."[51]

Rabbi Menakhem Mendel, the Besht's follower and friend, taught:

> The *Tzaddik* who is called Adam, does repentance when he realizes that he does not have *Devekut* with God, may He be blessed, i.e. [he must] unify [*le-dabek*] his thought in the light of *Ein-Sof* ... *since there is no other sin except when his thought is not unified with Him.*[52]

The third focal point that is unique to the Hasidic theory of repentance is *Simkhah*, namely the Hasidic *Mitzvah of Religious Happiness*. This *Mitzvah* has become the primary religious value in Hasidism since the time of the Besht. Hasidism perceives the religious and spiritual life of its people as a Divine pleasure. Thus, *Simkhah* is an affirmative Hasidic state of mind that permits the *hasid* to worship God with joy and to fulfill God's Will, who becomes joyous when His people worship Him with joy. The ideology behind this belief is bound up with the Hasidic conviction that the *hasid* continually struggles with his evil inclination, whose vicious agenda is to break the human's spirit by impelling him toward distress and sorrow, in order to destroy his soul and imprison her. In Hasidism, sorrow is a state of sin, and *Simkhah* is the corresponding state of repentance. The Hasidic *Simkhah* is the psychological source and the religious nourishment in the *hasid*'s approach to God and the world. It is the conscious state of mind that directs the *hasid* to stand before his God with a sense of thankfulness and completion. It is the source of the Hasidic dance and songs that have shaped the ritual life of the Hasidic families. Most of all, *Simkhah* is the principal Hasidic quality through which the *hasid* makes *Tikkun* and *Teshuvah*.

Rabbi Nachman of Bratslav taught:

> It is good for a human being that he teaches himself how to give life to himself through a melody [*Niggun*], for a melody is something great and very very high, and it has the power of pulling up man's heart to God, may He be blessed ... And the principal is [*Ve-ha-K'lal*]: that he must strongly overcome [his sorrow] with all his powers, and only be happy [*Same'akh*] forever. Since the nature of man is that he might be drawn down to melancholy and sorrow – due to the difficulties and

the harms of time – and he thus will be saturated with griefs [*Yissurim*], therefore he must force himself with great power to be always in *Simkhah* and make himself happy, and even with words of silliness [*Mille' de-She'ttuta*].⁵³

Thus, the Hasidic belief in the *Tzaddik*, in *Devekut*, and in *Simkhah* delineate the three central religious components that play the major role in the *hasid*'s path of return as he walks toward *Teshuvah*. Although Hasidism is nurtured by the classic teachings of Kabbalah and its symbolism, it does not consider repentance as merely a return from sin, nor even as a *Tikkun* of the worlds below and above. Instead, Hasidism expands the Kabbalistic concept of repentance by emphasizing the stature of the spiritual leader of the Hasidic community, the *Tzaddik*, whose exceptional strength assists the community to recover from the burden of sin. With the significant help of the *Tzaddik*, and through the continuing process of *Devekut* and *Simkhah*, the *hasid* perpetually makes the religious transition from the secular to the holy: from the world of *Yesh* back to the world of *Ayin*.

The Hasidic doctrine of *Teshuvah* has inspired not only the hundreds of thousands *hasidim* who belong to the myriad Hasidic circles but also many Jewish people and thinkers who have not identified themselves with the Hasidic world. One of these thinkers is the outstanding Jewish philosopher of the twentieth century, Rav Avraham Yitzkhak ha-Cohen Kook, who wrote: "Hasidism is forever a diadem and a crown for Israel ... we greatly need a pure, pre-eminent, and holy Hasidism in our time; and we are required to uplift ourselves so that we recognize from a healthy national feeling the special pertinence that [Hasidism] has for the entire nation."⁵⁴ When Rav Kook was inspired by the concept of *Simkhah* in Hasidism, he wrote: "The *Oneg* (pleasure) and the *Simkhah* are things that necessarily accompany every spiritual occurrence. When a man takes pleasure in the good and the righteous deed [that he does] and he is happy, then he becomes quick to fulfill those deeds and augment them every day to perfection ... *Oneg* and *Simkhah* in the heart accompany the good and the righteous deed ...."⁵⁵

Rav Kook expanded the Hasidic teachings on *Teshuvah* and instituted a new ideology of repentance at the center of his thought.⁵⁶ He perceived repentance as man's freedom from the chains of his being, but, even more importantly, he attributed to *Teshuvah* a new national ideology. In his *Orot Ha-Teshuvah* (*The Lights of Return*), Rav Kook developed the idea that the Zionist return of the Jewish people to *Eretz Israel* in the twentieth century marks the culmination of the freedom of each Jew. For Rav Kook, the return of the Jews to their homeland signified the genesis of national Jewish redemption and the commencement of the salvation of the world. The Jewish people's longing for their homeland, their unceasing desire to return to the Promised Land after 2,000 years of exile, and their hope of re-establishing their Jewish entity and identity in the land of their forefathers, says Rav Kook, are the biblical prophecies beginning to come true. Thus, the Zionist return of the Jewish people to Israel becomes, in Rav Kook's thought, the ultimate return, the ultimate *Teshuvah*.

In his *Orot Ha-Teshuvah* Rav Kook writes:

> *Teshuvah* occupies the greatest part of the Torah and in Life; personal and public hopes are built on it; it is the *Mitzvah* of God ... We must reveal this secret; that is, that the real *Teshuvah* of all Israel – the return to the Land of Israel – is becoming increasingly in our lives one of the great links ... listen dear brothers and put this golden key, the key of the true redemption, the *Teshuvah*, in your hearts; and a year of redemption and salvation, a year of faithful brotherly love will come upon us, soon, in our days, Amen.[57]

Conclusion

Repentance, as confronted by Jewish thought, has unquestionably become the fundamental thread in the fabric of Jewish life and ethics. As demonstrated above, the theme of repentance in Jewish thought has continuously changed and evolved. It has been conceptualized as the return of man from sin, the spiritual and intellectual cleaving to God, the penitent's yearning to enjoy the brilliance of the *Shekhinah* in the world to come, the Kabbalist's desire to return his soul to her pristine mother – the *Sefirah* of *Binah* – the cosmic return of the world to its utopian genesis – *Seder ha-Olam* – the *Tikkun* of the world below as well as the theurgical *Tikkun* of the world above, the *hasid*'s freedom from the chains of his own being, and even as the return of the secular Jews to Zion in our generation. However, the dominant common thread in the treasury of the *Teshuvah* literature has always been portrayed as *Return*. Therefore, it would be accurate to conclude that the notion of man's return to his source is the main ingredient of *Teshuvah*: indubitably, *the notion of return to the source is the religious component that stands at the heart of the Jewish faith.*

What is the nature of this crucial ingredient? It is bound up with the historical character of Judaism, which unceasingly requires that the Jew return to his past, to his origin and authenticity, and at the same time walk courageously in the path of the present while facing with hope the horizon in the future. The Jewish principal of return is deeply rooted in the nostalgic collective mind of the Jews, who have always perceived their faith as a fountain emerging from the great past of their forefathers. Judaism can be described, therefore, as a Divine dynamism that has unfolded its hidden layers throughout a chain of revelations. The greatest of all Jewish revelations was that of God revealing Himself to His chosen people when He gave them the Torah on Mount Sinai. However, even at the moment of this greatest historical revelation, the people of Israel sinned with the Golden Calf, from which we may learn that both sin and repentance are inherent in their nature.

KABALLAH AND THE ART OF BEING

The history of the Jewish people throughout its entire development has been confronted by an astounding dialectical current; that is, by the tendency to come near to God, toward the pure and the pristine, and by its opposite tendency to draw away from God, from the pure and the pristine. This current is entwined with another remarkable current, which is the historical paradox of the Jewish people, who were selected by God to be His chosen people, but during 2,000 years in exile have become His homeless people. Their particular history, on the one hand, and their spiritual destiny, on the other hand, have shaped their identity and ethics with an essential existential paradox that is unique in the history of humankind. For even when they stood far from God, even when they were rooted out of their homeland, even when they experienced pogroms and oppressions the Jewish people have always sought to fulfill their moral responsibility and Divine destiny. Hence, the classic texts on *Teshuvah*, written by the most prominent Jewish thinkers, do not only teach a lesson in repentance, they also reveal the existential answers that have sustained the Jewish spirit and have kept the Jews as a nation of distinctive identity – despite centuries of exile, persecution and genocide. These texts are the genuine spiritual and psychological documents that reflect the true *Pneuma* of the Jewish nation, a nation that has evolved and matured through the centuries. They reflect the teachings of Jewish spirituality as a Jewish way of life, for they taught the Jews how to survive in strenuous times; how to become actualized and fulfilled human beings; and how to flourish and live complete and healthy lives. Most importantly, these texts taught the Jews that there is always a way of return from every sin and a path of hope for every despair, for the gates of repentance are always open; *Teshuvah*, a gift from God, is the conclusive return to God.

There is an essential pledge in the Torah that shapes the spirit of Jewish life. It is the eternal covenant that was signed between the Creator and His chosen people. This covenant requires that God descend to His chosen people and save them, even when they sin against Him, and it demands that the Jewish people ascend to their God from the abyss of their sin, in order to be saved by Him. Therefore, the Jewish people cry out to God from the depth of their distress, and they continually search for that path by which they can return to Him.

In Kabbalah, man's search for God has become the fundamental component of the religious life. God's essence is found first and foremost in His esoteric process of creation, not in the mundane reality, but rather in the hyper-reality. When a man begins to explore the mystery of *Ein-Sof* the Creator – His perpetual act of emanation, His skill in creation, His love and His compassion – he learns how to follow the perfect models of existence and how to imitate the ultimate Art of Being. For every expression of God's creativity is bound up with His Art of Being, and His intention in creation is that this Art should be mirrored by man. The Kabbalists insist in their spiritual teachings that the Jewish people must create their own identity in accordance with God's creativity, for man is created in the image of God, and only by ascending to His lofty image can man discover his own creativity. Therefore, man must contemplate the Godly Art of creation, for the root of life and the secret of being are concealed in this Art. Hence, God's awakening to create the world, His desire to individuate Himself, His conscious aspiration to be recognized as the Creator, His search for the chosen people, His shift from thought to speech in creation, His expansion from singularity to plurality, His dealing with the broken worlds, and His repairing of the broken worlds, all of these acts are the essential components not only in God's Art of Being, but also in man's art of being. These creative acts, say the Kabbalists, attest to the dynamic God who perpetually actualizes Himself in order to bring the *Yesh* from the *Ayin*. Thus, the lesson that the Infinite God teaches to His chosen people is the understanding that Divine life can be implemented in this earthly life.

In our rapidly changing world, when every day we hear the dissonance of another advanced, computerized technology, lacking in spirit or individuality, we also encounter those people who listen to a different strain and yearn to discover an authentic *Niggun* within themselves. The inner song that has been in the hearts of the Jewish people ever since Abraham said to God *Hinneni*, at the time of the historical covenant, is echoed in the teachings of Kabbalah more than in any other Jewish school of thought. In Kabbalah we learn that when the Jewish people are eager to rediscover the legacy of their forefathers, they reveal anew their own authentic spirit, which – unlike the impermanent machines of our time – is certain, faithful, credible, real, and eternal. The Jewish encounter with its own authenticity is the major spiritual activity that sustains Jewish life. For centuries the continuing rediscovery of that authenticity has confirmed the true values and beliefs of the Jews; for generations it has strengthened the reality of the Jewish spirit. The teachings of Kabbalah and Jewish spirituality embody the *Practical Wisdom* and the vitality that this authenticity guarantees. These teachings are the enduring words of the Jewish sages who wrote for future generations: for you and me, for our children, and for the children of our children. These are the words of wisdom that heal the human body and mind, that affirm our true purpose of being. These words of wisdom empower the Jewish people with aspiration and dedication to live a life fulfilled. *The end of the matter, all having been heard: fear God and keep His commandments; for this is the whole of man.*[58]

TESHUVAH, Repentance

NOTES

1 THE MYSTERY OF CREATION

1. See G. Scholem, *Kabbalah* (New York, 1974), 88.
2. Mishnah *Hagigah* 2:1.
3. See Chapter 3, Kabbalah and language: thirty-two paths of wisdom.
4. *Mechilta*, *Pe'sakhim* 14: *Me'gilla* 29:1: Jerusalem Talmud, *Ta'anit* 1:1. On the exile of the Shekhinah (*Galut ha-Shekhinah*) in Jewish mysticism and Hasidism, see R. Schatz-Uffenheimer, *Hasidism as Mysticism* (Princeton University Press, 1980), 163–166.
5. R. Feynman, *Six Easy Pieces, Essentials of Physics* (Helix Books, 1996), 4.
6. See M. Idel, *Kabbalah – New Perspectives* (Yale University Press, 1988), 64–65.
7. See Hegel's "Independence and Dependence of Self-Consciousness," 178, 190, in *Phenomenology of Spirit*, translated by A. V. Miller (Oxford, 1977), 115.
8. M. Idel, op. cit., 39 ff.
9. See G. Scholem, *Major Trends in Jewish Mysticism* (New York, 1941), 122–123.
10. See M. Idel, "Universalization and Integration: Two Conceptions of Mystical Union in Jewish Mysticism," in *Mystical Union in Judaism, Christianity, and Islam*, M. Idel and B. McGinn (eds.) (New York, 1996), 27–57; G. Scholem, "*Devekut* or Communion with God," in *The Messianic Idea in Judaism* (New York, 1971), 203–227.
11. Genesis 1:1, 4, 5.
12. Genesis 1:27.
13. The phenomenon of the bisexuality of the gods has been present among various cultures in different forms, such as in the example of *Shiva*, the male, who appears united in a single body with *Shakti*, the female, his spouse – *Shiva* on the right side, *Shakti* on the left – who together form the manifestation known as *Adhanarisha*. See J. Campbell, "The Cosmogonic Cycle," in *The Hero With A Thousand Faces* (Princeton University Press, 1968), 225–294. The notion of Divine bisexuality is an essential component in theosophical Kabbalah, and is found even in pre-Kabbalistic literature. In the mystical teachings of the twelfth-century Ashkenazi Pietist, Eleazar of Worms, we find a unique dynamism in the Divine realm, accordingly the relation between the upper and the lower "glories" is based on bisexual theology. See E. R. Wolfson, "The Image of Jacob Engraved upon the Throne: Further Reflection on the Esoteric Doctrine of the German Pietists," in *Along The Path, Studies in Kabbalistic Myth, Symbolism, and Hermeneutics* (State University of New York Press, 1995), 1–62.
14. *Quis Rerum Divinarum Heres Sit*, 134, in *Philo of Alexandria, The Complete Life, The Giants, and Selections*, translated by D. Winston (New York, 1981), 97.
15. Ibid., 141–143, 97.
16. See Genesis 2:21–23, 5:1–2.

NOTES

17 Aristotle, *De Partibus Animalium*.
18 Ernest Cassirer, *An Essay on Man* (Yale, 1972), 25–26.
19 See Chapter 3, *Ein-Sof, Sefirot*, and *Atzilut*.
20 Genesis, 2:21–24.
21 Deuteronomy, 13:5.
22 *Sefer Mei'rat Enayim*, Munich Ms. 14, 140b. See also *Sefer Mei'rat Enayim* (Rabbi Isaac of Ako), A. Goldreich's edition (Jerusalem, 1984); A. Kaplan, "Rabbi Issac of Acco," in *Meditation and Kabbalah* (York Beach, Maine, 1984), 143.
23 Daniel 12:3.

2 A NOTE ON CREATION IN PHILOSOPHY, MYTHOLOGY AND GNOSIS

1 *The Guide for the Perplexed*, I: 52.
2 Ibid., I: 54.
3 See A. L. Ivrey, "Maimonides on Possibility," in *Mystics, Philosophers, and Politicians*, J. Reinharz and D. Swetshinski (eds.) (Duke University Press, 1982), 67–84; H. Davidson, "Maimonides' Secret Position on Creation," in *Studies in medieval Jewish History and Literature*, I. Twersky (ed.) (Harvard University Press, 1979), 16–40.
4 See S. Pines, "Translator's Introduction," *The Guide of the Perplexed*, Vol. I, cxxvii ff. (Chicago, 1963); A. Nuriel, "The Question of a Created or Primordial World in the Philosophy of Maimonides," in *Tarbiz* 33 (1964), 372–387.
5 See S. Klein-Braslavy, "The Creation of the World and Maimonides' interpretation of Gen. I–V," in *Maimonides and Philosophy*, S. Pines and Y. Yovel (eds.) (Martinus Nijhoff Publishers, 1986), 65 ff.
6 See S. Pines, "The Philosophic Sources of the Guide for the Perplexed," op. cit. lxxviii–xcii.
7 See Alfarabi, The Sources of Questions, as discussed in R. Hammond, in *The Philosophy of Alfarabi* (New York, 1947).
8 See S. Afnan, "Problems of Metaphysics," in *Avicenna* (Greenwood Press, 1980), 126–132; On Avicenna's influence on Maimonides see S. Pines, op. cit., xciii–ciii.
9 *Monologion* 8.
10 See Anselm, Introduction, in *Anselm of Canterbury: The Major Works* B. Davies and G. R. Evans (eds.) (Oxford, 1998), xii–xiii.
11 *Proslogion* 3. See Anselm, ibid., 88.
12 *Summa Contra Gentiles, Book Two: Creation*, translated by J. Anderson (University of Notre Dame Press, London, 1956), Chapter 17.
13 *Summa Contra Gentiles, Book One: God*, translated by A. Pegis (University of Notre Dame Press, London, 1955), Chapter 16.
14 See G. Scholem, *Jewish Gnosticism, Merkabah Mysticism, and Talmudic Tradition* (J.T.S., New York, 1965).
15 The Gnostic quotations in this Chapter are taken from K. Rudolph, *Gnosis*, translated by R. McLachlan Wilson (Harper & Row, 1987).
16 NHC II 4,94; 5,97; 5,99. *Gnosis*, ibid., 72.
17 NHC II 5,97. *Gnosis*, ibid.
18 *Hypostasis of the Archons, Gnosis*, ibid., 73.
19 NHC II, 5,99. *Gnosis*, ibid., 73.

NOTES

3 KABBALAH ON GOD'S INTENT AND LANGUAGE IN CREATION

1. *Zohar* III, *Raya Mehemna*.
2. On *Merkabah* literature see G. Scholem, *Major Trends in Jewish Mysticism* (New York, 1960), 40–79.
3. Chronicles 29:11.
4. S. Shokek, *Jewish Ethics and Jewish Mysticism in Sefer Ha-Yashar* (New York, 1991).
5. *Sefer Ha-Yashar* (Jerusalem, 1978), Chapter 1, selected paragraphs.
6. See S. Shokek, op. cit. "The Concept of God and Creation in *Sefer Ha-Yashar*," 39–81.
7. *Midrash Shemot Rabbah* 3:6.
8. *Midrash Tanhumah Shemot*, Parashat *tetze'*, 18.
9. Yehudah ha-Barceloni, commentary on *Sefer Ye'tzirah*, p. 175.
10. Ibid.
11. Jerusalem manuscript, Klausner 2/3 29b.
12. *Zohar*, part I, 2a. See I. Tishby, *The Wisdom of the Zohar* (Oxford University Press, 1989), Vol. I, 331.
13. *Ha-Kabbalah be-Gerona* (Academon, Jerusalem), 278.
14. *Zohar Hadash*, *Yitro* (Venice edition), 35b–35d.
15. *Zohar* I, 240b.
16. See I. Tishby (1989), "The Chain of the Sefirot," op. cit., 313–318.
17. See G. Scholem, *Major Trends in Jewish Mysticism* (New York, 1960), 223.
18. Deuteronomy 5:6.
19. On the creation from *nequdah* see I. Tishby, "The Process of Emanation," op cit., 309–313.
20. See G. Scholem, *Major Trends in Jewish Mysticism* (New York, 1960), 219.
21. Genesis 1:3.
22. Mishnah *Avot* 5:1.
23. Although God did not speak in the *first* act of creation, it is implied in the tradition of Judaism that the verse "In the beginning God created heaven and earth" (Genesis 1:1), refers to a creation through speech, and thus "In *Ten Sayings* the world was created." On *The Book of Formation*, see *Sefer Ye'tzirah*, A. Kaplan's edition (York Beach, Maine, 1993).
24. *Sefer Ye'tzirah* 2:6.
25. *Midrash Rabba* on *Be'Reshit* 1:1.
26. See "Rabbi Isaac the Blind of Provence," in *The Early Kabbalah*, edited by J. Dan, translated by R. Kiener (Paulist Press, 1986), 73 ff.
27. See I. Tishby (1989), "Thought, Voice, and Speech," op. cit., 325–327.
28. *Zohar* I, 16b–17a.
29. Genesis 2:20.
30. Genesis 32:29.

4 CREATION AND *IMITATIO DEI*: LURIANIC KABBALAH AND HASIDISM

1. *Pardes Rimmonim*, selected passages, 129a, 102b, 14b; See *Sha'ar Atzmut ve-Kellim*, Chapter 8; See also J. Ben Shlomo, *Torat Ha-Elohut Shel Moshe Cordovero* (Jerusalem, 1965, in Hebrew), Chapter 2.
2. See Moses Cordovero, "God is Unchanging," in *Ellmah Rabbati*, excerpted in L. Jacobs' *Jewish Ethics, Philosophy, and Mysticism* (New York, 1969), selected passages, 125–129.
3. Ezekiel 1:4–14.
4. *Sefer Etz Hayyim*, *Drush Iggulim ve-Yosher*, Chapter 2.
5. See J. Bradley, *Mach's Philosophy of Science* (Athlone, 1971), Chapter 6.

NOTES

6 I. Tishby, *Torat Ha-Ra ve-ha-Qelipah Be-Kabbalat ha-Ari* (Jerusalem, 1942, in Hebrew).
7 *Sefer Etz Hayyim, Heichal Adam Kadmon, Drush Iggulim ve-Yosher*, beginning of Chapter 1.
8 See I. Tishby (1942), op. cit.; G. Scholem, *Major Trends in Jewish Mysticism* (New York, 1946), 224–286; J. Dan, *Jewish Mysticism and Jewish Ethics* (University of Washington Press, 1986), 84–103.
9 *Midrash Rabba* 9:1.
10 *Masekhet Atzilut*, Section 4.
11 *Masekhet Atzilut*, ibid. For further discussion on *Masekhet Atzilut* See G. Scholem, "Sitra Ahra: Good and Evil in the Kabbalah," in *On the Mystical Shape of the Godhead* (New York, 1991), 62–63.
12 See G. Scholem, ibid., 84–85.
13 See, R. Schatz-Uffenheimer, *Hasidism as Mysticism* (Princeton University Press, 1993); M. Idel, *Hasidism Between Ecstasy and Magic* (State University of New York Press, 1995).
14 Maharal, *Netzakh Israel*, Chapter 1.
15 *Tanya, Sha'ar ha-Yikhud ve-ha-Emunah*, Chapter 7.
16 The *Sefirah – Yesod*, is the male *Sefirah* who usually has its counterpart as the female *Sefirah – Malkhut*, which may be coupled either with *Yesod* or *Tife'ret*.
17 See R. Elior, "The Kabbalistic Theosophy of *Habad* Hasidism," in *The Paradoxical Ascent to God* (State University of New York Press, 1993), 116; idem., "HaBaD: The Contemplative Ascent to God," in *Jewish Spirituality*, Vol. 14 (New York, 1989), 166–168.
18 *Maggid Devarav le-Ya'akov*, R. Schatz's edition, 21.
19 *Tanya, Sha'ar ha-Yikhud ve-ha-Emunah*, op. cit.
20 *Tanya, Iggeret ha-Kodesh*, Chapter 6; see R. Elior (1993), "Acosmism," op. cit., 49–72; R. Schatz-Uffenheimer, op. cit., 75, 261, 269.
21 The school of thought, called *Materialism*, can be understood as one of the best examples for the exact opposite of *Acosmism* in Hasidism. According to the school of *Materialism*, everything in the universe is made of matter, but the mind and the spirit are illusory, or can be somehow reduced to matter. See D. M. Armstrong, *A Materialist Theory of Mind* (Routledge, 1968): H. Robinson, *Objections to Physicalism* (Clarendon, 1993).
22 *Likutei Moharan*, II, Chapter 71.
23 *Tole'dot Ya'akov Yosef*, f. 66c, as quoted by M. Idel (1995) in his essay "Zaddiq as 'Vessel' and 'Channel' in Hasidism," op. cit., 193.
24 See M. Idel, "Reorganization of Kabbalah," ibid., 41.
25 See M. Idel, "Psychologization of Theosophy in Kabbalah and Hasidism," ibid., 227–238.
26 *Likutei Moharan* I, 17.
27 *Kedushat Levi*, beginning of *Be'Reshit*. See M. Hallamish, "The Doctrine of Creation," in *An Introduction to the Kabbalah* (State University of New York Press, 1999), 189–196.
28 *Be'er Mayyim Hayyim* on Genesis 1:26.
29 *Midrash Tehillim* on Genesis 1:1.
30 *Be'er Mayyim Hayyim*, on Genesis 1:26.
31 Introduction to Maimonides' *Laws Concerning Character Traits*, in *The Book of Knowledge, Hilchot De'ot*.
32 *Laws Concerning Character Traits*, Chapter 1.
33 Leviticus 19:2.
34 Deuteronomy 11:22–25.
35 *Siphre* on Deuteronomy 11:22.
36 *Sotah* 14.
37 Jerusalem Talmud, *Pe'ah*, 15b.
38 Rashi, Commentary on *Shabbat*, 133b.

NOTES

39 Exodus 33:18–19.
40 Exodus 33:20.
41 *The Guide for the Perplexed,* I: 54.
42 *Tomer Devorah,* Chapter 1.
43 Ibid., Chapter 5.
44 See M. Buber, "Imitatio Dei," in *Israel and the World, Essays in a Time of Crisis* (New York, 1963), 66–77.
45 See M. Idel, *Studies in Ecstatic Kabbalah* (State University of New York Press, 1988); idem., *The Mystical Experience in Abraham Abulafia* (State University of New York Press, 1988).
46 Ms. Sasson 56, f. 33a, as translated by M. Idel (1995) op. cit., 230. (Words in brackets are mine. S.S.).
47 Abulafia, *Sefer Gan Na'ul*, Ms. British Library, OR. 13136, f. 3a, based on M. Idel, ibid., 231.
48 See M. Idel, ibid., 232–233.
49 *Tole'dot Ya'akov Yosef*, Vol. 86a; See M. Idel, ibid., 234.

5 KABBALAH AND GOD'S INDIVIDUATION

1 On the term *mysterium tremendum* see Rudolf Otto, *The Idea of the Holy* (Oxford University Press, 1971), Chapter 4, 12–24.
2 Abraham Joshua Heschel, *God in Search of Man* (New York and Philadelphia, 1959), 136.
3 Genesis 2:18.
4 On healthy versus unhealthy narcissism and on narcissism as a developmental stage, see A. Morrison, editor, *Essential Papers on Narcissism* (New York University Press, 1986), 97, 109, 203, 208.
5 G. W. F. Hegel, "Self Consciousness," in *The Phenomenology of Spirit*, translated by A. V. Miller (Oxford University Press, 1952), 178.
6 Ibid., 221.
7 Ibid., 190.
8 *Sefer Ha-Rimmon (The Book of the Pomegranate)*, E. R. Wolfson's edition (Scholars Press, 1988), 181–182. See also G. Scholem, *Major Trends in Jewish Mysticism* (New York, 1941), 223.
9 Genesis 2:7.
10 Psalms 103–104.
11 Talmud, *Berakhot* 10a.
12 *Zohar Hadash, Be'Reshit* 5a.
13 Moshe Isserles, *Torat ha-Olah* (Prague 1569), 14, f. 19b d, as discussed by G. Scholem in his essay "Tselem: The Concept of the Astral Body," in *On The Mystical Shape of the Godhead* (New York, 1991), 259.
14 *Sefer Ha-Yashar*, Chapter one: "The Secret of the Creation of the World."
15 On individuation in Jungian psychology see J. Jacobi, *The Psychology of C. G. Jung* (Yale University Press, 1973), 107; A. Jaffe', *Was C. G. Jung A Mystic?* (Daimon Verlag, 1989), 57–102; R. Aziz, *C. G. Jung's Psychology of Religion and Synchronicity* (State University of New York Press, 1990), 17–18; E. Neumann, *The Origin and the History of Consciousness* (Princeton University Press, 1993), 411. R. Aziz, ibid,. lists three characteristics within Jungian individuation.

   1. The *ego* does not choose its goal but it is the one being led by the unconscious toward its goal.
   2. The *ego* denotes that the productive course of action for the individual is to move with the current of the spiritual growth, i.e. with individuation, and thus every individual simply submit to it because it is a natural process.

NOTES

3. The goal of individuation is the conscious realization of that which constitutes the center point and the meaning of the psyche. Therefore, in the course of individuation one seeks to facilitate the realization of the *self*. J. Jacobi, ibid., defines individuation as the parallel unfolding and maturation of both the psychic and the physical body of the human being. E. Neumann, ibid., claims that individuation is the "mastering of the dialectic between the *ego* and the collective unconscious."

16 See A. Jaffe', ibid., 60. It should be emphasized that Jung's understanding of God's individuation is profoundly rooted in Christian theology. In his Psychological *Approach to the Dogma of the Trinity* (*The Collected Works*, Vol. 11, par. 233), he claims that God's individuation involves suffering, and thus the Godly individuation is reflected in the "incarnation" of Christ, while a similar, existential human suffering, appears at the heart of the process of the human's individuation. Furthermore, in his *Answer to Job* (op. cit., par. 648), Jung says: "Yahweh's intention to become man, which resulted from his collision with Job, is fulfilled in Christ's life and suffering." See also C. G. Jung "On the Religious Function," in *The Basic Writings of C. G. Jung* (New York, 1993), 537–655; J. O. Dallett, *The Not-Yet Transformed God: Depth Psychology and the Individual Religious Experience* (York Beach, Maine, 1998), 103–122.

17 C. G. Jung, "Conscious, Unconscious, and Individuation," in *The Archetypes and the Collective Unconscious* (Princeton University Press, 1990(; *The Collected Works*, Vol. 9, 275–276; For a comprehensive study in Jung's psychology and terminology (including his definitions of his primary terms, such as analytical psychology, archetypes, ego, transformation, self, introvert–extrovert, anima–animus, shadow, and complex), see *The Collected Works of C. G. Jung* (Princeton University Press), Multiple Volumes.

18 See W. Benjamin in a letter to G. Scholem in "Walter Benjamin and Gershom Scholem," *Correspondence 1932–1940* (New York, 1989), 203; M. Buber, *The Eclipse of God: Studies in the Relation Between Religion and Philosophy* (New York, 1952), 78–86; and Jung's response to Buber, "A Reply to M. Buber, The Symbolic Life," in *Religion and Psychology* (*The Collected Works*, XVIII, 663 ff.); J. Dan, "The Myth and the Scholarship of Myth," in *Al ha-Kedushah* (*On Sanctity*) (Jerusalem, 1998, Hebrew), 162–171; See also E. Fromm's criticism of Jung, in his *Psychoanalysis of Religion* (Yale University Press, 1950), 20, and Jung's response to Fromm, in *Psychology and Western Religion* (Princeton University Press, 1984), 255–256. It should be emphasized that many of Jung's ideas are indeed in controversy among scholars. On Jung's theology, his relationship with the Nazis, his relationship with the Jews and his outlook of Judaism see F. McLynn, *Carl Gustav Jung: A Biography* (New York, 1996).

19 For example, one can deduce an explicit Jungian influence on G. Scholem in his *Major Trends in Jewish Mysticism*, when Scholem describes the process of the creation of the world in Kabbalah, and the transformation by which *Ein-Sof* emanates the ten *Sefirot*. Scholem uses explicit Jungian terms and calls the *Sefirah* of *Binah*, "the pure totality of all individuation" (p. 219). The seven lower *Sefirot* that are the manifestations of the qualities of God, he calls "the projection of the *archetypes* of the seven lower *Sefirot*" (p. 220). Individuation and *archetypes* are two classic Jungian terms especially when used in the context of creation, transformation, and growth, and were extremely popular Jungian terms during the time when Scholem's book was published (1941). Scholem participated in more then a few *Eranos Conferences* with Jung, whom he knew and whose analytical psychology was not unknown to him. The example before us merely demonstrates how the founder of the new contemporary scholarship of Jewish mysticism internalized components of Jungian psychology and terminology, but yet was reluctant to recognize Jung explicitly.

20 Jung, *Letters*, II (March 28, 1953, Amstutz). My comments on Jung's letters are based on their English translation in A. Jaffe's, *Was C. G. Jung A Mystic?* See also [Jung's] *Letters*, Adler G. and Jaffe' A. (eds.), translated by Hull R. F., Vol. I. 1906–1950, Vol. II. 1951–1961.

NOTES

21 *Letters* (January 5, 1952, Neumann).
22 *Letters*, II (February 16, 1954, Kirsch).
23 A. Jaffe', op. cit., 99–100. On Jung's analysis on Kabbalah and its symbolism, see "Adam as Totality," in *Mysterium Coniunctionis* (Princeton University Press, 1989, *The Collected Works*, Vol. 14), 438–456.
24 See above, Chapter 4, section I: "The *Creation Myth* in the Kabbalah of Cordovero and the Ari," p. 45.
25 See *Avodat ha-Levi*, *Va-Yehi*, Fol. 74a, as discussed by R. Elior in her essay "Wholeness as the Incorporation of Opposites," in *The Paradoxical Ascent to God* (State University of New York Press, 1993), 63–64.
26 See Jung (1990) "The Hermaphroditism of the Child," op. cit., 173–175.
27 On the anima-animus, see Jung (1990) "Conscious, Unconscious, and Individuation," op. cit., 284, 286–288.
28 On Language in Kabbalah, see above, Chapter 3, section III.
29 Genesis 1:2–3.
30 Genesis 1:4–5.
31 See Jung (1990) "Child God and Child Hero," op. cit., 167.
32 Jung emphasizes that wholeness of the personality requires two distinct simultaneous relationships, one with oneself and one with "the other." See C. G. Jung, *Psychology of Transference* (The collected Works, Vol. 16, par. 454). On Jungian integration see also E. A. Bennet, *What Jung Really Said* (New York, 1983), 171–174; V. Kast, *The Dynamics of Symbols, Foundations of Jungian Psychotherapy* (New York, 1992), 1–7.
33 See Jung (1990), op. cit., 279.

6 KABBALAH AND THE ART OF BEING

1 Aristotle, *Physics* II, 1–24. See J. Lear, *Aristotle, The Desire to Understand* (Cambridge University Press, 1998), 15.
2 Aristotle, *Physics* II, 22–24. See also R. McKeon's translation in *The Basic Works of Aristotle* (New York, 1966), 236.
3 *Midrash Rabba* 9:1.
4 Ecclesiastes 3:1.
5 Ibid. 3:1–9
6 *Avot* 3:1.
7 *The Duties of the Heart, Sha'ar ha-Ahavah*, Chapter 6.
8 Talmud, *Berachot* 33.
9 Rashi, Commentary on Genesis 22:1.
10 Genesis 22:2.
11 Ibid. 22:3.
12 See S. Kierkegaard, "Problema III," in *Fear and Trembling* (Princeton University Press, 1983), 115.
13 See W. James, "Mysticism," in *The Varieties of Religious Experience* (New York, 1963), 380. On Ineffability and other characteristics of mysticism and the mystical experience, see E. Underhill, *Mysticism* (New York, 1960), 81 ff.; W. R. Inge, *Mysticism in Religion* (Greenwood Press, 1976), 25 ff.; W. Wainwright, *Mysticism* (University of Wisconsin Press, 1981), 8 ff.; S. Katz, editor, *Mysticism and Religious Traditions* (Oxford University Press, 1983); M. Idel, *Kabbalah New Perspectives* (Yale University Press, 1988), introduction; M. Ostow, *Ultimate Intimacy, The Psychodynamics of Jewish Mysticism* (Karnak Books, 1995), 3 ff.; J. Dan, *Al ha-Kedusha* (Jerusalem, 1998, Hebrew), Chapters 3 and 6.
14 On the *noetic quality* in the religious experience, see W. James, ibid.

NOTES

15 *Pri Etz*, "Homily for Shabbat Teshuvah." See J. Dan, *The Teachings of Hasidism* (Behrman House, 1983) p. 73
16 *The Duties of the Heart*, *Sha'ar ha-Bitakhon*, Chapter 1.
17 Talmud, *Hagigah* 14b. See also *Tosefta*, *Hagigah* 2:3–4, and Jerusalem Talmud, *Hagigah* 2:1, 77a.
18 See Y. Liebes, *He'to' shel Elisha: Arba'ah she-Nichne'su la-Pardes ve-Tiv'ah shel ha-Mistika ha-Talmudit* (Jerusalem, 1990, Hebrew); M. Ostow, "Four Entered the Garden, Normative Religion Versus Illusion," op. cit., 129–143.
19 See M. Idel, *Language, Torah, and Hermeneutics in Abraham Abulafia* (State University of New York Press, 1991), 1–5.
20 See G. Scholem, *"Shi'ur Komah*: The Mystical Shape of the Godhead," in *On the Mystical Shape of the Godhead* (New York, 1991), Chapter 1.
21 *Avot* 1:1.
22 Psalms 4:5: See Maimonides' *The Guide for the Perplexed*, I:59. Maimonides claims that the highest level of praising God in prayer is in being silent.
23 Genesis 22:12.
24 *Metaphysics* I:I. *Vision* and *Sight* stand at the heart of the mystical experience in many pre-Kabbalistic and Kabbalistic texts. E. R. Wolfson's *Through A Speculum that Shines: Vision and Imagination in Medieval Jewish Mysticism*, is the best scholarly work that eruditely describes this phenomenon within Jewish spirituality. See for example the second Chapter in Wolfson's book, entitled: "Visions of God in Mystical Sources: A Typological Analysis," (Princeton University Press, 1994), 52–73.
25 See J. Lear, op. cit., p. xx.
26 "Looking," when referring to God or His acts, is also not permitted, even when other, similar, Hebrew words are used, such as *ra'ah* or *heebit*.
27 Genesis 19:17, 26.
28 Exodus 33:18, 20.
29 See P. Tillich, *The Courage To Be* (Yale University Press, 1980).
30 On Creativity in *Existentialism* see N. Langiulli (ed.), *The Existentialist Tradition* (Doubleday Anchor, 1971); J. Collins, *The Existentialists* (Greenwood Press, 1997).
31 *Sefer Ha-Yashar*, Chapter 1.
32 Rabbi Hayyim Vital, *Derush she-Nimsar le-Sagis* ("Homily that was Given to Sagis").
33 Genesis 2:20.
34 See *The Halakhic Man* (Philadelphia, 1983), 105. Part two of this magnificent book, entitled "Halakhic Man, His Creative Capacity," is an analysis of Jewish creativity in accordance with Jewish *Halachah*. Rabbi Soloveitchik also perceives repentance, *Teshuvah*, as "an act of creation – self creation." (p. 110).
35 See R. Feynman, *Six Easy Pieces, Essentials of Physics* (Helix Books, 1995), Chapter 4.
36 *Sefer Ye'tzirah*, 1:4.
37 Genesis 28:12–13, 16.
38 C. G. Jung tells us that our creativity is a pre-existing potentiality that actualizes itself, rather than a new invention. See *The Archetypes and the Collective Unconscious* (Princeton University Press, 1990), 280.
39 Jerusalem Talmud, *Pe'ah*, II: 6.
40 See Jung, "The Concept of the Collective Unconscious," in *The Archetypes and the Collective Unconscious*, 42 ff.
41 YHVH, when written in full spelling in Hebrew – Yod, He, Vav, He – has the numerical value 45, as does the name ADaM.
42 For further discussion on YHVH and ADAM see G. Scholem, "Kabbalah and Myth," in *On The Kabbalah And Its Symbolism* (New York, 1965), 104.

NOTES

43 The Maggid of Mazheritch, *Or HaEmet (The Light of Truth)*, 73b. See the analysis of R. Schatz-Uffenheimer on this subject, in *Hasidism as Mysticism* (Princeton University Press, New Jersey, 1993), 210–211.
44 Rollo May writes: "creativity occurs in an act of encounter, and is to be understood with this encounter as its center." See *The Courage to Create* (New York, 1975), 77.
45 The art of loving as intimately connected with the act of giving, is a theme well developed in Erich Fromm's *The Art of Loving* (New York, 1956).
46 See I. Tishby (1989) op. cit., "The Three Souls: the Nature and Status of Man," Vol. II, 677–714.
47 Deuteronomy 6:4–5.
48 *Shema* is recited in *Shakharit*, the morning prayer; *Arvit*, the evening prayer, and lastly in bed before going to sleep.
49 *The Duties of the Heart, Sha'ar ha-Ahavah*, Chapter 1.
50 *Sha'ar ha-Ahavah*, ibid. See also S. Shokek, "Rationalism and Spiritualization in the *Duties of the Heart*," in *Proceedings of the Eleventh World Jewish Congress* (Jerusalem, 1994, Hebrew), 17–23.
51 On Love of God in Kabbalah, see I. Tishby (1989), op. cit., Vol. III, 974 ff.: S. Shokek, *Jewish Ethics and Jewish Mysticism in Sefer Ha-Yashar* (New York, 1991), 195–246.
52 Genesis 4:1–2.
53 Maimonides' *The Book of Knowledge, Hilchot Teshuvah*, Chapter 10.
54 Leviticus 19:19.
55 See L. Fine, "The Pious Customs of Moses Cordovero," in *Safed Spirituality* (New York, 1984), 34–37.
56 See L. Fine, "The Pious Customs of Isaac Luria," ibid., 65–67.
57 Rollo May, *Existential Psychology* (New York, 1969), 11–12.
58 Exodus 24:7.
59 *Sefer Ha-Yashar*, Chapter 5.

7 WAITING FOR GODOT AND THE JEWISH ART OF WAITING

1 On the notion of suicide in *Waiting for Godot* see M. Esslin, "The Search for the Self," 36, and J. Fletcher, "Bailing out of Silence," 12. Both essays appear in H. Bloom (ed.) *Modern Critical Interpretations, Samuel Beckett's Waiting for Godot* (New York and Philadelphia, 1987).
2 E. Gans, "Beckett and the Problem of Modern Culture," ibid., 96.
3 See E. Becker, *The Denial of Death* (New York, 1973), especially Chapter one, entitled: "Human Nature and the Heroic," and part I, entitled: "The Depth Psychology of Heroism."
4 H. Bloom claims that " ... for Beckett, as for ... the Gnostics, the Creation and the Fall were the same event." op. cit, 3.
5 R. Gilman rightly emphasizes that Gogo and Didi are linked together by something "mysterious and elemental" which surpasses their friendship. Gogo and Didi, he suggests, are "under the obligation *to be two*, a pair, a social unit outside society." see "The Waiting Since," in Bloom (ed.), op. cit., 71.
6 See R. Cohn, "Waiting," in Bloom (ed.), op. cit., 43. B. O. States asserts that *Waiting for Godot* is an eschatological play in which Beckett has "observed the canons of Biblical style in choosing his parable from humble life (two tramps holding the Christian vigil, as opposed to two kings or philosophers)." See States' interesting article, "The Language of Myth," ibid., 88.
7 See R. Cohen, "Waiting," ibid., 47.
8 On the theological notions in *Waiting for Godot* see J. Fletcher, "Bailing out of Silence," in Bloom (ed.), op. cit., 21; M. Esslin, "The Search for the Self," op. cit., 33–35; E. Gans,

NOTES

"Beckett and the Modern Problem of Society," op. cit., 99–100. On the life and work of Samuel Beckett, see J. Knowlson, *Damned To Fame, The Life of Samuel Beckett*, especially Chapter 16, "Godot, Love, and Loss, 1953–55," (New York, 1996), 351–376.

9   Genesis 49:1.
10 See J. J. Collins, "The End of Days," in *Apocalypticism in the Dead Sea Scrolls* (London and New York, 1997), 56–58.
11 On resurrection and the eternal life of the righteous, see the book of Daniel 12:1–3. On the Dead Sea Scrolls' tradition on Daniel's prophecy see P. Flint, "The Daniel Tradition at Qumran," in *Eschatology, Messianism, and the Dead Sea Scroll*, C. Evans and P. Flint editors (Grand Rapids, Michigan/Cambridge, U.K., 1997), 41–60.
12 See M. Idel, *Messianic Mystics* (Yale University Press, 1998), 14–23. For selected articles on eschatology and messianism in Judaism (and Christianity) see L. Landman, editor, *Messianism in the Talmudic Era* (New York, 1979). In the latter see, for example, the learned essay of N. Schmidt, "The Origin of Jewish Eschatology," 38–50.
13 Talmud, *Sanhedrin* 97b. I discuss this Talmudical passage from a different point of view, in the beginning of Chapter 8: *"Teshuvah*: The Conclusive Return to God."
14 *Genesis Rabbah*, Chapter 85.
15 Talmud, *Sanhedrin* 98b.
16 On Moses and David as messianic figures see J. Klausner, "The Source and Beginning of the Messianic Idea," in Landman, op. cit, 27–33.
17 1 Kings, Chapters 18 and 19; 2 Kings, Chapter 2.
18 Malachi 3:23–24.
19 *Pesiqta Rabbati* 13a: Some of the selected Midrashic and Aggadic texts on the messianic tasks of Elijah were included in R. Patai's *The Messiah Texts* (Wayne State University Press, 1979), 131–144.
20 Adolph Jellinek, *Beth ha-Midrash*, Vol. 6, p. 96.
21 On Gog and Magog, and Armilus, see R. Patai, op. cit., 145–155, 156–164.
22 On the "Two Messiahs" see G. Scholem, *The Messianic Idea in Judaism* (New York, 1971), 18; R. Patai, op. cit., 165–170.
23 See M. Idel (1998), op. cit., 58–100.
24 *The Zohar (The Book of Enlightenment)*, was attributed to the second century Jewish sage, Rabbi Simeon bar Yohai, but was apparently written in thirteenth century Spain by the Kabbalist Rabbi Moses de-Leon. See I. Tishby, *The Wisdom of the Zohar* (Oxford University Press, 1989), Vol. I., "General Introduction: The Structure and Literary Form of the *Zohar*," 1–126.
25 See Y. Liebes' most stimulating essay, "The Messiah of the *Zohar* or Rabbi Simeon Bar Yohai as a Messianic Figure," in *Studies in the Zohar* (State University of New York Press, 1993), 1–84; See also M. Idel (1998), "Concept of the Messiah in the Thirteenth and the Fourteenth Centuries: Theosophical Forms of Kabbalah," op. cit, 101–125; J. Dan, "The Emergence of Messianic Mythology in Thirteenth Century Kabbalah in Spain," in *Occident and Orient: A Tribute to the Memory of A. Schreiber* (Budapest/Brill, Leiden, 1988), 57–68; R. Patai, "The Bird's Nest," op. cit., 84–89.
26 See M. Idel (1998), "Messianism and Kabbalah: 1470–1540," 126–153.
27 See G. Scholem (1971), "The Messianic Idea in Kabbalism," op. cit., 37–48; M. Idel (1998), "From Italy to Safed and Back, 1540–1640," 154–182.
28 See G. Scholem, *Sabbatai Sevi The Mystical Messiah* (Princeton University Press, 1973); idem (1971), "Redemption Through Sin," op. cit, 78–141; M. Idel (1998), "Sabbateanism and Mysticism," 183–211; Y. Liebes, *Studies in Jewish Myth and Jewish Messianism* (State University of New York Press, 1993).
29 See M. Buber, *The Origin and Meaning of Hasidism* (New York, 1960); G. Scholem (1971), "The Neutralization of the Messianic Element in Early Hasidism," op. cit., 176–256: M.

NOTES

Idel (1998), "Hasidism: Mystical Messianism and Mystical Redemption," op. cit., 212–247.

30 *The Thirteen Principles of the Jewish Faith* are recited in *Sha'kharit*, the daily morning prayer, after *Alleinu*.

31 See Maimonides' *Mishneh Torah*, the end of *Hilchot Melachim*,("The Laws of Kings"). For an analysis of Maimonides' concept of the Days of the Messiah see G. Scholem, "Messianism, A Never Ending Quest," in *On the Possibility of Jewish Mysticism in Our Time* (Philadelphia and Jerusalem, 1997), 106–107.

32 Talmud, *Sanhedrin* 93.

33 Maimonides' introduction to *Pereq Heleq*, in his introduction to the Commentary on the Mishnah.

34 *Ma'asse' deRabbi Yehoshua' ben Levi*, A. Jellinek, *Beth ha-Midrash*, op. cit., 2:50.

35 *Pesiqta Hadta*, A. Jellinek, *Beth ha-Midrash*, op. cit., 6:43–44. For selected Rabbinic texts on waiting, see R. Patai, op. cit., 42–53. On the unbreakable covenant between God and his chosen people see "God, Israel, and Shekhinah," in *Zohar, The Book of Enlightenment*, D. Matt's edition (Paulist Press, 1983), 153–162.

36 See M. Idel (1998), "Messiah and Malkhut, and Messiah and Keter," op. cit., 110–118.

37 Talmud, *Pe'sakhim* 54a. See also *Genesis Rabbah* 1:4.

38 Moses de-Leon, *Sheqel Ha-Kodesh* (London, 1911), 23–26, translated by D. Matt in *The Essential Kabbalah* (Harper, San Francisco, 1996), 70.

39 It should be emphasized that the Jewish mystics understood the word *mah* not only as "what" but also as "essence," since the Hebrew word "*mah*" is the short phrase for the Hebrew word "*mahut*," which literally means essence. Thus *Sefer Ye'tzirah* (1:8) taught concerning the *Sefirot*, "*Esser Sefirot b'li-mah*"; that is, "Ten *Sefirot* without [*b'li*] essence [*mah*]." Here the word "*mah*" refers to the material essence; i.e. since the *Sefirot* are spiritual and Divine, they lack any material essence; they are *b'li mah*.

40 On the controversy regarding the messianism of Abulafia see M. Idel (1998), op. cit., 59–60.

41 On the mental illness of Sabbatai Sevi see G. Scholem (1973), op. cit, 125–138.

42 *Toward A Meaningful Life, The Wisdom of the Rebbe*, Menakhem Mendel Schneerson (New York, 1995).

43 Ibid., p. 282.

44 Ibid., p. 283.

45 *New York Times*, July 8, 1997, A5.

46 Ibid. The text cites: "Rabbi Chaim Vital, *Arba Mei'os Shekel Kesef*."

47 Ibid. The text cites: "Jer. Talmud *Berachot*, chap. 2, *Halachah* 4."

48 Ibid. Bold and italic words appear in the original.

49 The wounds of the Sabbatean movement were so deep in the European Jewish communities that they left a painful scar even within some Hasidic circles in the eighteenth century. See Y. Liebes, "Ha-Tikkun Ha-Kelali of R. Nahman of Bratslav and Its Sabbatean Links," in *Studies in Jewish Myth and Jewish Messianism* (1993), 115–150.

50 G. Scholem (1973) op. cit., 208. On Nathan of Gaza see G. Sholem (1973) op. cit., 199 ff.

51 See G. Scholem (1973) "Sabbatai Sevi, The Movement in Europe," op. cit., 461 ff.

52 Two major Jewish groups left the Jewish faith and converted to other religions following their Messiah: The *Do'nmeh* converted to Islam in 1683, and the *Frankists* to Catholicism in 1759. See G. Scholem (1971), "Redemption Through Sin," op. cit, 78–141.

53 *Midrash Shir ha-Shirim Rabbah*, Chapter 2.

54 See, for example, Maharal of Prague, *Netzakh Israel*, Chapter 24.

55 *Va-Yoel Moshe, Ma'amar Sheloshet ha-Shevuo't* ("The Three Oaths Tractate"), Chapter 19.

NOTES

56 The Messiah, according to ancient Jewish tradition, is one of the seven things that pre-existed the creation of the world. See *Midrash Tehillim*, Buber, Psalm 90, 196a.

57 R. Schatz-Uffenheimer demonstrates in her research how in the Hasidic teachings of the Maggid of Mazheritch and Rabbi Hayyim Haykl of Mudbar, the Lurianic concepts of "breaking" (*shevirah*) and "repairing" (*tikkun*) are psychologized. Here the expression of the Lurianic "contraction" (*tzimtzoom*) became the human "contraction," whereas the individual *hasid* withdraws into the depth of his psyche. See *Hasidism as Mysticism* (Princeton University Press, 1993), Chapter 13, notably 209–210,

58 See K. E. Grozinger, *Kafka and Kabbalah* (New York, 1994), p. 96.

8 *TESHUVAH*: THE CONCLUSIVE RETURN TO GOD

1 Talmud *Sanhedrin* 97b.
2 Maharal of Prague, *Netzakh Israel*, Chapter 31.
3 *Netzakh Israel*, Chapter 2.
4 Among the vast number of classic texts that were written on *Teshuvah*, or at least had designated a Chapter or a discussion to *Teshuvah*, I would like to mention those that have greatly influenced Jewish ethics but were not included in the scope of this Chapter. These encompass the following medieval Hebrew ethical works: *Sefer Ha-Olam Ha-Katan* of Rabbi Yoseph Ha-Tzaddik; *Sefer Higyon ha-Nefesh ha-Atzu'vah* of Rabbi Avraham Bar Hiyya; *Sefer Ha-Kuzarri* of Rabbi Yehudah ha-Levy; *Sefer Ma'alot ha-Midot* of Rabbi Ye'khie'l of Rome; *Sefer Kad ha-Kemakh* of Rabbenu Bachya Ben Asher; the treatises on repentance of the Kabbalists of Gerona, Nachmanides, Rabbi Ezra and Rabbi Azriel; *Sefer Menorat ha-Maor* of Rabbenu Yitzkhak Abua'b; *Hibbur Ha-Teshuvah* of Rabbi Menakhem ha-Mei'ri; *Sefer Sha'ar ha-Razzim* of Rabbi Todrous Abulafia; and *Sefer Ha-Iqarrim* of Rabbi Yoseph Albo. The following Safedian, Lurianic, and post-Lurianic texts also include significant discussions on *Teshuvah*: *Sefer Tomer Devorah* of Rabbi Moses Cordovero; *Tikkuney Teshuvah* of Lurianic Kabbalah; *Sefer Ha-Hezyonot* of Rabbi Hayyim Vital; *Sefer Harredim* of Rabbi Elie'zer Azkari; *Sefer Reshit Hokhmah* of Rabbi Eliyahu de-Vidas; *Tikkuney Teshuvah* of the school of Sabbatai Sevi; *Sefer Orkhot Tzaddikim*; *Sefer Messilat Yesharim*, and *Sefer Derech HaShem* of Rabbi Moshe Hayyim Luzzato. Among the *Hasidic* treatises that hold important influential discussions on *Teshuvah*, I would like to mention the *Tanya* of Rabbi Shneur Zalman of Liadi; *Likkutey Moharan* of Rabbi Nachman of Bratslav; and *Maggid Devarav le-Ya'akov* of Rabbi Dov Baer, the Maggid of Mazheritch. Likewise, my analysis in this Chapter does not include the inspiring educational treatises on *Teshuvah* written by the *Mussar* Movement, founded by Rabbi Yisrael Salanter, nor does it examine the *Teshuvah* literature in twentieth century Jewish thought in the works of Hermann Cohen, Franz Rosenzweig, Ha-Rav Yoseph Dov Soloveitchik, and Rabbi Menakhem Mendel Schneerson of Lubavitch. Some of these works have appeared in English translation. They are listed here for those who wish to expand their knowledge on *Teshuvah* in the classic Hebrew texts.
5 See S. Shokek, "Rav Saadia Gaon: The Beginning of Repentance in medieval Jewish Thought – The Transition from *Halachah* to Philosophy," in *Repentance in Jewish Ethics, Philosophy and Mysticism* (New York, 1995, Hebrew), Chapter 1.
6 See S. Shokek (1995), "Rabbenu Bachya Ibn Paquda: Spiritual Repentance in *The Duties of the Heart*," op. cit., Chapter 2.
7 See S. Shokek (1995), "Rabbenu Jonah of Gerona: The Height of Spiritual Repentance," op. cit., Chapter 5.
8 Maimonides uses the Hebrew word *reshut* that I translate here as "permission." The word denotes the "freedom to make choices."
9 *Berachot* 17.
10 *Berachot* 17.

NOTES

11 See Maimonides, *Mishneh Torah*, *Sefer Ha-Mada'*, *Hilchot Yesodey ha-Torah*, Chapter 4.
12 Maimonides, *Mishneh Torah*, *Sefer Ha-Mada'*, *Hilchot Teshuvah*, selections, Sections 5, 6, 8.
13 Isaiah 41:8.
14 *Hilchot Teshuvah* 10.
15 See *The Guide for the Perplexed*, I: 1.
16 See S. Shokek (1995), "Maimonides' Intellectual Repentance," op. cit., Chapter 3: I. Gruenwald, "The Concept of *Teshuvah* in the Teachings of Maimonides and Rav Kook," in *The World of Rav Kook's Thought*, B. Ish Shalom and S. Rosenberg (eds.) (Avi Chai, 1991), 283–304.
17 See I. G. Marcus, *Penitential Theory and Practice Among the Pious of Germany – 1150–1250* (Ph.D. Dissertation, J.T.S. 1975); J. Dan "A Note on the History of *Teshuvah* Among Ashkenaz Chasidim," in *The World of Rav Kook's Thought*, 271–282.
18 Isaiah 57:19.
19 See S. Shokek (1995), "The Book of the Righteous: The Religious Status of the Penitent and the Righteous," op. cit., Chapter 6; Idem, "Status of *Baale' Teshuvah*," in *The World of Rav Kook's Thought*, 305–321.
20 *Sefer Ha-Yashar*, Chapter 10.
21 *Sefer Ha-Yashar*, ibid.
22 *Midrash Tehillim*, Buber, Psalm 90, 196a.
23 *Perush Ha-Aggadot* L'Rabbi Azriel, I. Tishby's edition (Jerusalem, Academon, 1978, Hebrew), 96.
24 *Zohar*, I, 129a–130b.
25 See S. Shokek, "The Affinity of *Sefer Ha-Yashar* to the Kabbalistic Circle of Gerona," in *The Beginning of Jewish Mysticism in Europe: Mekhkarey Yerushalayim be-Makhashevet Yisrael*, J. Dan, editor (Jerusalem, 1987, Hebrew), Vol. 6 (c–d), 337–366; Idem, *Jewish Ethics and Jewish Mysticism in Sefer Ha-Yashar* (New York, 1991).
26 *Midrash Tehillim*, Verse 90.
27 *Pirqey de-Rabbi Eliezer*, Chapter 3.
28 *Zohar*, I, 90a, *Sitre' Torah*. See I. Tishby, "Creation," in *The Wisdom of the Zohar* (Oxford University Press, 1989), Vol. II, 568.
29 In a few passages in the *Zohar* Repentance is described as the symbol of the *Sefirah Tife'ret*, or the *Sefirah Malkhut*. See I. Tishby (1989), "Repentance," op. cit., Vol. III., 1501–1507.
30 See M. Hallamish, "The Doctrine of *Shemittot*," in *An Introduction to the Kabbalah* (State University of New York Press, 1999), 201–205.
31 The numerical value of the Hebrew letter *nun* is 50.
32 The etymological root of the English word "Jubilee" is the Hebrew word *Yovel*.
33 See, S. Shokek (1995), "The *Zohar*: Repentance as Theosophic Symbolism in Kabbalah," op. cit., Chapter 7.
34 Genesis 2:10.
35 Joseph Gikatila, *Sha'arey Orah*, "The Eighth Gate."
36 *Zohar*, part 3, 141, *Idra Rabba*.
37 The Maharal of Prague, *Ne'tivot Olam* (*The Paths of the World*), "*Ne'tiv ha-Teshuvah*," Chapter 2. See S. Shokek (1995), "Maharal of Prague: Mending the Cosmos through Repentance," op. cit., Chapter 9.
38 On the *Creation Myth* in Lurianic Kabbalah, see Chapter 4, "The *Creation Myth* in the Kabbalah of Cordovero and the Ari."
39 Eliyahu de-Vidas, *Reshit Hokhmah* (*The Beginning of Wisdom*), "*Sha'ar ha-Teshuvah*," Chapters 1–2, excerpts.
40 See G. Scholem, "Gilgul: The Transmigration of Souls," in *On the Mystical Shape of the Godhead* (New York, 1991), 197–250.

NOTES

41 Rabbi Hayyim Vital, *Sefer Ha-Likkutim*, on the verse: *"Ovri be-Emeck ha-Bacha,"* (Psalms 84:7).
42 See S. H. Dresner, *The Tzaddik* (London, 1960); A. Green, "The Zaddik as Axis Mundi in Later Judaism," in *The Journal of the American Academy of Religion*, 45 (1977).
43 The title "Rebbe" in Hasidic terminology means: the Rabbi of Rabbis.
44 Rabbi Menakhem Mendel, *Ben Porat Yoseph*, Le'ch Le'cha. See S. Shokek (1995), "Hasidism: Repentance as Communion with God, Righteousness, and Religious Felicity," op. cit., Chapter 10.
45 Leviticus 16:21.
46 See Chapter 1, *"Devekut* and the Breaking of the One into the two."
47 See G. Scholem, *"Devekut* or Communion with God," in *The Messianic Idea in Judaism* (New York, 1971), 203–227.
48 Based on *Tikkuney Zohar, Tikkun* 57, *"Le't Attar Pannuy Minne'."*
49 The Besht's Commentary on Deuteronomy 11:16. See R. Schatz-Uffenheimer, *Hasidism as Mysticism* (Princeton University Press, New Jersey, 1993), 293.
50 Tractate *Ma'cot*, 7:b.
51 *Tzava'at ha-Ribash*, 8:b.
52 *Tole'dot Ya'akov Yoseph*, 113:d.
53 *Tikkun ha-Lev: Stories, Dreams, Conversations*, P. Sadeh (ed.) (Jerusalem and Tel Aviv 1981, Hebrew), 199, 188. See also *Likutei Moharan, "Bo el Paro'*,*"* 64:5: M. Buber, *The Tales of Rabbi Nahman* (New York, 1956).
54 *Eder ha-Yakar*, the opening of section 5.
55 "The *Oneg* and the *Simkhah*," in *Iqvey ha-Tzon*.
56 See *The World of Rav Kook's Thought*, ibid., notably the essays of S. Rosenberg, "Introduction to the Thought of Rav Kook," 16–127; E. Schweid, "Repentance in Twentieth-Century Jewish Thought," 349–372; B. Ish Shalom, "Religion, Repentance and Personal Freedom," 373–419. See also B. Ish Shalom, *Rav Avraham Itzhak HaCoen Kook, Between Rationalism and Mysticism* (New York, 1993); B. Z. Bokser (translator) *Abraham Isaac Kook, The Lights of Penitence, The Moral Principles, Lights of Holiness, Essays, and Poems* (New York, Ramsey, Toronto, 1978).
57 The opening of *Orot Ha-Teshuvah*, *"Ha-Teshuvah ve-ha-Shalom."*
58 Ecclesiastes 12:13.

GLOSSARY

Acosmism No-cosmos; the Hasidic concept of God being everywhere, to the extent that there is nothing else but God
Adam Kadmon Primordial Adam; also, the ten *Sefirot*
Adnut Mastership
Adon Master
Aggadah Stories and commentaries in the Mishnah and the Talmud that are not *Halachah*
Akharit ha-Yamim End of the Days
Akhdut Unity; singularity
Alliyah Ascent
Aqeddah The story of the binding of Isaac (Genesis 22)
Armilus A Satanic creature who kills "Messiah son of Joseph" in a battle in which the army of Israel is defeated by Gog and Magog
Assiyah Within the Godly act of the creation, four worlds are created simultaneously; they are known in Hebrew as the worlds of *Atzilut* ("Emanation"), *Be'riah* ("Creation"), *Ye'tzirah* ("Formation"), and *Assiyah* ("Making")
Atzilut See *Assiyah*
Atzmut/be-Etzem Substance; substantial, with permanence
Avodah Zarrah Idolatry
Ayin Nothingness; also the name of the first *Sefirah*, *Keter*
Be'riah See Assiyah
Bi'at ha-Mashi'akh Coming of the Messiah
Binah Understanding: third *Sefirah*, also called *Teshuvah*, repentance, Supernal Mother, Feminine
B'rit Milah Circumcision
Cosmogony The processes that led to the Creation of the world
Cosmology The arrangement emerging from the Creation of the world, the cosmos
Devekut Communion with God. Man's yearning to become One with God
Ein-Sof Infinite; the hidden God of the Kabbalah who emanates the *Sefirot*
Elohim Akherim Other gods, idolatry

GLOSSARY

Enantiodromia   The desire to unite the opposites; C.G. Jung
Eretz Yisrael   The Land or (State) of Israel
Eschatology   The concept of and about the End of the Days
Ex nihilo   From Nothingness, the belief that the world was created from nothingness
Gadlut   A mental state of "greatness"
Galut   Exile
Gematria   Numerical value of the Hebrew letters
Ge'ullah   Redemption
Gevurah   Judgment, fifth *Sefirah*, also called *Deen*
Gilgul/Gilgulim   Transmigration of the soul
Gnosis/Gnosticism   Ancient religion that believed in the kingdom of two gods; influenced early Jewish mysticism and Kabbalah
gnosis   Mystical knowledge
Gog   See *Armilus*
Halachah   The Jewish law, see *Mishnah* and *Talmud*
Hanhagot   Mystical literature on religious behavior (sixteenth-century Safed)
Hasid/Hasidim   Pious man, pious people; Hasidism
Hasidism   A religious movement of pietism, founded in the eighteenth century by the Besht
HaVaYaH/YHVH   Being; Existence; Was-Is-Will Be; the Tetragrammaton, the Ineffable Divine name
Haverim   Comrades; Kabbalists belonging to Rabbi Simeon bar Yokhai's circle according to the *Zohar*
Heichal   Palace; also, one of the names of *Binah*
Hesed   Lovingkindness; fourth *Sefirah*
Hishtavut   Equanimity; a method of communion with God, in thirteenth century Kabbalah
Hitbodedut   Isolation; a form of communion with God, see *Devekut*
Hitbonenut   Visualization; a form of communion with God, see *Devekut*
Hitore'rut   Awakening; God's and man's urgency to rise up and create
Hitpashtut   Expansion; God's expansion into the *Sefirot*; Lurianic Kabbalah
Hitzitz   Stared intensely; gazed, in the Talmudic story on the four who entered the *Pardes*
Hokhmah   Wisdom; second *Sefirah*, also called *Reshit*, beginning, and *Yesh*, Being, and Supernal Father, Masculine
Hypostasis   A Divine entity; *Sefirah* or angel of God
Imitatio Dei   Imitation of God; following God's ways
Individuation   Spiritual and psychological growth of every individual (C. G. Jung)
Ineffability   The characteristic of a personal mystical experience that cannot be conveyed in words (W. James)
Kabbalah   Tradition; Jewish mystical movement based on ancient Jewish mysticism, emerges in twelfth-century Europe

GLOSSARY

Katnut   A mental state of "smallness"
Kavanah   Inward intention, especially during prayer
Kavanat ha-Lev   Inwardness of the heart
Ken Tzippor   The Bird's Nest; the *Zoharic* concept on the abode of the Messiah
Keter   Crown; the highest *Sefirah*, also called *Ayin*, nothingness, and *Hefetz*, will
Kisse' Eliyahu   The chair of Elijah
Kohanim   Jewish Priests
Leshem Yikhud Kudshah Brich Hu u-Shekhinteh   For the sake of the unification of the Holy One, blessed be He, and His *Shekhinah* (Isaac Luria)
Maanin Tevirin   Broken Vessels; *Zohar*
Ma'asse' Be'Reshit   The account of Creation
Madregot   Steps; also, *Sefirot*
Magog   See *Armilus*
Mezuzah   Torah verses placed on the threshold of the doors of Jewish houses
Midrash   Jewish literature of commentaries on the Torah, and other Jewish holy books
Mikre'   Accident; not substantial, with no permanence
Mishnah   Earliest code of Jewish law, composed in the first and second centuries
Mitnagdim   Opponents of Hasidism
Mitzvah/Mitzvot   Jewish precept; Jewish laws
Mitzvot Asse'   The Jewish laws of action; affirmative *Mitzvot*
Mysterium tremendum   The core of the mystical experience; the encounter with the Holy (R. Otto)
Nefesh   One of five aspects of the human soul that descend from the world of the *Sefirot*, also *Rua'kh*, *Neshamah*, *Hayya*, and *Yekhidah*
Neffilat ha-Tzaddik   The descent of the Tzaddik; Hasidism
Neshamah   See *Nefesh*
Niggun   A Hasidic melody or song
Nissui'n   Marriage
Nitzotzot   Sparks; the lights that were imprisoned by the material world after the *Shevirah*
Noetic quality   An active experience of illumination tinged with great significance (W. James)
Olam ha-Ba   The world to come
Olam ha-Zeh   This (earthly) world
Oneg   Religious pleasure (Hasidism)
Or she-Ain Bo Makhashavah   A Light that does not contain thought
Or she-Yesh Bo Makhashavah   A Light that contains thought
Oz   Courage; the daring to be and the fortitude to create
Pakhad   Human fear
Pardes   Orchard; the garden of the king; the domain of the Divine
Pleroma   The Godly world in its fullness; the angelic and sefirotical hyper-reality

GLOSSARY

Pneuma   Spirit; Fire; the core of the mind and the heart
Qelipah   The Shell; the symbol of materiality and evil in Lurianic Kabbalah
Ribbuy   Plurality
Rua'kh   See *Nefesh*
Sandaq   Godfather
Seder ha-Olam   The order of the world; Maharal of Prague
Sefirah, Sefirot   Divine emanation (emanations), manifested by *Ein-Sof*: *Keter, Hokhmah, Binah, Hesed, Deen, Tife'ret, Netzakh, Hod, Yesod,* and *Malkhut*
Sefirat ha-Yovel   The *Sefirah* of Jubilee, *Binah*
Shaa'r ha-Nun   The Gate of Fifty, *Binah*
Shabat Shabaton   The Sabbath of Sabbaths, *Yom ha-Kippurim*
Sha'kharit   The daily morning prayer
Shefa   Abundance; flow
Shekhinah   The Divine Presence; the tenth *Sefirah* called *Malkhut*; Feminine
Shem Meshutaf   Equivocal term; an identical name that bears two different meanings
Shemitot   Kabbalistic concept of cosmological cycles of life; each cycle exists for seven thousand years in each of the seven lower *Sefirot*, until the world rests in *Binah* in the fiftieth-thousand year
Shevirah   The destruction of the harmony in the world of God after the *Tzimtzoom*. The myth of the breaking of the worlds (or the breaking of the vessels) during the Creation; Lurianic Kabbalah
Shiur Komah   Measure of the heights of God; also, one of the books of ancient Jewish mysticism, in the literature of *Heichalot* and *Merkavah*
Sibbat ha-Sibbah   The cause of a cause, the reason of a reason; Maharal of Prague
Simkhah   Religious happiness; Hasidism
Sod ha-Hayyim   The secret of life
Summum Bunum   The Highest Good
Talmud   Code of Jewish law composed between the third and the sixth centuries in two forms, Jerusalem Talmud and Babylonian Talmud
Tefillin   Phylactories; boxes containing words from the Torah that traditionally observant Jews wear during their morning prayers
Telos   The ultimate goal
Teshuvah   Repentance
Theogony   The origin of God: The occurrences in the mind of God before the Creation
Theurgy   Mending the harmony in the world of God through inward intention and good deeds in the earthly world
Tife'ret   Beauty; sixth *Sefirah*, also called *Kadosh Baruch Hu*, the Holy One, blessed be He, Masculine
Tikkun   The Kabbalistic most elevated *Mitzvah*, to repair the worlds below and above through good deeds and by fulfilling the commandments; Lurianic Kabbalah

GLOSSARY

Torah The five Books of Moses; Genesis, Exodus, Leviticus, Numbers, Deuteronomy
Tzaddik A Righteous man; also, the title of a Hasidic spiritual leader
Tzaddik ha-Dor The Righteous of the generation; Hasidism
Tzelem Elohim The image of God
Tzeruf Combination; a method of communion with God through meditative combination of the Hebrew letters
Tzimtzoom The Kabbalistic myth of God's withdrawal; the cosmogonial act of God in the Creation; God's contraction in order to create space for the Creation; Lurianic Kabbalah
Tzinorot ha-Nishbarim The broken vessels; a metaphor for the broken worlds after the *Shevirah*; Lurianic Kabbalah
Tzitzit Fringes that observant Jews attach to their garments, especially on the prayer shawl worn during morning prayers
Unio mystica The concept of Communion with God without boundaries
Unum argumentum The ultimate argument; the final proof
Yediat HaShem Knowledge of God
Yekhidah See *Nefesh*
Yemot ha-Mashi'akh Days of the Messiah
Yeridah Descent
Yeridah Tzorech Alliyah Religious descent for the sake of Ascent
Yesh Being; the material, created world; also, the name of the second *Sefirah*, *Hokhmah*
Yesod Foundation; ninth *Sefirah*, associated with Righteousness
Ye'tzirah Formation or Making, see *Assiyah*
Yikhud Union of the human soul with the *Shekhinah*
Yira'h Religious awe
Yissurim Grief
Yom ha-Kippurim The Day of Atonement
Zeh Eli ve-Anvehu "This is my God and I will glorify Him," Exodus 25:2.

BIBLIOGRAPHY

Abraham Isaac Ha-Cohen Kook (1978) *The Lights of Penitence, The Moral Principles, Lights of Holiness, Essays, and Poems*, Bokser B. Z. (translator), Paulist Press: New York, Ramsey, Toronto.
Afnan, S. (1980) *Avicenna*, Greenwood Press: Westport.
Anselm (1998) *Anselm of Canterbury: The Major Works*, Davies B. and Evans, G. R. (eds.), Oxford University Press: Oxford.
Aquinas, Thomas (1955) *Summa Contra Gentiles, Book One: God*, Pegis A. C. (translator), University of Notre Dame Press: London.
—— (1956) *Summa Contra Gentiles, Book Two: Creation*, Anderson J. E. (translator), University of Notre Dame Press: London.
Aristotle (1966) *The Basic Works of Aristotle*, McKeon R. (translator), Random House: New York.
Armstrong, D. M. (1968) *A Materialist Theory of Mind*, Routledge: London.
Aziz, R. (1990) *C. G. Jung's Psychology of Religion and Synchronicity*, State University of New York Press: New York.
Becker, E. (1973) *The Denial of Death*, Free Press: New York.
Beckett S. (1954) *Waiting For Godot*, Grove Press: New York.
Benjamin, W. and Scholem G. (1989) *Correspondence 1932–1940*, Schocken Books: New York.
Bennet, E. A. (1983) *What Jung Really Said*, Schocken Books: New York.
Ben-Shlomo, J. (1965) *Torat Ha-Elohut Shel Moshe Cordovero*, Mosad Bialik: Jerusalem (Hebrew).
Bloom, H. (ed.) (1987) *Modern Critical Interpretations: Samuel Beckett's Waiting for Godot*, Chelsea House Publications: New York and Philadelphia.
Bradley, J. (1971) *Mach's Philosophy of Science*, Athlone Press: London.
Buber, M. (1952) *The Eclipse of God: Studies in the Relation Between Religion and Philosophy*, Harper: New York.
—— (1956) *The Tales of Rabbi Nahman*, Horizon Press: New York.
—— (1960) *The Origin and Meaning of Hasidism*, Horizon Press: New York.
—— (1963) "Imitatio Dei," in *Israel and the World: Essays in a Time of Crisis*, Schocken Books: New York.
Campbell, J. (1968) *The Hero With A Thousand Faces*, Princeton University Press: Princeton.
—— (ed.) (1971) *The Portable Jung*, Viking: New York.
Cassirer, E. (1946) *Language and Myth*, Harper and Brothers: New York.
—— (1972) *An Essay on Man*, Yale University Press: New Haven.
Collins, J. (1997) *The Existentialists*, Greenwood Press: Westport.
Collins, J. J. (1997) *Apocalypticism in the Dead Sea Scrolls*, Routledge: London and New York.

BIBLIOGRAPHY

Dallett, J. O. (1998) *The Not-Yet Transformed God: Depth Psychology and the Individual Religious Experience*, Nicolas Hays: York Beach.

Dan, J. (1968) *Torat ha-Sod shel Hasidut Ashkenaz*, Mosad Bialik: Jerusalem (Hebrew).

—— (1983) *The Teachings of Hasidism*, Behrman House: West Orange, NJ.

—— (ed.) (1986) *The Early Kabbalah*, Kiener R. (translator), Paulist Press: New York; Ramsey: Toronto.

—— (1986) *Jewish Mysticism and Jewish Ethics*, University of Washington Press: Seattle.

—— (1988) "The Emergence of Messianic Mythology in Thirteenth Century Kabbalah in Spain," in Dan R.O. (ed.) *Occident and Orient: A Tribute to the Memory of A. Schreiber*, Budapest, Brill, Leiden.

—— (1998) *Al ha-Kedushah*, Magnes: Jerusalem (Hebrew).

Davidson, H. (1979) "Maimonides' Secret Position on Creation," in Twersky I. (ed.) *Studies in Medieval Jewish History and Literature*, Harvard University Press: Cambridge, MA.

Dov Baer of Mazheritch (1976) *Maggid Devarav le-Ya'akov*, [Korets 1784], Schatz-Uffenheimer R. (ed.), Magnes: Jerusalem.

Dresner, S. H. (1960) *The Tzaddik*, Abelard Schuman: London.

Elior, R. (1993) *The Paradoxical Ascent to God*, State University of New York Press, New York.

—— (1989) "HaBaD: The Contemplative Ascent to God," in Green A. (ed.) *Jewish Spirituality*, Vol. 14, New York.

Eliyahu De-Vidas (1972) *Reshit Hokhmah*, [Venice 1579], Jerusalem (Hebrew).

Evans C. and Flint P. (eds.) (1997) *Eschatology, Messianism, and the Dead Sea Scroll*, Wm B. Eerdmans Publishing Co.: Grand Rapids, MI, Cambridge.

Feynman, R. (1996) *Six Easy Pieces, Essentials of Physics*, Helix Books: Reading.

Fine L. (1984) *Safed Spirituality*, Paulist Press: New York; Ramsey: Toronto.

Fromm, E. (1950) *Psychoanalysis of Religion*, Yale University Press: New Haven, CT.

—— (1956) *The Art of Loving*, Bantam Books: New York.

—— (1988) *To Have or to Be*, Harper & Row: New York.

—— (1997) *The Art of Being*, Continuum: New York.

Gikatila Joseph (1883) *Sha'arey Orah*, Warsaw (Hebrew).

Green, A. (1977) "The Zaddik as Axis Mundi in Later Judaism," *Journal of the American Academy of Religion*, 45.

Grozinger, K. E. (1994) *Kafka and Kabbalah*, Continuum: New York.

Hallamish, M. (1999) *An Introduction to the Kabbalah*, State University of New York Press: New York.

Hammond, R. (1947) *The Sources of Questions: The Philosophy of Alfarabi*, Hobson Book Press: New York.

Hegel, G. W. F. (1977) *Phenomenology of Spirit*, Miller A. V. (translator), Oxford University Press: New York.

Heschel, A. J. (1959) *God in Search of Man*, Jewish Publication Society of America: New York and Philadelphia.

Hirsch S. R. (translator) (1989) *Avot, The Chapters of the Fathers*, Feldheim Publishers: New York [1979] (Hebrew/English).

Idel, M. (1988) *Studies in Ecstatic Kabbalah*, State University Press of New York: New York.

—— (1988) *The Mystical Experience in Abraham Abulafia*, State University Press of New York: New York.

—— (1988) *Kabbalah – New Perspectives*, Yale University Press: New Haven.

—— (1991) *Language, Torah, and Hermeneutics in Abraham Abulafia*, State University Press of New York: New York.

BIBLIOGRAPHY

—— (1995) *Hasidism Between Ecstasy and Magic*, State University Press of New York: New York.
—— (1996) "Universalization and Integration: Two Conceptions of Mystical Union in Jewish Mysticism," in Idel M. and McGinn B. (eds.) *Mystical Union in Judaism, Christianity, and Islam*, Continuum: New York.
—— (1998) *Messianic Mystics*, Yale University Press: New Haven.
Inge, W. R. (1976) *Mysticism in Religion*, Greenwood Press: Westport.
Ish Shalom, B. (1993) *Rav Avraham Itzhak HaCoen Kook: Between Rationalism and Mysticism*, State University Press of New York: New York.
—— and Rosenberg S. (eds.) (1991) *The World of Rav Kook's Thought*, Avi Chai (English translation of the Hebrew edition, Jerusalem, 1985).
Jacob Joseph of Polnoy (1954) *Ben Porat Yoseph*, New York (Hebrew).
—— (1966) *Tole'dot Ya'akov Yoseph*, Jerusalem (Hebrew).
Jacobi, J. (1973) *The Psychology of C. G. Jung*, Yale University Press: New Haven.
Jacobs, L. (1969) *Jewish Ethics, Philosophy, and Mysticism*, Behrman House: New York.
Jacobson, R. S. (1995)*Toward A Meaningful Life: The Wisdom of the Rebbe, Menachem Mendel Schneerson*, William Morrow: New York.
Jaffe', A. (1989) *Was C.G. Jung A Mystic?* Daimon Verlag, Einsiedeln: Switzerland.
James, W. (1963) *The Varieties of Religious Experience*, University Books: New York.
Jellinek, A. (1938) *Beth ha-Midrash*, Bamberger et Vahrman: Jerusalem (Hebrew).
Jung C.G. (1990) *The Collected Works*, Read H. and Fordham M. (eds.), Multiple Volumes, Princeton University Press: Princeton.
—— *Letters*, Selections from C. G. Jung, Vol. 1, 1906–1950, and Vol. 2, 1951–1961. Bollingen series, XCV.
—— (1990) "Conscious, Unconscious, and Individuation," in *The Archetypes and the Collective Unconscious*, in Read H. and Fordham M. (eds.) *The Collected Works*, Vol. 9, Princeton University Press: Princeton.
—— (1993) *The Basic Writings of C. G. Jung*, Staub De Laszlo V. (ed.), Modern Library: New York.
Kaplan, A. (1984) *Meditation and Kabbalah*, Samuel Weiser: York Beach.
Kast, V. (1992) *The Dynamics of Symbols: Foundations of Jungian Psychotherapy*, From International Publishing Corp.: New York.
Katz, S. (ed.) (1983) *Mysticism and Religious Traditions*, Oxford University Press: New York.
Kierkegaard, S. (1983) *Fear and Trembling*, Princeton University Press: Princeton.
Klein-Braslavy, S. (1986) "The Creation of the World and Maimonides' interpretation of Gen. I–V," in Pines S. and Yovel Y. (eds.) *Maimonides and Philosophy*, Martinus Nijhoff Publishers: Dordrecht.
Knowlson, J. (1996) *Damned To Fame: The Life of Samuel Beckett*, Simon & Schuster: New York.
Lear, J. (1998) *Aristotle: The Desire to Understand*, Cambridge University Press: New York.
Landman L. (ed.) (1979) *Messianism in the Talmudic Era*, Ktav Publishing House: New York.
Langiulli, N. (ed.) (1971) *The Existentialist Tradition*, Doubleday Anchor: Garden City, NY.
Liebes, Y. (1990) *He'to' shel Elisha: Arba'ah she-Nichne'su la-Pardes, ve-Tiv'ah shel ha-Mistika ha-Talmudit*,The Hebrew University: Jerusalem (Hebrew).
—— (1993) "Ha-Tikkun Ha-Kelali of R. Nahman of Bratslav and Its Sabbatean Links," *Studies in Jewish Myth and Jewish Messianism*, State University of New York Press: New York.
—— (1993) "The Messiah of the *Zohar* or Rabbi Simeon Bar Yohai as a Messianic Figure, *Studies in the Zohar*, State University of New York Press: New York.
Maharal of Prague (1980) *Ne'tivot Olam*, Yahadut: B'nei Brak (Hebrew).

BIBLIOGRAPHY

—— (1980) *Netzakh Israel*, Yahadut: B'nei Brak (Hebrew).
—— (1980) *Tife'ret Israel*, Yahadut: B'nei Brak (Hebrew).
Marcus, I. G. (1975) *Penitential Theory and Practice Among the Pious of Germany – 1150–1250* (PhD Dissertation), Jewish Theological Seminary of America: New York.
Maslow A. V. (1994) *Religion, Values, and Peak Experiences*, Viking Press: New York.
Matt, D. C. (1983) *Zohar, The Book of Enlightenment*, Paulist Press: New York; Ramsey: Toronto.
—— (1996) *The Essential Kabbalah*, Harper: San Francisco.
May, R. (1953) *Man's Search for Himself*, Norton: New York.
—— (1969) *Existential Psychology*, Random House: New York.
—— (1975) *The Courage to Create*, Norton: New York.
—— (1983) *The Discovery of Being*, Norton: New York.
McLynn, F. (1996) *Carl Gustav Jung: A Biography*, St Martin's Griffin: New York.
Moses ben Maimon, *Mishneh Torah* (Various editions in Hebrew and English).
—— *The Guide for the Perplexed* (Various editions in Hebrew and English).
Moses Cordovero (1944) *Tomer Devorah*, Tel Aviv (Hebrew).
—— (1974) *The Palm Tree of Deborah*, Jacobs L. (translator), Sepher Hermon Press: New York.
—— (1994) *Or Ne'erav*, Robinson I. (translator), Yeshiva University Press: New York.
—— (1962) *Pardes Rimmonim*, [Cracaw 1592], Jerusalem (Hebrew).
Moses de-Leon (1988) *Sefer Ha-Rimmon* (*The Book of the Pomegranate*), Wolfson E. R. (ed.), Scholars Press: Atlanta.
—— (1911) *Sheqel Ha-Kodesh*, London (Hebrew).
Moshe Isserles, *Torat ha-Olah*, Prague 1569 (Hebrew).
Morrison, A. (ed.) (1986) *Essential Papers on Narcissism*, New York University Press: New York.
Nachman of Bratslav (1969) *Likutei Moharan*, Jerusalem (Hebrew).
Neumann, E. (1993) *The Origin and the History of Consciousness*, Princeton University Press: Princeton.
Nuriel, A. (1964) "The Question of a Created or Primordial World in the Philosophy of Maimonides," *Tarbiz* 33, Jerusalem.
Ostow, M. (1995) *Ultimate Intimacy, The Psychodynamics of Jewish Mysticism*, Karnac Books: London.
Otto, R. (1971) *The Idea of the Holy*, Oxford University Press: New York.
Patai, R. (1979) *The Messiah Texts*, Wayne State University Press: Detroit.
Philo (1981) *Philo of Alexandria, The Complete Life, The Giants, and Selections*, Winston D. (translator), Paulist Press: New York; Ramsey: Toronto.
Pines, S. (1963) "The Philosophic Sources of the Guide of the Perplexed," in *The Guide of the Perplexed*, Vol. I., University of Chicago Press: Chicago.
Rapoport-Albert A. (ed.) (1996) *Hasidism Reappraised*, Vallentine Mitchell: London.
Robinson, H. (1993) *Objections to Physicalism*, Clarendon: Oxford.
Rudolph, K. (1987) *Gnosis: The Nature and History of Gnosticism*, McLachlan R. Wilson (translator), Harper & Row: San Francisco.
Sadeh, P. (ed.) (1981) *Tikkun ha-Lev: Stories, Dreams, Conversations*, Schocken Books: Jerusalem and Tel Aviv (Hebrew).
Schatz-Uffenheimer, R. (1993) *Hasidism as Mysticism*, Princeton University Press: Princeton.
Schneur Zalman of Liadi (1993) *Tanya, Likutei Amarim* [Vilna 1990], Bilingual edition, Otzar, Hasidism: New York.
Scholem, G. (1941) *Major Trends in Jewish Mysticism*, Schocken Books: New York.
—— (1965) *Jewish Gnosticism, Merkabah Mysticism, and Talmudic Tradition*, Jewish Theological Seminary of America: New York.
—— (1965) *On The Kabbalah And Its Symbolism*, Schocken Books: New York.

BIBLIOGRAPHY

―― (1971) *The Messianic Idea in Judaism*, Schocken Books: New York.
―― (1973) *Sabbatai Sevi: The Mystical Messiah*, Princeton University Press: Princeton.
―― (1974) *Kabbalah*, Qadrangle: New York.
―― (1991) *On The Mystical Shape of the Godhead*, Schocken Books: New York.
―― (1997) "Messianism, A Never Ending Quest," *On the Possibility of Jewish Mysticism in Our Time*, Jewish Publication Society of America: Philadelphia and Jerusalem.
Sefer Etz Hayyim (Rabbi Hayyim Vital), Korets, 1784 (Hebrew).
Sefer Ha-Emunot ve-Ha-De'ot (Rav Saadia ben Joseph Al Fayumi), Leipzig (1864) (Hebrew).
Sefer Ha-Rokea'kh (Rabbi Elazar of Worms), Jerusalem (1960) (Hebrew).
Sefer Ha-Yashar (attributed to Rabbenu Tam), Eshkol: Jerusalem (1978) (Hebrew).
Sefer Haredim (Rabbi Eliezer Azkari), [Venice 1601], Jerusalem (1980) (Hebrew).
Sefer Hasidim, Margaliot (ed.) Jerusalem (1964) (Hebrew).
Sefer Hovot ha-Levavot (Rabbenu Bachya Ibn Paquda), Jerusalem (1928) (Hebrew).
Sefer Mei'rat Enayim (Rabbi Isaac of Ako), Goldreich A. (ed.) Jerusalem (1984) (Hebrew).
Sefer Sha'arey Teshuvah (Rabbi Jonah Gerondi), Jerusalem (1966) (Hebrew).
Sefer Ye'tzirah (anonymous), Kaplan A. (ed.), York Beach, Maine (1993) (Hebrew/English).
Shokek, S. (1991) *Jewish Ethics and Jewish Mysticism in Sefer Ha-Yashar*, The Edwin Mellen Press: Lewiston, NY.
―― (1995) *Ha-Teshuvah be-Sifrut ha-Musar ha-Ivrit, ba-Philosophia ha-Yehudit u-va-Kabbalah* (*Repentance in Jewish Ethics, Philosophy, and Mysticism*), The Edwin Mellen Press: Lewiston, NY (Hebrew).
Soloveitchik, B.J. (1983) *The Halakhic Man*, Jewish Publication Society of America: Philadelphia.
Tillich, P. (1980) *The Courage To Be*, Yale University Press: New Haven.
Tishby, I. (1957, 1961) *Mishnat ha-Zohar*, 2 Vols, Jerusalem (Hebrew).
―― (ed.) (1978, 1982) *Perush Ha-Aggadot L'Rabbi Azriel*, Magnes: Jerusalem (Hebrew).
―― (1984) *Torat Ha-Ra ve-ha-Qelipah Be-Kabbalat ha-Ari*, Magnes: Jerusalem (Hebrew).
―― (1989) *The Wisdom of the Zohar*, 3 Vols, Oxford University Press: New York.
Underhill, E. (1960) *Mysticism*, Dutton: New York.
Wainwright, W. (1981) *Mysticism*, University of Wisconsin Press: Brighton.
Wolfson, E. R. (1994) *Through A Speculum that Shines: Vision and Imagination in Medieval Jewish Mysticism*, Princeton University Press, Princeton.
―― (1995) "The Image of Jacob Engraved upon the Throne: Further Reflection on the Esoteric Doctrine of the German Pietists," in *Along The Path, Studies in Kabbalistic Myth, Symbolism, and Hermeneutics*, State University of New York Press: New York.
Zohar, Margaliot R. (ed.) 3 Vols, Jerusalem (1984) (Hebrew).
―― Sperling H. and Simon M. (eds.), 5 Vols, London (1931–4).
Zohar Hadash, Margaliot R. (ed.) Jerusalem (1978) (Hebrew).

INDEX

Abraham Abulafia 6, 60
Abraham ben Eliezer ha-Levi 114
Abraham Isaac HaCohen Kook 144–5
Adam 36, 93
Afnan, S. 150
Alfarabi 16–17
Anselm 17–19
Aqeddah 83–4, 86
Aquinas 19–20
Ari, Isaac Luria 40–1
Aristotle 9, 79, 87–8
Armstrong, D. M. 152
art of being 1, 78, 99–101
Asher Lemelin Reutlingen 114
Assara Ma'amarot 33
atoms 5
Atzilut 3, 24–25
Augustine 19
Averroes 17, 19
Avicenna 17
Awakening (*Hitore'rut*) 47, 50–1, 72, 78–81
Ayin and *Yesh* 34–36, 63, 79
Aziz, R. 153–54
Azriel of Gerona 26

Bachya Ibn Paquda 15, 82, 97, 129
Becker, E. 157
Beckett, S. 103
Ben Porat Yoseph 141
Benjamin, W. 154
Bennet, A. 155
Besht, Israel Ba'al Shem Tov 49, 115
Beyond Good and Evil 80
Binah 32, 84
Bloom, H. 105, 157
Boxer, B. Z. 162
Bradley, J. 151
breaking (of the One into the two) 7–11

B'rit Milah 95
Buber, M. 153, 154, 158

Campbell, J. 13
Cassirer, E. 9
chain of being 65–6
Christianity 17–20
Cohn, R. 157
Collins, J. 156
Collins, J. J. 158
courage (art of being) 81–8
Creation: in Christianity 17–20; esoteric, exoteric 13; in Gnosis 21–22; in Islam 16–17; Kabbalistic myth 2; of man 66; in mythology 20–21; theogony, cosmogony, cosmology 2
creativity 88–94
Critique of Pure Reason 34

Dallet, O. J. 154
Dan, J. 151, 154, 155, 158
Devekut: Aristotelian, Neoplatonic, Hermetic 7–8; biblical 8–11; *hishtavut, hitbonenut, hitbodedut, tzeruf* 12; *unio mystica* 8
Dibbur 36
Dresner, S. H. 162
Duties of the Heart 82

Elior, R. 152
Eliyahu de-Vidas 139–40
Emunah 84
Enantiodromia 71
Eoolin, M. 157
Existentialism 98
Ezekiel 41
Ezra of Gerona 26

173

INDEX

Feynman, R. 149, 156
Fine, L. 157
Fletcher, J. 157
Flint, P. 158
Fromm, E. 154, 157

Gallut 50
Gans, E. 157
Ge'ullah 50
Gikatila Joseph 136–7
Gilgamesh 20
Gilman, R. 157
Gnosis 21–2
God: artisan 9, 63, 89; bisexuality 74; consciousness 72–3; *Ein Sof* 24, 43; *Elohim, HaShem* 29–30; First Cause, First Being 16; *individuation* 68–76; intent in creation 26–31; love 96–7; masculine and feminine 10; for recognition 46, 64–4; shift from *ayin* to *yesh* 62–76; shift from silence to voice 35; transformation 75–6; YHVH, *Was-Is-Will Be* 93
Goldreich, A. 150
Green, A. 162
Grozinger, K. E. 160

Halakhic Man 90
Hallamish, M. 152, 161
Hanhagot 97
Hasidism: acosmism 53; *devekut* 42; eschatology 120–1; HaBaD 50–52; *katnut and gadlut* 53; *nefilat ha-tzaddik* 141–2; *niggun* 144; *simkhah* 143–4; *tzaddik* 54–5, 140–1; *tzimtzoom* 53; *yeridah* and *alliyah* 143
Hayyim Vital 114, 140
Hegel, G. W. F. 7, 149, 153
Heschel, A. J. 153
Hesed 59
Heichalot and *Merkabah* 85
Hitore'rut 47, 50–1, 72, 78–81
Hitpashtut 50
Hokhmah 118

Idel, M. 7, 59, 149, 152, 153, 155, 159
Imitatio Dei: in Kabbalah 58; in Maimonides 56; in Midrash 55–7; in Torah 56
individuation 68–70
ineffability 83
Inge, W. R. 155
integration 73
Isaac of Ako 12
Isaac the Blind 26, 35

Ish-Shalom, B. 162
Islam 16–17
Ivrey A. L. 150

Jacob's dream 91–2
Jacobi, J. 154
Jacobson, Rabbi Simon 119–20
Jaffe', A. 71, 153, 154, 155
James, W. 155
Jellinek, A. 158
Jung, C. G.: analytical psychology 154, 155; *anima-animus* 74; collective unconscious 92–93; individuation 70; on Lurianic Kabbalah 71; union of opposites 73–74

Kabbalah: existential element 3–5; four worlds of creation 3; language and speech 31–36; *mitzvot* 44; Provence and Gerona 6; psychological element 5–7; self-discovery 98–100; theosophical, theurgical, ecstatic 1
Kafka, F. 125
Kant, E. 34
Kast, V. 155
Katz, S. 155
Kavanah 95
Kirkegaard, S. 83–4
Klein-Braslavy, S. 15–16
Knowlson, J. 158

law of conservation of energy 90–1
Lear, J. 156
Levi Yitzkhak of Berdichev 55
Liebes, Y. 156, 158, 159
Lights of Return 145
Likutei Moharan 54–5, 143–4, 162
Logos 34, 75
loving (art of being) 94–8
Lurianic Kabbalah 47–8

Ma'asse Be'Reshit 16
Mach's Principle 43
Maharal of Prague 127–8, 138
Makhashavah 36
man: *animal rationale, animal symbolicum, animal dualismus* 9; micro cosmos 9
Marcus, I. G. 161
Masekhet Atzilut 48
Matt, D. 159
May, R. 98, 157
McLynn, F. 154
Menakhem Nakhum of Chernobyl 115

INDEX

Menakhem Mendel Schneerson 119–21
Messianism: Abulafia 112; *Aggadah* and *Midrash* 116–17; *A'kha'rit ha-yamim* 109; Hasidism 115, 119–22; Kabbalah 117–18; light of Messiah 113; Lurianism 114; Sabbateanism 114–15; two Messiahs 112; *Zohar* 113–14
metamorphosis 43, 75
Mitnagdim 49
Monologion 17–18
Moses ben Maimon 15–16, 96–7, 115–16
Moses ben Nachman 26
Moses Cordovero 38–40, 58–59
Moses de-Leon 32
mythology (in creation): Babylonian 20; Egyptian 20; Greek 20–21

Nachman of Braslav 54, 143–4
narcissism 63
Nathan of Gaza 48, 122–3
Nefesh (*Rua'kh, Neshamah, Hayya, Yekhidah*) 66
Neoplatonism 2, 7–8
Nequdah (primordial point of creation) 30, 32
Neumann, E. 153, 154
Nietzsche, F. 80
Nitzotzot 44
noetic quality 83
Noumenon 34
Nuriel, A. 150

Or she Ain-Bo Makhashavah 48–9
Or she Yesh-Bo Makhashavah 48–9
Ostow, M. 155
Otto, R. 153

Pardes: domain of the spirit 1; the "four who entered" story 84–8
Patai, R. 159
Philo 9
Pines, S. 150
Pleroma 41, 91, 105
Plutarch 20
Proslogion 18

Qelipah 44–5

Ratzo va-Shov 41, 42–3
Reshit Hokhmah 139–40
Ribbuy and *Akhdut* 50
Rosenberg, S. 162
Rudolph, K. 150

Saadia ben Joseph 15
Sabbatai Sevi 122–3
Sadeh, P. 162
Schatz Uffenheimer, R. 152, 157, 160
Schmidt, N. 158
Schneur Zalman of Liadi 50
Scholem, G. 122–3, 149, 150, 151, 152, 153, 154, 156, 158, 159, 161
Schweid, E. 162
Sefer Ahavah 95
Sefer Ellimah Rabbati 39–40
Sefer Etz Hayyim 40, 64, 114
Sefer Ha-Hezyonot 114
Sefer Ha-Mal'ach ha-Meshiv 114
Sefer Ha-Rimmon 32, 65–66
Sefer Ha-Yashar 26–30, 64, 67–8, 89, 100
Sefer Pardes Rimmonim 38–9, 64
Sefer Sheqel Ha-Kodesh 118
Sefer Yo'tzirah 33
Sefirot 24–6, 32–3
Shekhinah: divine feminine presence 113; in *Gallut* 44; *Malkhut* 25
Shema (prayer) 95
Shi'ur Komah 86
Shlomo ben Abraham Adret (Rashba) 112
Shlomo Molcho 114
Shokek, S. 151, 160, 161
Soloveitchik, J. 90
States, B. O. 157
Submission (to God) 88
Summa Contra Gentiles 19–20
Symbiosis (God's and man's co-existence in Kabbalah) 5

Tanya, Likutei Ammarim 65
Teshuvah: ascetic 132–3; *Ba'al Teshuvah* 133; Hasidism 140–4; intellectual 130–2; Kabbalistic symbolism 134–40; Maharal 138; in Rav Kook 144–5; spiritual 129–30; in *Talmud* 127–9; *Yom ha-Kippurim* 137; *Zohar* 134–35
Thirteen Attributes of Mercy 58
Tikkun 44, 139–40
Tillich, P. 156
Tishby, I. 151, 152, 157, 157, 161
Tomer Devorah 58–9
Tzimtzoom: Lurianic Kabbalah 45–6; *Tzimtzoom* and *Shevirah* 89–99; *Tzimtzoom, Shevirah, Tikkun* 42–4
Tzitzit 95

Underhill, E. 155
unification of opposites 75–6

INDEX

Va-Yoel Moshe 124

Wainwright, W. 155
Waiting for Godot: awareness and unawareness 107; dream and reality 108; eschatological philosophy 103–9; speech and immobility 107–8
Wolfson, E. R. 149, 156

Ya'akov Yosef of Polnoy 60
Yehudah ha-Barceloni 29–30
Yehudah Hayyat 67, 114
Yira'h 82
Yitzkhak Aitzik Yehudah Safrin 115
Yoel Teitelbaum 124
Yonah Gerondi 129–30

Zohar 6, 24, 30, 31, 35, 64